Postcolonial Literature and the Biblical Call for Justice

Postcolonial Literature and the Biblical Call for Justice

EDITED BY

SUSAN VANZANTEN GALLAGHER

UNIVERSITY PRESS OF MISSISSIPPI

Jackson

Print-on-Demand Edition

The paper in this book meets the guidelines for permanence and durability of the Committee on Production Guidelines for Book Longevity of the Council on Library Resources.

Library of Congress Cataloging-in-Publication Data

Postcolonial literature and the biblical call for justice / edited by
Susan VanZanten Gallagher.
      p.   cm.
    Includes bibliographical references and index.
    ISBN 1-60473-016-1
    ISBN 13: 978-1-60473-016-6
    1. Christianity and literature.   2. Literature, Modern—History and literature.
3. Justice in literature.   4. Imperialism in literature.   5. Colonies in literature.
I. Gallagher, Susan V.
PN49.P678   1994
809'.93382—dc20   94-17078
                                                                    CIP

British Library Cataloging-in-Publication data available

for

JOSEPH

and all his brothers and sisters around the world
with my love

Contents

Acknowledgments

My thanks goes to the Conference on Christianity and Literature for originally launching me on this project. Able secretarial and research assistance was provided by Sherry Smith, Chris Wheeler, Star Maeder (at Calvin College); Sage Rogers and Mark Barnes (Seattle Pacific University). Clarence Walhout, Mark Walhout, and Alan Jacobs remain my most faithful and perceptive readers; their support and encouragement have been invaluable.

The contributors to this volume have all been delightful people with whom to work. I appreciate their cheerfulness, willingness to revise, and prompt responses to my queries. As communal scholars, they have all been exemplary.

Finally, my gratitude to John, my partner in life, in parenting, and in love.

Postcolonial Literature and the Biblical Call for Justice

Introduction
New Conversations on Postcolonial Literature

SUSAN VANZANTEN GALLAGHER

This volume contains a collection of essays on a variety of topics associated with the biblical call for justice in relationship to postcolonial literatures from a number of different traditions. Although the Bible addresses many other aspects of life that such literature also addresses—such as personal and social identity—and although postcolonial literature includes many facets other than a relationship to justice, we have chosen this conjunction of topics for a number of reasons. The contributors to this volume share both a common excitement about the numerous flourishing postcolonial traditions and a common commitment to the ethically compelling nature of biblical justice. Historically, we find many powerful and provocative interconnections between the two. Our collective discussion functions to develop a new way of talking about postcolonial literature; it adds a previously silenced or overlooked voice to the ongoing cultural conversation.

In many ways, the questions this volume raises are, at the very least, paradoxical; at the most, contradictory. What, after all, is postcolonial literature? Is the term *postcolonial* a historical label or one based on a political position? Are we not ourselves committing an act of cultural imperialism even to suggest that we can affix this label to such a multiplicity of literatures that have been produced in a number of markedly different historical contexts, by people of different classes, religions, and genders? What social, economic, and cultural conditions characterize colonialism? And why discuss postcolonial works in the context of the call for justice articulated in the Scriptures of the Christian tradition, a tradition itself often associated with the evils of colonialism?

Some of these questions echo important critical conversations occurring today. A growing interest in postcolonial literature has prompted much theorizing about appropriate critical approaches, heated discussions of the relationship between postcolonialism and postmodernism, explorations of the way that indigenous cultures influence postcolonial texts, and numerous studies of individual traditions and authors. The unquestionable vitality of writing emerging from the so-called Third World—Africa, Asia, Latin America—is evidenced not only by the recent awarding of the Nobel Prize to such authors as Gabriel García Márquez (in 1982), Wole Soyinka (1986), Naguib Mahfouz (1988), Nadine Gordimer (1991), and Derek Walcott (1992), but also by these authors' international success. Publishers and scholars alike have demonstrated a new interest in promoting the works of such authors, and the academy's growing concern with multiculturalism has also prompted increased study of literature that falls outside the mainstream of the Western tradition.

The popular label of *postcolonial literature* has numerous meanings. Although in common usage it seems to refer to any world literature from outside the traditional Western canon, other definitions are more restricted. In historical terms, *postcolonial* refers to a national culture after the departure of an imperial power. Bill Ashcroft, Gareth Griffiths, and Helen Tiffin define the term in more narrow geographical terms as "writing by those peoples formerly colonized by Britain," although they admit that their discussion of postcolonial literature also has relevance to countries colonized by other European powers. However, they extend "postcolonialism" historically to include "all the culture affected by the imperial process from the moment of colonization to the present day" (1, 2). Their definition results in the rather unusual classification of canonical American literature as postcolonial, while native American literature falls outside their boundaries.

For many theorists, postcolonial literature is defined by its common political posture. According to Linda Hutcheon, postcolonial texts not only originate in countries that have experienced colonization but also possess a distinct political agenda and theory of agency, both of which function to combat marginalization and to assert the "denied or alienated subjectivity" of the Other ("Circling" 168). Ashcroft, Griffiths, and Tiffin see postcolonial texts as "foregrounding the tension with the imperial power, and . . . emphasizing their differences from the assumptions of the imperial centre" (2). Stephen Slemon also goes beyond a historical definition to define the particular function of postcolonial literature: he focuses on "a specifically anti- or *post*-colonial *discursive* purchase in culture" ("Modernism's" 6). Postcolonial literature, for Slemon, is anticolonial discourse, a discourse that distances itself from and subversively refuses the tradition of the colonizer.

Some of the difficulties inherent in both the historical and functional definitions of *postcolonial* were strikingly manifested at the 1992 convention of the Modern Language Association during a session aptly entitled, "What Does It Mean to Teach 'Postcolonial' Literature?" The panel presentations included accounts of teaching Latin American, native American, South African, and Indian literature. Much of the discussion following the initial presentations concerned the term *postcolonial*. A Nigerian writer in the audience objected to what he perceived as the political nature of the label, which he felt too quickly categorized his work. "Why not just call me a Nigerian author?" he asked. Another member of the audience, a black woman from South Africa, had a different kind of objection: "You can't say that South Africa is a *post*colonial state, and neither is the United States [for native Americans]. Lots of people are still living in colonial situations." The session leader quickly had to point out the quotation marks surrounding *postcolonial* in the session title as an admission of the problematic nature of the term.

Such comments highlight the practical and ethical difficulties of talking about postcolonial literature. By affixing one label to a multiplicity of literatures that have been produced in a number of markedly different historical contexts by people of different classes, religions, and genders, are we guilty of cultural insensitivity? While definitions such as those previously given can be useful for discussing many of the works emerging from a colonial history, this volume will use a historical definition. We will define *postcolonial literature* as writing that emerges from peoples who once were colonized by European powers, now have some form of political independence, but continue to live with the negative economic and cultural legacy of colonialism. Consequently, it is literature from those who, historically, have been the oppressed, the marginalized, the Others of the world. We do not include works that originate in the settler colonies that formed in the United States, Canada, or Australia, except for works from the remnant of those indigenous peoples who were either physically annihilated or completely marginalized when the colonizers' languages and cultures were successfully transplanted. However, we do include works from the countries of Latin America, where the history of colonialism, as we shall shortly discuss, contributed to a chaotic political and economic postcolonial period. Our definition also encompasses writing from Africa, Asia, and the Middle East, as well as the literary productions of native Americans and the indigenous people of New Zealand.

Insisting on opposition to colonialism as a necessary quality of postcolonial literature poses many problems, and we are wary of such an approach. As a matter of fact, some postcolonial writers do adopt certain aspects of the legacy of colonialism, such as the recent new global enthusiasm for democracy; others accept certain formal aspects of colonial culture. The Kenyan writer Ngũgĩ wa Thiong'o, for example, has accused some of his fellow African writers, such as Chinua Achebe, of too easily adopting European forms and languages to create the Afro-European novel rather than revitalizing the African novel. Thus, Ngũgĩ concludes, Achebe accommodates, rather than opposes European culture (*Decolonising* 70). Yet other readers have praised Achebe as a leading postcolonial writer in his vivid exposure of the devastating moral and social effects of colonialism. Such disagreement highlights an important issue: to what degree must writers reject colonialism and its cultural products before they are oppositional enough to be termed postcolonial, in Slemon's sense?

Secondly, while all postcolonial works originate in and emerge from colonial history, they are not necessarily bound to treat that history overtly or even thematically, although many do. A claim to the contrary has been made by Fredric Jameson, who argues in "Third World Literature in an Era of Multinational Capitalism" that all of what he calls "Third World fictional texts" are necessarily national allegories, even when they appear to be traditional realistic fiction.[1] His comments have caused quite a controversy, with one critic citing Jameson's "disturbing arrogance, even . . . paternalism based on [his] own privileged status as a highly reputed, first-world, white, male theorist who must now take on the 'white man's burden' to theorize about third-world literature."[2] Jameson's argument ignores historical specificity under the banner of what he terms his "sweeping hypothesis." While we might want to grant that any work brought out in postcolonial conditions—from a particular author, country, or press—has a different kind of social existence and resonance than those produced by a John Updike or an Anthony Burgess, to claim that all such works are inherently allegorical seems to be a manipulative overgeneralization that denies works and authors the ability to function independently from Western critical power.

Nonetheless, while granting that many different reactions to the colonial situation exist, we can still identify some frequently appearing motifs in postcolonial literature, motifs that find their origin in some of the common elements of colonial history. That history is first and foremost a history of economic and political exploitation, as Albert Memmi's classic definition emphasizes (149). As an economic practice, colonialism sought to control the production of wealth, but in so doing it also controlled the production of culture. Ngũgĩ notes that colonialism relied on military conquest and political dictatorship to maintain its economic control, "but its most important area of domination was the mental universe of the colonised, the control, through culture, of how people perceived themselves and their relationship to the world" (*Decolonising* 16). Either by denying the existence of indigenous culture or by denigrating its value, colonialism marginalized the cultures of the colonized. Further marginalization occurred by means of the dominant culture. Edward Said points out, for example, the "formidable structure of cultural domination" of the Arab people in Western discourse about the East in *Orientalism,* where he demonstrates how Eastern Others were trivialized into exotica (25). Without a recognized culture, colonized peoples were deemed less civilized, less advanced, perhaps even less human.

Some of these crucial dynamics of colonialism are elaborated by the Martiniquan psychiatrist Frantz Fanon in *The Wretched of the Earth,* which has become a classic text for postcolonial studies. Colonialism, in Fanon's psychological terms, consists of the unequal relationship of oppressor and oppressed, a relationship in which the oppressor dominates not only physically and economically but also culturally and morally. Culturally, the settlers write the history, positing precolonial barbarism and refusing to acknowledge any significant indigenous cultural achievements. Fanon terms colonialism "a Manichean world," in which the settler refuses to recognize or acknowledge the indigenous culture and "paints the native as a sort of quintessence of evil" (33). According to Fanon, this Manichean dichotomy allows the colonizer to assume moral superiority and implicitly justifies the political, economic, and cultural domination.

Within these common dimensions of economic and cultural domination, postcolonialism takes numerous and significantly different forms. The postcolonial situation of Kenya, for example, differs from that of Ghana, and the postcolonial productions of native Americans are hardly identical with, or even strikingly similar to, those of Nicaraguan writers. Colonialism shows different faces in different parts of the globe, and its progeny come in different shapes, colors, and forms. Any discussion of postcolonialism, then, is a discussion of the difference and multiplicity as well as of the commonality of oppression and injustice. The essays in this volume demonstrate both this multiplicity—in the variety of works, traditions, and approaches they include—and this commonality—in the echoes and reverberations that appear throughout.

Thus, in addition to identifying some of the common struggles of the postcolonial writer, we need also to outline briefly some of the significant historical differences among postcolonial conditions. The complex history of colonialism has two main narratives: in the first wave of European activity, as it took place primarily in the Americas, the colonizer's language and culture were transplanted and "the indigenous inhabitants were either annihilated or marginalized"; in the second, occurring primarily in Africa and Asia, "cultural imposition took place on the homeground of the colonised people and the lines between colonised and coloniser were more clearly drawn" (Brydon 3). In the first scenario, the settlers eventually dominate the population as well as politics and culture, establishing a settler society that replaces the indigenous society. In the second, the colonial power imposes its methods of governing, its economy, its language and its culture upon an indigenous people who remain a significant sector of the population. The essays in this volume address literature reflecting both of these narratives, each of which includes numerous individual stories.

The Americas, with their complex and intricate histories of colonialism, have given birth to numerous postcolonial traditions; two that this volume discusses are the magical Marxist voice of Latin America and the besieged voice of the surviving native Americans. All of the Americas experienced numerous waves of European invasion from the fifteenth to the eighteenth century. Yet the subsequent manifestations of colonialism were markedly different. As Chevigny and Laguardia point out, the United States was settled by individuals who were themselves escaping from various forms of European domination, while the colonization of Spanish America was carried out by people working on behalf of the mother country, striving both to extend its rule and enrich themselves. While the primarily Protestant United States settlers had a strong sense of individualism, the Catholic Spanish-American settlers thought in corporate, semifeudal terms. A developing nation of small independent farms and farmers, the United States conducted an aggressive campaign to eradicate the native population, leaving only a remnant of native Americans behind to struggle with the questions raised by the imposition and threat of European culture. But the

Spanish, once they had subjugated the indigenous peoples, incorporated them into the feudal hierarchy as manual laborers on the large plots of land held by the wealthy upperclass, using them to produce the raw materials that were sent back to the mother country (4–9). Many of the original inhabitants were killed in the wars of occupation and by imported European disease, but the offspring of Indian and Spanish intermarriage, termed *mestizos*, rapidly contributed to the new oppressed class of rural poor.

The independence and growing international power of the United States also kept its southern neighbors in dependent positions. Chevigny and Laguardia describe how the United States quickly developed its political structures, drawing on a long tradition of Western individualism and democracy, in essence formalizing an already given political autonomy. But the Spanish Americas were torn by political chaos in the post-Napoleonic era and, without autonomous governing systems in place, underwent a series of leftist revolutions, experiments in democracy, and right-wing dictatorships throughout the nineteenth and twentieth centuries (6–10). With no economic basis for industrialization and existing primarily as suppliers of raw material, the countries of Central and South America experienced a continuing dependence on economically secure countries and international financiers. Even today their political and economic instability continues to cast them in the role of the oppressed, the colonized, by forces both within (a Somoza dictatorship, for example) and without (multinational corporations). As one observer notes, "Central America has yet to overcome its colonial legacy, with its disturbance of social structures—of traditional patterns of life pertaining to land, labor, and community—and its resulting economic dependence on export agriculture. Even today there is hardly a break with the past of the Spanish domination in the way in which poor peasants and the working classes are treated by the wealthy and powerful elite" (Spykman et al. 43).

We find different kinds of stories in Africa, the Middle East, and the far East. In most of this hemisphere, European powers—including the British, Germans, Russians, French, Dutch, Belgians, and Portuguese—began extending their colonizing activities and economic control primarily in the sixteenth and seventeenth centuries, expanded their empires significantly in the post-Napoleonic era, and began decolonization in the twentieth century, particularly following World War II and the United Nations Charter's rebuke to the colonial system. Again, we find many variations on a central motif.

In both Asia and Africa, the colonialism begun in the age of exploration continued with a new surge of imperial expansion in the late nineteenth century. Britain firmly controlled the colonization of India, but the continent of Africa was subject to the competing forces of numerous European countries. Prompted to various degrees by militant nationalism, dreams of wealth, the humanitarian concerns of a David Livingstone, and the land hunger of King Leopold of Belgium, the European powers eventually partitioned the continent among themselves. Encountering a brilliant patchwork of indigenous economic and social structures—ranging from nomadic tribes to absolute monarchies already engaged in extensive international trade—the European colonizers imposed their political and administrative control in a variety of ways (Gann and Duignan 1: 6–14). Throughout Africa, Europeans assumed political, economic, and cultural superiority, instigating population transfers, segregating living spaces, developing export products, and imposing Western dress, education, and culture. Colonial rule, frequently characterized by demands for reform but not for abolishment, continued throughout most of Africa and Asia until the process of decolonization and the emergence of independent African and Asian countries began in the years following World War II.[3]

The impact of colonialism on northern Africa and the Middle East has been similarly disruptive. The Arab people witnessed a massive expansion of European economic and political power throughout the nineteenth century with the incursion of European trade, technology, and armies. With the defeat of Algeria in 1847, European countries began their formal political rule of the region, and the previously powerful Ottoman Empire became increasingly subject to European influences and control. During the period between the world wars, the Ottoman Empire was effectively dismantled, and Britain and France emerged as the sole power brokers in the central countries of the Muslim world, a role which the United States and the Soviet Union eventually took over. After the destruction of the Ottoman Empire, the Arab people turned to nationalism as a means of finding political stability and identity, and the subsequent history of the Middle East has been one of opposing nations, world-power politics, and rising Muslim fundamentalism (Hourani 263–351).

The process of colonialism in Africa and the East in some ways had a vastly different impact than did that process in the Americas. In only a few instances, such as the San (or Bushman) population of southern Africa, were the indigenous people eliminated or forcibly removed and a new settler society developed. We can also find a few cases of the creation of a new underclass by means of intermarriage similar to the formation of the mestizos, such as the government-classified "coloureds" of South Africa. But for the most part, in countries as diverse as Zambia, Egypt, and India, colonialism functioned to create a two-tiered society in which European bureaucrats, financiers, and technicians ruled and administered, and in which indigenous people provided the labor. Although a few vital settler colonies became established—with Rhodesia and South Africa as the most notable and troublesome examples—for the most part, decolonization in Africa and Asia brought with it a physical withdrawal of most of the colonizers. The confused political and depleted economic situation that colonialism left behind is starkly attested in the turbulent recent histories of many former colonies of Africa, Asia, and the Middle East.

The seeds that were planted throughout the world in the colonial period continue to bear fruit in the radically inequitable world economy that is its legacy. The economic oppression under which a great deal of the world today lives can be seen as a direct consequence of colonialism: "Europe did not 'discover' the underdeveloped countries; on the contrary, she created them. . . . Nearly all of the people encountered in today's underdeveloped areas were members of viable societies which could satisfy the economic needs of the community. Yet these societies were shattered when they came into contact with an expanding Europe" (Griffin 72, 75). And the major industrial nations continue to draw on the resources of these underdeveloped and less powerful nations in a variety of ways. Twentieth-century colonialism appears in new forms: in East-West power struggles played out on a Middle-Eastern gameboard, in the intricacies of the international arms market, and in the exploitative labor practices of multinational corporations.

Cultural and psychological domination also continues. Despite the growing interest in postcolonial literatures, many critics working in this field continue to feel marginalized. Diana Brydon argues, "Some of the most exciting writing in English this century has come not from Britain or the United States but from other parts of England's fragmented empire. Yet this literature has gone largely unrecognised, its value misconstrued by readings that sought to bring it into line with inappropriate standards of the Anglo-American literary establishment" (2). Particular instances of cultural oppression are only too easy to find. Edward Said has extended his examination of Western discourse about the East, arguing in the context of the Gulf War of 1991 that the Western media continues to present a distorted picture of the Arab as irrational, blood-hungry, and barbaric ("Tragic"). The blacks in South Africa continue to be written as Other in contemporary history and discourse, which often characterizes indigenous people as less than human, as caricatured manifestations of evil or bestiality. And racism and prejudice against African Americans and native Americans still permeates American society, despite thirty years of civil rights agitation and legal reform.

Postcolonial literature, then, is literature that emerges from and is frequently opposed to these conditions of colonialism. While granting that some postcolonial literature may not be overtly opposed to Western culture and values, we should also note that a prominent motif of much postcolonial literature is revelation of and protest against the multiple instances of injustice located in colonialism. However, other injustices may be identified as arising from indigenous traditions and practices. A common opposition to oppression—no matter what the source—unites the particular works that are discussed in this volume. Yet each work arises within a unique context and so also maintains cultural specificity. Latin America's colonial legacy is dominated by oppressive economic and physical conditions, so its literature is often concerned with issues of social and distributive justice, as several of our contributors elaborate. But while economic injustice is also of concern to other postcolonials, the difficulty of expressing a cultural identity emerges far more strongly in postcolonial writing of Africans and native Americans. A desire for ontological justice, recognition as human beings, and an affirmation of the complexities and positive contributions of an indigenous culture more frequently characterize these works.

Much critical conversation about postcolonial literature today is caught up in debate over the relationship of the three "posts": poststructuralism, postmodernism, and postcolonialism. The exact definitions of and distinctions between poststructuralism and postmodernism are frequently blurred in such discussions, but for our purposes we shall define *poststructuralism* as the theory, established most notably by Jacques Derrida, that questions the implicit universalist claims of Western epistemology by deconstructing linguistic and philosophical authority and by dismantling the notion of agency. Poststructuralist theory, then, often is used to explain *postmodernism,* a writing practice that subverts and questions authority by means of a particular rhetoric and form. In *A Poetics of Postmodernism,* Linda Hutcheon argues that postmodern art paradoxically both employs and questions culturally accepted conventions of discourse and representation, demonstrating a "contradictory dependence on and independence from that which temporally preceded it and which literally made it possible." Postmodernism, according to Hutcheon, is primarily characterized by intertextual parody, using the strategies of the dominant culture to challenge its discursive practices from within (18, 20–21).

A conjunction of similar writing strategies and forms lends credence to the comparisons among poststructuralism, postmodernism, and postcolonialism: much postcolonial literature, like poststructuralist criticism, rests upon dismantling, unmasking, or questioning the concepts of hierarchy and otherness. Proclaiming the value of the marginal in its very existence, much postcolonial literature challenges the master-narratives of history. These shared concerns result in many similar formal techniques: much postcolonial literature, along with postmodernism, rejects realism, employs irony and allegory in a refiguration of history, refuses textual closure, and attacks the binary constructions of concepts and language. Magic realism—with its interweaving of the fantastic, the dreamlike, and the sharply realistic—has been a topic of particular interest to those critics concerned with the conjunction of postmodernism and postcolonialism (see Slemon, "Magic").

Yet despite these theoretical and formal similarities, most scholars of postcolonial literature oppose a complete identification of postcolonialism with postmodernism or poststructuralism. Helen Tiffin, for example, cautions against "the reinscription of non-European realities into a dominant European system," and concludes, "the post-modern label should, I feel, be resisted, and while Euro-American post-structuralist theories offer exciting possibilities to post-colonial theoreticians, it would be dangerous if they were to be accepted without rigorous interrogation from post-colonial perspectives" (171). Tiffin's resistance, however, is qualified, and her subsequent discussion of some of the similarities paradoxically indicates her own interest in the "exciting possibilities" offered by postmodernism. Somewhat more adamant is Simon During's claim that "the play of passions we call postcolonial . . . name and disclaim postmodernism as neo-imperialist. And they do so by accepting and using those practices and concepts (representation, history, evaluation) which postmodernism most strenuously denies" ("Postmodernism" 369).

Many critics of postcolonial literature feel what Ketu H. Katrak terms a "social responsibility" to respond seriously to problems of oppression and dominance, but simultaneously experience a paralyzing confusion in light of their embrace of poststructuralism (157). In attempting to avoid cultural imperialism, Slemon finds himself arguing for a double standard: "postcolonial criticism . . . would draw on post-structuralism's suspension of the referent in order to read the social 'text' of colonialist power and at the same time would reinstall the referent in the service of colonized and post-colonial societies" ("Modernism's" 9). In the interest of justice, Slemon would allow referentiality and mimetic truth claims to function in non-Western texts but not in Western texts.

But as Tiffin, During, and others point out, most postcolonial writers are deeply committed to the notion of the subject; having been denied the position of subject in discourse for so long by the practices of colonialism, postcolonial writers want to affirm their humanity, their consciousness. Similarly, such writers often rely on the mimetic and referential quality of a text, reflecting in realistic detail the conditions of life in South Africa, Argentina, or Pakistan. Perhaps most significantly, they still affirm, in the face of poststructuralist theory, the possibility of truth claims. In their more postmodern works, the unmasking and dismantling of authority is merely a strategy, a means of fulfilling a political agenda to retrieve identity in the face of cultural imperialism. By questioning colonial authority, post-colonial writers do not necessarily question *all* authority. Rather, they set out to dismantle a specific historically grounded discourse in the hopes of demonstrating that an alternative discourse is possible. Kwame Anthony Appiah contends that postcolonial African novels are misleadingly post-modern in their rejection of realism. "[Their] basis for that project of de-ligitimation is very much not the postmodern one: rather, it is grounded in an appeal to an ethical universal; indeed it is based, as intellectual responses to oppression in Africa largely are based, in an appeal to a certain simple respect for human suffering" (152). Authors such as Yambo Ouologuem (from Mali) are "hardly likely to make common cause with a relativism that might allow that the horrifying new-old Africa of exploitation is to be understood—legitimated—in its own local terms" (152). Postcolonial writ-ers, Appiah believes, reject the master narratives of modernity while hold-ing on to a "provisional, historically contingent, antiessentialist" humanism (155). In these theoretical assumptions and ethical motivations, most post-colonialism is radically different from poststructuralism.

The critical concentration on the relationship of the three "posts" has perhaps unnecessarily limited our ways of thinking about postcolonial lit-erature. While ultimately refusing the connection, many critics still play the game, repeatedly analyzing the formal similarities of postcolonial and postmodern literature. Katrak notes the "insidious trend" of "theoretical gymnastics"—using fashionable methods of criticism either "to validate postcolonial literature, even to prove its value through the use of complicated Eurocentric models" or "to succumb to the lure of engaging in a hegemonic discourse of Western theory . . . often for the sole purpose of demonstrating its shortcomings for an interpretation of postcolonial texts" (158). One of the dangers of such gymnastics is the distorted emphasis on certain kinds of postcolonial writing at the expense of others. Timothy Brennan admits, "Even as 'third world' authors receive attention and even acclaim in the book reviews and in the academy, the ones so chosen for notoriety are usually those whose stylistic and thematic 'complexities' fit comfortably within established critical norms" (4–5).

However, a number of significant forms and strategies exist in post-colonial writing. Much postcolonial literature is far more realistic than postmodern in its formal strategies. South African black writers, for ex-ample, frequently turn to social realism, oral poetry, and participatory drama as a means of consciousness raising in the struggles in the townships. In fact, realism is considered such a crucial element of South African op-positional writing that those authors such as J. M. Coetzee who eschew both traditional and social realism are often criticized as being irresponsible and politically naive.[4] For many black readers in South Africa, the more diffuse postmodern tendencies of a Coetzee appear esoteric, distanced, and irrelevant, while André Brink's novels of psychological realism are much more pertinent. Autobiography and biography—providing voices of wit-ness and testimony—are additional texts that are often relegated to the back burner of discussion rather than put in the large pot in which poststructur-alism is brewing. And even when postcolonial texts play with other texts in postmodern fashion, the intertextual references and revisions may be em-ployed to affirm the source and expand its implications, rather than to parody it, as in Nicaraguan poet Ernesto Cardenal's poetic revision of the Psalms discussed in this volume.

Postcolonial literature has also given rise to many new forms and genres of literature. The unique concerns of postcolonial people, as Barbara Har-low suggests, subvert previously valid generic conventions, creating new forms ("Narrative"). Similarly, referring to the new genres that emerged in Europe in the Middle Ages, John Beverley argues, "We should expect an age such as our own—also one of transition or the potential for transi-tion from one mode [of] production to another—to experience the emer-gence of new forms of cultural and literary expression that embody, in more or less thematically explicit and formally articulated ways, the social forces contending for power in the world today" ("Margin" 12). Harlow describes such new genres in Palestinian literature: the communiqué and prison report; Beverley discusses a specific kind of Latin American narrative text called *testimonio*. These are a few of the formal considerations that may be overlooked in the focus on postcolonial irony, allegory, and subversive intertextuality.

A poststructuralist analysis of postcolonial literature, then, can result in ethical conundrums, logical inconsistencies, and an unnecessarily restricted canon. In refusing authorial subjectivity and textual referentiality to postcolonial texts, in privileging postmodern parody and intertextuality, and in embracing a complete relativism, poststructuralism at times seems to reenact the oppressions of colonialism, turning into a critical imperialism that once again manipulates Others by refusing to take them on their own terms.

Another common conversation about postcolonial literature concerns its relationship to indigenous culture. For many postcolonial people, as Fanon points out, the search for a precolonial, national culture is a crucial part of psychological liberation, a means by which they assert their complex humanity in the face of the destruction of that culture and history by Western forces: "This passionate search for a national culture which existed before the colonial era finds its legitimate reason in the anxiety shared by native intellectuals to shrink away from the Western culture in which they all risk being swamped. Because they realise they are in danger of losing their lives and thus becoming lost to their people, these men, hot-headed and with anger in their hearts, relentlessly determine to renew contact once more with the oldest and most pre-colonial springs of life of their people" (169–70). One such critical attempt appears in *Toward the Decolonization of African Literature* by Chinweizu, Onwuchekwa Jemie, and Ihechukwu Madubuike, which aims "to end all foreign domination of African culture" by exposing the "dominant and malicious eurocentric criticism" of its poetry and prose and positing an alternative "afrocentric" criticism. Criticizing the slavish imitation of European modernism by many writers, these critics claim that "African literature *is* an autonomous entity separate and apart from all other literatures. It has its own traditions, models, and norms" (4).

The question of autonomy is a crucial one also for those postcolonial critics who wish to abjure an imperialistic criticism. Defining postcolonial literature as a form of counterdiscourse, always speaking against the European center, always reacting to the conditions of colonialism appears, somewhat ironically, to confirm its marginality. Europe remains the center; colonialism remains the force against which postcolonialism can emerge only in reaction. Do postcolonial writers have the ability to craft their own questions, their own forms, their own analyses, from their own point of view? Can the Manichean binary oppositions of colonialism ever be undone?

While such questions are valuable reminders of the morally shaky ground of the Western critic, the sins of the past cannot simply be undone or wished away. The historical reality of colonialism, with its massive impact on colonized societies, cultures, and people, cannot be denied. In the Americas, many indigenous cultures have been decimated, and, as Annamaria Carusi notes, original, precolonial African culture is "virtually irrecoverable" (85). Wole Soyinka calls the search for an authentic African culture "Neo-Tarzanism" and asserts that his Africa includes "precision machinery, oil rigs, hydro-electricity, my typewriter, railway trains (not iron snakes), machine guns, bronze sculpture, etc." (38). The "nativist nostalgia" found in *Toward the Decolonization of African Literature*, says Appiah, is actually "a reverse discourse" of racism, accepting Western ideologies of nationhood, language, and literature (59). Furthermore, denying the syncretism of the modern world and insisting on escaping history to return to a precolonial indigenous world ultimately proves more marginalizing than liberating. Graham Huggan comments,

> The tendency of some of the more extreme nationalist critics to wish away the existence of a European cultural heritage, however distorting and/or debilitating that heritage may have been, seems not only to divest post-colonial writing of much of its oppositional power in exposing and critiquing the material conditions which govern its cultural production, but also to risk corralling nation- or race-based literature into separate, jealously protected territories which resist intrusion to the extent that they become accessible only to those "exclusive insiders" possessed by virtue of birthright or immediacy of experience of an intimate knowledge of their own "field." (20–21)

In order for some form of cross-cultural communication and understanding to exist, we need ways to dialogue that are not completely dependent upon culturally specific experience, yet we also must not fall into the common error that assumes Western values to be equivalent to transcendent values, an error that Appiah calls *pseudouniversalism* or "Eurocentric hegemony *posing* as universalism" (58). The difficulty that Western critics face is how to recognize true universality in a way that avoids repressing oppositional voices or trivializing historical contexts and differences.

Several critics have spoken recently of a process of mutual interaction as a way out of this dilemma. Simon During calls the products of the interaction between colonizer and colonized "post-culturalism" and sees such work as celebrating "the productive energy of mutual misrecognitions and forgettings" ("Waiting" 47). Brydon provides a useful trope that suggests such interaction without necessarily employing binary oppositions: instead of the imperial metaphor of the tree trunk and branches, she proposes a model of cross-cultural interaction as imaged in a multirunnered rhizome, in which numerous shoots cross and re-cross each other (3). This kind of interaction is potentially possible because of the polyvalent quality of both the postcolonial and the colonial experience. We have already noted some of the multiplicity inherent in postcolonialism, but many critics who are quick to note that one should not overgeneralize about the colonial mind as opposed to the imperialistic mind forget that the concept of the imperialistic mind is also "a fiction that imposes wholeness on what is not a whole" (Brydon 1). While fundamentally structured around the dichotomy of oppressor and oppressed, colonialism, as a wide-ranging social practice, also has other, potentially more beneficial, aspects. And we should not forget the existence of oppositional voices—that every culture has a counterculture, or, as Marxism has taught us, that a residual tradition always exists in the midst of the hegemonic, or dominant. Colonial culture had its own internal dissidents, one powerful example of which is found in the biblical tradition of justice. Rather than working from an exclusively binary opposition of colonial and postcolonial culture, we may want instead to envision a mutual dialogue between the two in which each has contributions to make, confessions to proffer, and forgiveness to grant.

For Western critics, one way to achieve such dialogue is to listen to postcolonial critics in order to better critique and challenge our own pseudo-universal notions. Postcolonial critics, particularly in Africa, have not shown much interest in postmodernism (which does remain an important strand of concern for some Latin American writers). Many postcolonials repeatedly emphasize the need to approach and understand their literature within its own context, not as a poor imitation of Western art. The Nigerian novelist Chinua Achebe decries the ignorance of Western critics who continue to see the African writer as "an unfinished European." In an influential indictment of what he terms "colonialist criticism," Achebe warns "that the European critic of African literature must cultivate the habit of humility appropriate to his limited experience of the African world and purged of the superiority and arrogance which history so insidiously makes him heir to" (*Hopes* 73). Such postcolonial critics ask us to examine genuine local differences more closely before leaping to conclusions about universalism.

To begin, a deeper understanding of indigenous forms will help develop a more profound notion of aesthetic achievement. Although a return to precolonial culture is a Rousseauean romance, many different kinds of indigenous cultures continue to flourish in Latin America, Asia, the Caribbean, and Africa—colonial opposition, denial, and disapproval notwithstanding. As Appiah testifies, "The fact is that most of us who were raised during and for some time after the colonial era . . . all experienced the persistent power of our own cognitive and moral traditions: in religion, in social occasions as the funeral, in our experience of music, in our practice of the dance, and, of course, in the intimacy of family life" (7 – 8). Such vital traditions inform much postcolonial literature, and useful studies have explored such issues as the contributions of African and Amerindian folk culture to Caribbean literature (Brathwaite, "African Presence"), the poetic productions of the Aztec world (León-Portilla), or the impact of Yoruba masquerades and traditional poetry on the plays of Wole Soyinka (Beier 243 – 54).

Understanding literature in its context means not only acknowledging the contributions of indigenous forms but also understanding the social role of the African artist. In the dominant Western view, individuality defines the person, but the dominant African view holds that personal life depends on and is a product of the community (see Menkiti). Consequently, rejecting the European concentration on individual expression and experience, many African artists believe they have a responsibility to serve the community as a teacher. Achebe sees his role as "to help my society regain belief in itself and put away the complexes of the years of denigration and self-abasement" (*Hopes* 44). Given the economic chaos and political corruption of their societies, Latin American critics are similarly interested in the consequences of the social practice of writing, sometimes using Marxist and neo-Marxist theory in their analysis of literature as a vehicle for social change. Western critics are thus challenged to reconsider the function of literature and our methods of talking about it. Other common postcolonial debates—such as the debate over the advisability of employing an indigenous tongue rather than the colonizer's language—help us better to understand postcolonial peoples' concerns for justice and identity.[5] While not embracing a total relativism that makes communication and interaction impossible, we need to make more of an effort to understand postcolonial literature within its own context and to acknowledge that the universal manifests itself only in the particular.

"Since it is too late for us to escape each other," Appiah writes, "we might instead seek to turn to our advantage the mutual interdependencies history has thrust upon us" (72). One of postcolonial literature's greatest possibilities lies in a dialogical consideration of the strengths and weaknesses, the benefits and dangers, appearing in both the indigenous culture and the colonial experience, as well as in the resulting postcolonial mix. However, given the harsh and oppressive realities of colonialism, true dialogue requires that Western readers be willing at this time to listen seriously and respectfully to postcolonial voices.

This volume attempts to encourage such a dialogue by reflecting on some of the multiple relationships existing between postcolonial literature and the biblical call for justice. Our contributors often participate in earlier conversations concerning postmodernism, indigenous culture, and the question of language; but we consider these issues in the light of postcolonial literature's relationship to the prophetic biblical text, which calls societies and individuals to new ways of life. Like the Bible, the works discussed here are prophetic art. Originating in contemporary events, prophetic art is "simultaneously its echo and mirror but also possesses an awakening prophetic power which can have far-reaching and profound effect" (Kadinsky 6). Postcolonial literature echoes and mirrors the realities of the postcolonial world, but it also attempts to awaken its audience, asking—both in its thematic concerns as well as in its very existence—for greater justice in the twentieth-century world.

The reflections on postcolonial literature and the prophetic biblical text appearing here may perhaps seem incongruous to some readers for whom colonialism and Christianity are synonymous, so we should address this objection at the outset. Without question, the agents and agencies of Christianity all too frequently aided and abetted some of the worst instances of colonial oppression. Many devout colonizers, acting on behalf of their mother nation, did see their activities as a means of carrying out God's purposes. Throughout the history of colonialism, the White Man's Burden—however Kipling might have defined it—was frequently understood as a moral responsibility to transform native economies, societies, and cultures. In many cases, such an ideology served either to mask or at least to endorse the political and cultural domination needed to support Fanon's Manichean dichotomy. Throughout Central and South America, Africa, and Asia, the colonial condition was repeatedly constructed by a complex mixture of economic interests, moral responsibility, and power politics, or "gold, God, and glory" (see Winks). Yet feelings of moral superiority, although frequently couched in religious rhetoric, were not always explicitly informed by Christianity. Historians have noted how racist ideology, the contemporary understanding of Darwinian evolution, a secular belief in the superiority of Western culture and thought, and even a repressed sexual energy all contributed to the formation of the notion of Western moral responsibility. Many late Victorians who had lost their belief in Christianity during the age of "the disappearance of God" adopted a moralistic imperialism as a kind of surrogate faith.[6]

Civil administrators might have been prompted by either a secular or a Christian belief in moral responsibility, but another important aspect of colonization included the influx of missionaries into colonies, missionaries with a drive to convert the natives both to Christianity and, frequently, to a Western way of life. Accompanying the history of political colonization is the history of missionary activity, as the Catholic church sent missionary priests to the New World and as the growth of evangelicalism in the late eighteenth and early nineteenth century gave birth to the great American and British missionary societies that set out to evangelize Africa and Asia. Christian missionary activity often was a crucial element of colonization, transforming cultures and societies as well as religions. It is precisely such blind cultural egotism that Herman Melville criticizes in *Omoo,* in his account of Tahitian women absurdly clad in Western dress by narrow-minded missionaries. Similarly, in Africa, "the missionaries often inculcated a policy which paralleled that colonial policy which . . . assumed as a necessary precondition for the development of Africa the creation of an African middle class which would fit into the world of the European" (Dickson 79). Fanon caustically compares the Christianity that wipes out native culture to DDT that destroys yellow fever and concludes, "the triumphant *communiqués* from the missions are in fact a source of information concerning the implantation of foreign influences in the core of the colonised people" (34).

But while undoubtedly contributing to colonial expansion and frequently acting as an ally with the colonizing forces, missionaries also often worked to oppose the government and its abuses, the excesses of their own religious agencies—as the film *The Mission* depicts—as well as the oppressive aspects of the indigenous culture. Historians generally agree that the late nineteenth-century growth in missionary activity in Africa was in great measure prompted by a moral desire to provide restitution for the oppression created by the Western slave trade. But the positive contributions of missionaries in Africa go beyond their influence in stopping slavery; Christian missionaries frequently worked against oppression by mediating in internecine warfare, protesting against unjust labor practices instigated by colonial powers, encouraging the abolition of female circumcision, dealing with the social problems caused by alcoholism and refugees, and providing medical care and education for the indigenous people. The institution of mission schools was of special importance, for despite its chauvinistic cultural limits, such education eventually provided the means by which significant indigenous leaders were formed. The political leaders who were to take the lead in the postwar decolonization process were invariably educated in mission schools. And the leading figures in literature, such as Ngũgĩ, also first struggled with the issue of finding a voice with the benefit of their mission school educations.

That education, as Ngũgĩ notes, was carefully circumscribed. Contemporary novels included in school libraries were carefully chosen "so as not to expose the young minds to dangerous, undesirable and unacceptable moral and political influence" (*Decolonising* 69). Yet that education repeatedly exposed the embryonic author to the powerful stimulus of the Christian literary tradition as found in the Bible, the Book of Common Prayer, and John Bunyan's *The Pilgrim's Progress*—three of the most influential texts commonly cited by African writers. Latin American writers developed a similar familiarity with the texts of Holy Scripture. While missionaries often exhibited a great cultural intolerance, they did make one extremely significant contribution to the development of indigenous culture: because of the need to speak native tongues for evangelical work, missionary societies often devoted themselves to a systematic study of indigenous languages and literatures. Groves calls such linguistic study one of the missionaries' greatest contributions to Africa, noting that it gave the Africans the feeling that their culture was worthy of respect and study (484). In 1926, prompted by missionary initiative, an International Institute of African Languages and Cultures was formed to conduct linguistic, literary, ethnographical and sociocultural studies (Baëta 434). Similar linguistic and cultural studies were encouraged on other mission fields, and today the Wycliffe Bible Translators organization continues to provide extensive linguistic training for its missionaries, who study oral indigenous languages and transcribe them into written form.

Although employed as a tool of imperialism and oppression, Christianity, through missionary activities, also sometimes served to battle imperialism and oppression. Christianity occasionally offered a countercultural voice in opposition to the hegemony of colonialism. In this fight against in-

justice, Christians were being true to their biblical roots. The call for justice is articulated in many forms in the Bible. The Exodus story begins
with the divine command to "let my people go," and follows the people
of Israel out of bondage, through the wilderness, and into the Promised
Land, thus providing a mythology and rhetoric for oppressed people
across the globe. The prophetic words of Isaiah speak eloquently against
oppressors:

> Ah, you who make iniquitous decrees,
>   who write oppressive statutes,
> to turn aside the needy from justice
>   and to rob the poor of my people of their right,
> that widows may be your spoil,
>   and that you may make the orphans your prey! (10:1−2)

Isaiah calls Israel not to meaningless religious ritual but to active work
against physical oppression:

> Is not this the fast that I choose:
>   to loose the bonds of injustice,
>   to undo the thongs of the yoke,
> to let the oppressed go free, and to break every yoke?
> Is it not to share your bread with the hungry,
>   and bring the homeless poor into your house;
> when you see the naked, to cover them,
>   and not to hide yourself from your own kin? (58:6−7)

In the New Testament, Jesus, "the prince of peace," issues a similar command to care for the poor and the oppressed. In his ministry, he embraced
the Others of the Hebrew world: women, simple fishermen, those with
mental illnesses or leprosy, and the ethnically alienated Samaritans. Furthermore, the heavenly kingdom envisioned in the apocalyptic texts of
Daniel and Revelation is one in which justice reigns and nations are united
with nations.

During the process of colonization these biblical narratives and images
permeated the world. In *Exodus and Revolution*, Michael Walzer discusses
how the story of deliverance from oppression embodied in Exodus has
served as the origin and controlling metaphor for most of the liberation
movements in the political history of the West. "The Exodus is a story,"
he says, "a big story, one that became part of the cultural consciousness of
the West—so that a range of political events . . . have been located and
understood within the narrative frame it provides" (7). However, as a part

of the cultural consciousness of the West, the biblical call for justice as rendered in Exodus and other texts has sometimes paradoxically served as a tool of oppression. Look, for instance, at the way the rhetoric of Exodus was employed by the Puritan settlers of North America or by the Afrikaner theologians of South Africa. As we have seen, the power of Western religious discourse to grant legitimacy and moral certitude to many of the excesses and evils of colonization cannot be overlooked.

While some, such as Forrest G. Wood, have consequently argued that Christianity is fundamentally racist and oppressive in ideology, organization, and practice, many people—both members of colonizing nations and victims of colonization—believe that Christianity and the biblical text embody an ideal of justice that is fundamentally opposed to oppression. As many of our contributors demonstrate, biblical rhetoric frequently has been appropriated by many colonized peoples as particularly appropriate to and empowering for their situations. The American slave Frederick Douglass, for example, after defying the brutal treatment of a slave-breaker, speaks of his new-found psychological freedom as "a glorious resurrection, from the tomb of slavery, to the heaven of freedom." Such appropriation is not a mindless absorption of the dominant culture but rather a careful discernment of cultural limits. After repeatedly finding the so-called "Christian" slave owners in the southern United States the most cruel and reprehensible masters, Douglass could still insist on a crucial difference between "the Christianity of this land, and the Christianity of Christ" (113, 153). Fanon draws a similar distinction when he says, "The Church in the colonies is the white people's Church, the foreigner's Church. She does not call the native to God's ways but to the ways of the white man, of the master, of the oppressor" (34). But, given the cultural context of understanding, how can we understand God's ways, or the Christianity of Christ? Can Christianity be comprehended outside of the Western cultural tradition of which it is so crucial a part?

One such attempt has been made by the Catholic priest Vincent J. Donovan, who was sent to work among the Masai people of Africa in the 1960s. Conscious of the previous missionary imposition of Western customs and culture, Donovan rejected ties to mission schools and hospitals, choosing instead to live among the Masai and to attempt to communicate the essential message of the Bible without cultural trappings. Yet he soon realized that the means of salvation came *through* culture: "As I began to ponder the evangelization of the Masai, I had to realize that God enables a people, any people, to reach salvation through their culture and tribal, racial customs and traditions. . . . I had no right to disrupt this body of customs, of traditions. It was the way of salvation for these people, their way to God" (30). Giving up a Western cultural interpretation in order to see the meaning of the Bible in the context of Masai culture opened up new ways of understanding for Donovan. What he calls his "rediscovery of Christianity" through the eyes of the Masai demonstrates the value of cross-cultural dialogue for enlightening Western thought.

Other new perspectives on Christianity have emerged in the past two decades by means of the growth and development of different Third-World, or liberation, theologies. Such theologies explore new ways to understand the Bible, to practice Christianity, to be the church. Often originating within communities of oppressed or postcolonial people, such theologies share a commitment to social justice, emphasize the contextual nature of theological understanding, and call for new views to be expressed "from the underside," from the perspective of the oppressed (Thistlethwaite and Engel 1–20). Liberation theologies have emerged from the various contexts experienced by African Americans, women, Latin Americans, Africans, and Asians. But in each case, "theologians throughout the world who felt a call to speak more relevantly to their age and generation freed themselves from traditional dogmatic and systematic theology and focused on life issues. Instead of telling people what questions to ask and then furnishing them with the answers, theologians began to listen to the questions people were asking and then seek the answers" (Oduyoye 3). Simultaneously affirming both solidarity and variety, sharing a common method and commitment, liberation theologies provide new ways of understanding the Christian tradition and of putting that tradition into action.

Perhaps the best known of liberation theologies is that developed in Latin America, a theology emphasizing the need for liberation from the structures of unjust economic domination and exploitation. The proclamations of the Conference of Latin American Bishops—particularly in Medellín in 1968—Gustavo Gutiérrez's *A Theology of Liberation* (1971), and Juan Segundo's *The Liberation of Theology* (1975) first defined and called for a new kind of theology that spoke to the Latin American postcolonial situation. Viewing economic oppression as a structural manifestation of sin in the world and often drawing on Marxist analysis to provide a theoretical explanation for the existence of injustice, these liberation theologians call for both economic and existential freedom for the Others of the world. Gutiérrez writes, "The goal is not only better living conditions, a radical change of structures, a social revolution; it is much more: the continuous

creation, never ending, of a new way to be a man, a *permanent cultural
revolution*" (*Theology* 32).

In Africa, with its different colonial history, liberation theology has been
more concerned to identify the problems that arose when Western Christians confused the material and the spiritual to embrace an imperialistic
Christianity that fused the political and the religious. Allan Boesak, a black
South African theologian of the Reformed tradition, distinguishes sharply
between the state and Christianity, a distinction that is tragically obscured
in his country: "It is my conviction that, for a Christian, obedience to the
state or any earthly authority is always linked to our obedience to God.
That is to say, obedience to human institutions (and to human beings) is
always relative. The human institution can never have the same authority
as God, and human laws must always be subordinate to the word of God"
(35). Such convictions prompt new readings of the Bible from African
perspectives. The demanding task of the African theologian, Dickson says,
is not simply to pass on Western theology but rather to look at Scripture
anew in the light of African culture (7–8). Like Douglass, these theologians are attempting to embrace the Christianity of the Bible rather than
the Christianity of Europe.

These liberation theologies, among others (such as those provided by
feminist theologians), suggest one fertile flowering of the multirunnered
rhizome, one way that silenced voices have dialogued with the traditional
biblical text. Several of the contributors to this volume, especially those discussing Latin American texts, draw on such liberation theologies, although
our contributors differ in their critique of the relationship of Marxism and
liberation theology. Others understand the biblical call for justice in light
of the Reformed tradition, which from the time of John Calvin has stressed
the importance of "world-formative" Christianity, a Christianity devoted
to reforming the distorted and unjust structures of the social world.[7] As
developed by the turn-of-the-century Dutch theologian Abraham Kuyper,
this tradition has emphasized the necessity for structural change, for the
reformation of society to better reflect God's ideals: "When rich and poor
stand opposed to each other, [God] never takes His place with the wealth-
ier, but always stands with the poorer. . . . We shall not be satisfied with
the structure of society until it offers all human beings an existence worthy
of man. Until then, the structure must remain the object of our *criticism*"
(27, 57 n).

The Calvinist tradition has long advocated political activism, as Michael
Walzer chronicles in *Revolution of the Saints* (1965). South African theo-

logians and pastors opposed to apartheid, such as Allan Boesak, are some
of the most recent and prominent examples of this long Reformed tradition
of resistance. Perhaps the most articulate contemporary development of this
perspective is provided by Yale philosopher Nicholas Wolterstorff in *Until
Justice and Peace Embrace* (1983). "The saints are responsible for the structure of the social world in which they find themselves," Wolterstorff writes,
"That structure is not simply part of the order of nature; to the contrary, it
is the result of human decision, and by concerted effort it can be altered.
Indeed, it *should* be altered, for it is a fallen structure, in need of reform.
The responsibility of the saints to struggle for the reform of the social order
in which they find themselves is one facet of the discipleship to which their
Lord Jesus Christ has called them" (3). Similar to various liberation theologies, Reformed theology claims that sin and salvation encompass both
social as well as individual reality. But Wolterstorff views the biblical call
for justice within the larger context of *shalom*, the Hebrew word for *peace:*
"Shalom is the human being dwelling at peace in all his or her relationships: with God, with self, with fellows, with nature" (69). Such peace,
Wolterstorff continues, involves not only the absence of hostility but also
an enjoyment and delight in harmonious relationships. Biblical texts that
call for justice participate in this larger call for *shalom*, and the *shalom*
perspective "incorporates but goes beyond the salvation perspective of the
liberation theologians" to include "the pursuit of increased mastery of the
world so as to enrich human life" (72). Justice, thus understood, involves
the freedom to create works of art and to explore intellectually.

In examining a variety of postcolonial works in the context of the biblical
call for justice, the contributors to this volume draw on these various theological perspectives. Common motifs include how biblical justice challenges poststructuralism, the tensions and conflicts that occur in a synthesis
of Christianity and indigenous cultures, and the ethical and aesthetic dilemmas faced by authors and critics who oppose injustice. Moving progressively from the Americas to Africa, and appropriately concluding in the
tumultuous Middle East, these essays identify numerous ways in which
biblical justice has informed and been informed by postcolonial literature.
    The volume opens with a confrontation between postmodernism and
postcolonial literature in Ed Block's "Experience, Existence, and Mystery:
Biblical Ideas of Justice in Postcolonial Fiction." Block argues that much
postcolonial literature, with its concern for a justice that is compatible with
biblical notions, is much more profound and ethical than postmodernist

fiction. Defining two forms of biblical justice—distributive justice and existential justice—Block examines these concepts with examples from Nadine Gordimer, Milan Kundera, Mario Vargas Llosa, and Gabriel García Márquez. Novels focusing on distributive justice oppose specific material forms of injustice and represent the redressing of evils wrought by oppression. Novels of existential justice suggest the mysterious sense of beatitude experienced in performing acts of justice for their own sake, in spite of their futility and often negligible effects. Experiential novels generally deal with specific regions and sociopolitical causes, in the realist tradition, while existential novels focus less on specific places or causes to explore a sense of mission or vocation and the depth of love that motivates particular characters in the quest for justice. Throughout his discussion, Block perceives that authors may give voice to ineffable notions of justice without necessarily working from an expressly Christian horizon.

Distributive justice is the primary concern of Ernesto Cardenal, the Nicaraguan poet discussed in Terry DeHay's "The Kingdom of God on Earth: Ernesto Cardenal's *Salmos*." DeHay's essay examines the life and thought of this ordained priest and minister of culture in the Sandinista government, analyzing how Cardenal's belief in liberation theology emerges in his *Salmos*, a revision of the Psalms to reflect the struggle for justice in Latin America. Examining such devices as his contemporary language, concrete images, and significant changes in tone and themes from the Psalms, the essay shows how Cardenal criticizes the oppressor and praises the communal strength and commitment of the people. DeHay employs Raymond Williams's theory of hegemony and the residual to explain Cardenal's curious merging of Christianity and Marxism, and she convincingly demonstrates the powerful cross-fertilization occurring between the Hebraic Psalms and modern Nicaraguan life.

Biblical imagery and motifs pervade Latin American writing. In Chapter 3, "Biblical Justice and the Military Hero in Two Novels of Gabriel García Márquez," Lourdes Elena Morales-Gudmundsson demonstrates how this imagery functions in the work of perhaps the most prominent Latin American novelist. Citing García Márquez's interest in the Bible "as a primitive and gutsy text" and his familiarity with liberation theology, Morales-Gudmundsson shows how he draws on the durable structures, symbols, and themes of the Bible in two novels that expose the fundamental sinfulness at the heart of the human struggle for power. With a formal analysis of *No One Writes to the Colonel* and *The Autumn of the Patriarch*, Morales-Gudmundsson reveals how the Colombian novelist uses biblical and liberationist concepts as a way to build his own theology of justice.

Another theology of justice—this time feminist in nature—is discussed by Claudia Marie Kovach in "Mask and Mirror: Isabel Allende's Mechanism for Justice in *The House of the Spirits*." Kovach's analysis of the central female characters in Allende's novel moves away from the distributive justice of Cardenal and García Márquez (which we might characterize as more masculine) toward Block's notion of existential justice, in a meditation on the psychological and spiritual dimensions of the characters. A basic requirement for distributive justice, she notes, is individual conversion, a recovery of identity that comes from connectedness to family and culture. Allende's novel depicts the physical and psychological oppression meted out to women in Latin America, and Kovach argues that the recovery and reconstitution of these lost identities is one of the primary responsibilities of liberationists. Drawing on the work of feminist theologian Elisabeth Schüssler Fiorenza, Kovach suggests that justice can arise through a community of women who reunite the fragments of self and community through repeated memories, solidarity, and equality. The female characters in *The House of the Spirits* serve as such rememberers and mediators, bringing together the rational and the irrational, the mirror and the mask, the poor and the rich, enacting a call to justice even in the midst of their oppression.

Allende's novel includes disturbing scenes of rape and torture—a deeply troubling twentieth-century reality of oppression, as Amnesty International continues to remind us. Lois Parkinson Zamora takes up the issue of political torture in "Deciphering the Wounds: The Politics of Torture and Julio Cortázar's Literature of Embodiment." Zamora outlines a critical approach to what she terms *la literatura de denuncia*, literature that impugns political torture, using the phenomenological theories of Maurice Merleau-Ponty to examine the way the "lived body" takes an active part in conferring meanings upon the world and the ways in which literature projects that participation. She then shows how the Argentinean writer Cortázar strives to make material the immaterial pain of the victim, to shape the physical matter of history with language, and to assign it significance. The essay relates the literary project of embodiment, in which the flesh is made word, to the Christian concept of incarnation, in which the word is made flesh. Suggesting that in Latin American religious culture the physicality of Christ and his suffering has maintained a higher degree of significance than in Anglo-American culture, Zamora concludes with an account of the peasant art of Solantiname and Cortázar's response to that art. His literary exploration of the relation between physical suffering and ontological significance thus links his late fiction to biblical concepts of being and justice.

Solantiname contains, as Zamora elaborates, a fertile mix of peasant art with biblical images, but religious colonization is not always so fruitful; instead, it can result in troublesome tensions, as our next couple of contributors explore. In "Charles Eastman, Nicholas Black Elk, and the Construction of Religious Identity," Bradley J. Monsma demonstrates, in a close analysis of the paradigmatic cases of two native American authors, not only what is lost when a writer capitulates to the colonizer's dichotomies but also what can be gained by refusing such dichotomies. While Charles Eastman attempts to assimilate, adopting both the religion and the cultural values of the colonizer, Nicholas Black Elk embraces Christianity but still retains his Lakota identity and beliefs. Black Elk works to construct an identity from the multifaceted complexities of both his native American world and the colonizer's Anglo-Christian world, thus adding to and expanding both traditions. The differing religious negotiations of Eastman and Black Elk, Monsma concludes, inform some of the current political struggles of native Americans today.

Another look at the tensions implicit in religious colonization appears in John C. Hawley's "We Wretched of the Earth: The Search for a Language of Justice." Noting that missiology too often has joined the side of oppression by discouraging the use of indigenous languages and cultures, Hawley discusses how the act of embracing the conqueror's religion is frequently more restricting than liberating, as the examples of Jose Maria Arguedas and Ngũgĩ wa Thiong'o demonstrate. How can Christianity find a language that liberates rather than oppresses? Drawing on both liberation theologians and the literary theories of Mikhail Bakhtin, Hawley concludes that the poor are the most eloquent teachers of the language modern Christianity needs.

Further application of the theories of Mikhail Bakhtin occurs in my essay, "The Dialogical Imagination of Chinua Achebe." After examining Achebe's complex inheritance of indigenous and European languages, literary forms, and definitions of art, I explicate the numerous voices, or strata of discourses, that appear in *Things Fall Apart*, Achebe's most famous novel. This classic postcolonial novel exemplifies Bakhtin's notion of polyphonic discourse both in its form and in the thematic implications of that form for issues of postcolonialism and Christianity. Ultimately, I argue, Achebe's heteroglossia suggests a dialogical rather than hierarchical interaction in which each tradition questions both itself and the other, especially with respect to the idea of justice.

The mediation between indigenous culture and the colonizer's religion in

Africa is explored further by Oliver Lovesey in "'The Sound of the Horn of Justice' in Ngūgī wa Thiong'o's Narrative." Delineating the struggle that Ngūgī faced in accepting the colonizer's language, literary forms, and religion, Lovesey looks at Ngūgī's curious adoption of biblical narrative and Bunyanesque allegory in two of his recent novels. Since Ngūgī's intended readers for *Devil on the Cross* and *Matigari* (both written in Gikuyu) are the peasants of his homeland, who are deeply familiar with biblical stories, in these works Ngūgī turns to the Bible for images and narratives. Lovesey's analysis shows how Ngūgī's radical use of biblical narrative draws on that narrative's metaphysical, transformative power and demands an active community response to calls for truth, justice, and liberation.

Chapter Ten, "Comrade Jesus: Postcolonial Literature and the Story of Christ," by Norman R. Cary, takes one particular biblical narrative—the story of Christ—and examines how it has been appropriated in a similar fashion by a number of different postcolonial writers. Cary gives a detailed reading of two Christ narratives that appear in Ngūgī's earlier novel, *A Grain of Wheat*, and also analyzes Augusto Roa Bastos's *Son of Man*, Roger Mais's *Brother Man*, and Naguib Mahfouz's *Children of Gebelaawi*. He concludes that these varied authors have replaced the European Christ story, which they associate with religious and cultural subjugation, with an indigenized Christ, whom they associate with liberation and justice.

Justice is integrally connected to the notion of history, as all four authors Cary discusses show in their choice of the historical narrative of Christ to provide a structural pattern for their works. In South Africa, justice and history are even more closely related, as is evidenced by the distortions of history practiced by the white South African government. In "The Nightmare of History Revisited: André Brink's *An Instant in the Wind*," Alan Jacobs analyzes the strategies of one Afrikaner novelist who wishes to repudiate the dominant mode of history practiced by his community. Jacobs's essay provides a brief account of the tradition of Afrikaner self-interpretation and typological view of history and then explores the alternative view of history presented by Brink. Beginning with an obscure historical incident in which a white woman and runaway slave find themselves alone in the interior of the Cape region, Brink constructs a novel illustrating a philosophy of history that radically opposes Afrikaner thinking. His alternative, Jacobs shows, is a romantic individualism, positing a self independent of any social Other, and so ironically confirms the inevitability of tragedy in South African history. Brink provides an inadequate escape from history,

Jacobs argues, concluding that perhaps it is time for a reassessment of the work of Alan Paton, who may be a more successfully "connected critic," in Michael Walzer's terms.

The question of what a committed criticism should entail is examined most fully in the volume's concluding essay, Mark Walhout's "The *Intifada* in Criticism: An Ecumenical Perspective on the Walzer-Said Exchange." Walhout examines an exchange between two eminent cultural critics, the Jewish writer Michael Walzer and the Palestinian writer Edward Said. After reviewing the modes of criticism practiced by each, the essay then analyzes their vehement published debate over Walzer's *Exodus and Revolution*. A key focus of that debate concerns the role of the biblical conquest of the promised land and the founding of the modern Jewish state. Both authors believe that the critic should be connected with a particular people and their fate, but Walzer and Said differ in their belief as to how one should choose and manifest that connection. Walhout points out the failure of the two to achieve genuine dialogue, argues for the importance of a communal commitment, and concludes that true justice depends on how the critic works out that commitment.

The differing literatures and issues addressed throughout this collection suggest the tremendous variety within the field of postcolonial literature. Unquestionably other literatures could be included: the epic poetry of Derek Walcott; the cross-cultural fiction and essays of V. S. Naipaul; the flourishing African-American literary tradition; or Indian writers such as Anita Desai, Mannu Bhandari, and Krishna Sobti. Even the list of what has been omitted from such a volume must remain tentative. The postcolonial world contains an embarrassment of riches, a wealth of new nations, old peoples, and productive traditions. This collection celebrates that diversity.

Yet it also reveals that a recurring theme and concern in postcolonial literature is a call for justice, a concern with community and equality, a development of lost or suppressed cultural potential. Given the diversity of authors and traditions discussed here, the recurrence of such concerns demonstrates a commitment to the ideal of justice that crosses cultural barriers and is shared by numerous people in very different historical circumstances. That ideal also emerges as a major concern within the biblical tradition, particularly as understood and elaborated by various liberation theologies. The dialogues and exchanges that ensue between postcolonial people and the Christian tradition provide the common thread that appears in the rich tapestry of postcolonial literatures discussed here, and this collection serves to encourage that dialogue and continued mutual edification.

Finally, *Postcolonial Literature and the Biblical Call for Justice* provides some new and useful ways to talk about postcolonial literature; it allows us to hear some unrecognized voices within the heteroglossia of postcolonialism and so functions to highlight some conflicts and paradoxes within the history of colonialism and Christianity. The biblical call for justice is an often unrecognized voice within the cultural dialogue. Paying attention to such a voice is, in the very act of criticism itself, an act of justice. The authors of the essays in this anthology, from within a number of different personal religious traditions, share a common dedication to the elimination of injustice and oppression and thus take their stand as committed critics in today's poststructural world.

1

Experience, Existence, and Mystery
Biblical Ideas of Justice in Postcolonial Fiction

ED BLOCK, JR.

We live in an era that denigrates both the significance of the responsible individual agent and moral codes applicable across diverse cultures. In such an era, the concept of justice—what Chaim Perelman has called "one of the world's most highly respected notions" (5)—has the potential to transcend the disparate interests of a pluralistic world. Ideas of justice, whether derived from the Judeo-Christian tradition or other cultures' conceptions, have the potential of initiating a dialogue and thereby greater understanding of what writers in disparate national literatures are seeking to affirm. At such a time the Christian critic has a unique opportunity to contribute to the discussion of justice by focusing on the different biblical senses and uses of the concept. In what follows I shall suggest that a concern with exploitation, oppression, colonization, and acculturation (or the obliteration of cultural difference through a homogenizing of life habits and values) unites a variety of postcolonial literatures. My examples, drawn not only from the literatures of Africa and the Americas but also from Eastern Europe, will seek to show that justice as a category of understanding helps us transcend the usual boundaries set for understanding postcolonial literature.

What first attracts attention to this class of works that have justice as a uniting element is their difference from many novels of developed Western countries. The sense of difference in these novels is not the poststructuralist difference of exoticism, perversity, or "illegibility." Their alterity results from a sense of weight and seriousness. Like Dantean comedy, they acknowledge, even celebrate, existence and mystery even in the midst of seemingly overwhelming misery. Their effect resembles the ethical/spiritual claim that the tradition of British and continental fiction possessed until that claim was eroded by skeptical poststructuralist theory and practice. In part these works manifest the struggle for justice in the way they represent human beings in their identification with the particularities of place, cause, vocation, and love. By means of these categories I shall explore the way in which the multiform struggle for justice is found in a variety of postcolonial novels.

By *place* I mean a sense of abode, or more broadly a situation, a rootedness in the particularities of individual cultures and mores. *Cause* is a way to class those events or conflicts which are of a life-and-death seriousness to the characters rooted in place, and to which they almost matter-of-factly devote or even give their lives. *Vocation* refers to an attitude or disposition, a sense of particular mission that the people of these works manifest, vocation to particular causes being one significant but not exclusive form. Medicine, politics, and ethnology are other important vocations, but almost equally important are vocations in farming, engineering, parenting, and romantic loving. A sense of vocation lends nobility but also uniqueness to these characters. *Love,* in these novels, has multiple meanings: from importunate and lawless erotic love to a deepening sense of familial, maternal, and even patriotic love. But love is always a mysterious force, not because of its obsessiveness, aggression, and perversity, but because of its origins, depth, strength, and almost preternatural staying power.

In the works to which I refer, biblical justice takes two related forms. For clarity's sake we can distinguish in biblical authors from Ezra to John two kinds of justice: "distributive" (and its related "retributive") justice, and the more mysterious and more awesome justice of God, often found in the image of "Yahweh, the sun of righteousness."[1] The first can be exemplified negatively by the following passage from the prophet Amos: "they sell the righteous for silver, and the needy for a pair of sandals—they who trample the head of the poor into the dust of the earth, and push the afflicted out of the way" (2:6−7). In his criticism of specific injustices the prophet implies a call for distributive justice, which here means giving the poor and the needy what they require, their due. To be just means opposing the attitudes that make such exploitation possible. Justice means treating the poor, as well as those who are already right-minded, not as commodities to be sold. Implicit in these injunctions is a respect for individual persons.

Of the second kind of justice the Psalmist says: "As for me, I shall behold your face in righteousness; / when I awake I shall be satisfied beholding your likeness" (Ps. 17: 15). It is more difficult to infer from this passage the meaning of the justice of Yahweh than it is to see distributive justice in the book of Amos. But the justice of Yahweh means something like dwelling in righteousness, in the virtues implied by the passage from Amos, to such an extent that righteousness, or justice, is its own reward. In some fashion the righteous individual enjoys a vision of goodness, a vision of Yahweh. It is a reality only dimly suggested by the richness enfolded in the concept of *shalom*. Experientially, perhaps, this sense of justice is that furtive glimpse of beatitude that reveals itself when we have done any good deed for its own sake, and God's. To take another example, in the book of the prophet Malachi we find these words: "For you who revere my name the sun of righteousness shall rise, with healing in its wings" (4:2). Once again, poetic expression signifies an almost ineffable experience. The justice of Yahweh is simultaneously like the sun rising and like a bird (it would be the Holy Spirit in a later, New Testament tradition) descending with "healing in its wings."

John R. Donahue, a contemporary theologian of biblical justice, summarizes: "The justice of God is both gift and mystery and the attempt to crystallize it by human standards can result in destroying the proper relation with Yahweh. To be just is to be open to the world as gift and God as mystery" (71). A final example from the Psalms shows how both ideas of justice often combine in a single text for a single effect. Psalm 146 is basically a hymn of praise:

Praise the LORD!
Praise the LORD, O my soul!
I will praise the LORD as long as I live;
    I will sing praises to my God all my life long.
Do not put your trust in princes,
    in mortals, in whom there is no help.
When their breath departs, they return to the earth;
    on that very day their plans perish.
Happy are those whose help is the God of Jacob,
    whose hope is in the LORD their God,
who made heaven and earth, the sea, and all that is in them;

who keeps faith forever;
    who executes justice for the oppressed;
    who gives food to the hungry.   (1−7)

This Psalm expresses a love of life realized from the very beginning in
an attitude of loving praise of Yahweh. The first lines express an almost
boundless sense of gratitude at the mystery of Yahweh's justice. This sense
surpasses, seems not even to rest upon, specific deeds of distributive justice,
to which the remaining lines nevertheless refer. To this abiding predisposition ("all my life long") the passage contrasts a life of earthly attainments,
influence, power. The ground of this abiding happiness comes in the trust
that the Psalmist places in Yahweh, "who keeps faith forever." This faith
in Yahweh, however, is linked immediately with Yahweh's help for the
oppressed who may indeed include the speaker, the Psalmist himself. The
justice of Yahweh forms the unconsciously accepted ground from which the
assertions of Yahweh's distributive justice proceed. This Psalm compre-
hends both the biblical ground of distributive justice and the justice of
Yahweh. It is a justice born of divine and human love. Not worldly wealth
and influence, but life itself, and life lived according to the laws of Yahweh,
are what make life worth living. To live according to this inner conviction
and vision is to live justly.

From this complex unity of the two kinds of justice we may infer that
for a literary work to reflect biblical ideas of distributive or retributive
justice, that work's concerns for the oppressed must not be conceived of
merely in political or social terms. Novels that emphasize biblical ideals of
justice begin with respect for personhood but translate that predisposition
into actions that serve to affirm the poor, to ameliorate the lot of the oppressed, or to oppose the forces of injustice. The ground of such concern
must be a confident and affirmative love that acknowledges and accepts.
The widows, the orphans, the poor, and the marginalized must be seen as
human beings deserving of respect and love. The mystery of their personhood must be acknowledged. They cannot be conceived of purely as forces
in global or regional struggles for power, dominance, or even equality.

In much postcolonial literature we find just such affirmation and action.
One thinks of the white and black characters in Athol Fugard's dramas,
talking to each other, sharing their ordeals, and seeking a sense of common
justice. In *"Master Harold"*. . . *and the Boys* (1982), young white Hally is
suffering through his alcoholic father's hospitalization. In the course of a
rainy afternoon in St. George's Tea Room, he learns to appreciate and

acknowledge the wisdom and sense of justice of the black employees, Willie and Sam. For Sam, a ballroom dancing championship is a metaphor for the ideal of a harmonious life:

> SAM: For as long as the music lasts, we are going to see six couples get it right, the way we want life to be.
> HALLY: But is that the best we can do, Sam . . . watch six finalists dreaming about the way it should be?
> SAM: I don't know. But it starts with that. Without the dream we won't know what we're going for.   (46)

Even when, in his pain and anger at having betrayed his own ideals, Hally leaves the Tea Room for the hospital, he will not forget that image or the story Sam has told of an earlier shared experience, when he responded to Hally's plea for help in fetching his father:

> SAM: Remember? He was dead drunk on the floor of the Central Bar . . . You went in first by yourself to ask permission for me to go into the bar. Then I loaded him onto my back like a bag and carried him back to the boarding house . . . A crowded Main Street with all the people watching a little white boy following his drunk father on a nigger's back! I felt for that little boy . . . Master Harold.   (58–59)

Sam's reminder is a plea not only for justice but love, and simple fellow-feeling for another human being.

An active commitment to distributive justice may also involve solitary commitment to a specific course of action: in short, a vocation, within a particular nation or historical period. Such a witness to justice, ahead of and often in the face of the community, may involve isolation or rejection; it often involves profound sacrifice. The Bible, the New Testament particularly, gives us a paradigm in the lives of the prophets and the life of Jesus.

As an example of the isolated individual pursuing his or her vocation for the realization of distributive justice, I would single out Mario Vargas Llosa's *The Real Life of Alejandro Mayta* (1986), in which the narrator tries to discover the whereabouts of Mayta, a Lima-bred Peruvian revolutionary who had struggled to mount a coup against the government by mobilizing the Andean peasants. The coup had failed, and Mayta's young lieutenant was killed. Mayta himself had disappeared. After a prolonged search that uncovers the details of the coup attempt and Mayta's lonely labor for the poor, the narrator finds the protagonist released after an ordeal in prison, still working for social change on a humbler scale. Mayta continues to live out his life in prophetic fashion, even after his grand gesture, the coup, has failed. Although the narrator seems uncomprehending and his final vision of Mayta is contradictory, the tale of justice is wiser than its urbane and almost skeptical teller. The image of Mayta organizing a food kiosk in prison is humble yet eloquent in its manifestation of what the atheist Vargas Llosa could not have said had he wanted to. "'We created genuine revolution,' he assures me with pride. 'We won the respect of the whole place. We boiled the water for making fruit juice, for coffee, for everything. We washed the knives, forks, and spoons, the glasses, and the plates before and after they were used. Hygiene, above all. A revolution, you bet'" (294). Care and concern for the prisoner bespeaks a commitment to justice. The self-sacrificial image of Mayta adumbrates that of Christ in the gospel. Mayta's vocation, lived out in the particular circumstances of Peru in the 1950s, manifests the biblical ideal of long-suffering struggle to achieve distributive justice.[2]

Endorsing Mayta's turn from political struggle to something like community involvement, scholars of biblical justice say that justice derives as much from keeping faith with a community and struggling to maintain that community as it does from any direct, political action. Donahue writes, "To live in Old Testament terms is to be open to relationships. For the Israelite death is not simply the cessation of life but the end of a relation to Yahweh, to fellow Israelites and to the land. In most general terms justice is fidelity to this threefold relationship by which life is maintained" (77). Justice, then, establishes, maintains, and renews community. From Donahue's words we might conclude that to be a voice of justice, a work must embody one or more of the following: (1) the voice of a particular people, (2) the prophetic voice of a person, or (3) a situation that cries out for justice.

Novels that manifest the struggle for distributive justice are often relatively easy to classify because of their emphasis on place and cause. To determine whether a particular work reflects the biblical idea of Yahweh's justice is more difficult. However, the Book of Job and the Beatitudes can be good touchstones. Here the themes of persevering in one's vocation and abiding in love also assume greater importance. Furthermore, if a work reflects a hesitant attitude toward all human ideas of justice, without slipping into nihilism, skepticism, or relativism, it may be interpreted as reaching toward that dark center of visionary awareness that understands human limits without denying a more profound respect in which justice is to be achieved or is, in fact, already being achieved despite its apparent absence or defeat. If the work sides with the poor, the oppressed, and those animated by an intangible ideal like peace or justice, then such a work at least implicitly illuminates biblical themes of justice.

The concern for distributive justice is most prominent and manifests itself in themes having to do with political and prophetic causes in particular places and times. For example, *The Real Life of Alejandro Mayta* analyzes the plight of the Peruvian poor. Mongane Serote's *To Every Birth Its Blood* (1983) and Nadine Gordimer's *A Sport of Nature* (1988) envision the overthrow of South African apartheid. In contrast, the concern for the justice of Yahweh manifests itself in themes that reverence the individual and his or her ability to act responsibly, justly, and humanely, in spite of overwhelming odds. These novels frequently have an almost eschatological vision of justice. They also emphasize those personal and, in Milan Kundera's words, "suprapersonal" (*Art* 158) attitudes, predispositions, and habits that allow individuals to treat each other as part of a community indebted to and informed by similar ideals of justice and love. While a rootedness in place may be present, and sensitivity to causes at least implicit, vocation and love are the most prominent themes. Gabriel García Márquez's *Love in the Time of Cholera* (1988) preaches no overt political lesson but intimates that love (even in the steaming degeneracy of a fictive city resembling Cartagena, Colombia) is a transcendent power of transformation and endurance. Vargas Llosa's *The Storyteller* (1989), imagining no primitivist utopia, nevertheless envisions the personal devotion of a white outsider to the preservation of a primitive tribe's difficult but authentic way of life and its relation to the earth, its religion, and its values. Speaking with Mascarita, the outcast linguist-turned-storyteller, the narrator asks what four hundred years of oppression mean to him: "'That these cultures must be respected,' he said softly, as though finally beginning to calm down. 'And the only way to respect them is not to go near them. Not touch them. Our culture is too strong, too aggressive. It devours everything it touches. They must be left alone'" (98, 99). Such a vocation to prevent acculturation bespeaks a devotion to an at least arguably transcendent ideal of justice.

In its concern for the two types of justice, postcolonial fiction may distinguish itself structurally as well. Gordimer's *My Son's Story* (1990) is set in the townships of South Africa and maintains a predominantly realistic structure and style, despite its innovative treatment of viewpoint and chronology. But other works are more inclined to "imaginative," even fantastic structure and style, in which we can see an intimation of God's mysterious justice. It seems appropriate that *Love in the Time of Cholera* manifests (despite its historical foundation) a quality of "magic realism" or that *The Storyteller* has about it an almost mythic quality. In such novels the concern for justice may then express itself in highly oblique ways. One might note, first of all, an inclination to parable and other hyperbolic genres. In the short fiction of the late Argentinian exile Julio Cortázar, for instance, the critique of oppression occurs by means of parables like "A Small Paradise" in *A Certain Lucas* (1984). Here an almost impassive narrator describes the populace of a fictive, almost fairy-tale country, ruled by a general, oppressed by its colonels, and addicted to millions of "little gold fishes" coursing through their blood. Cortázar's commitment to justice and truth is transparent despite the impassive narrator and the parabolic style. García Márquez's short tale "A Very Old Man with Enormous Wings" is also a subtle critique of social and religious mores, couched in the form of fantasy. As Michael Wood notes, "García Márquez's legends and tall tales, allow [him] to depict not only the social and material world shared by so many novels, but the same world infiltrated by ghosts and lies and unshakable memories" (34). One further way to identify such a novel, then, is to look for incursions of fantasy, hyperbole, or parable.

Besides affecting genre and structure, an intense concern for the forms and effects of oppression can also strain the style of some postcolonial fiction into a distinctly surrealistic mode, conveying the sense of incomprehensible mystery that surrounds, invades, and forms the matrix within which exiles, fugitives, and the oppressed must exist. Again, Cortázar's fictions are a principal example. Surrounding the ironically unreal story of the political kidnapping of a pair of penguins, *A Manual for Manuel* (1978) builds a surreal tale of outcasts and exiles. Parts of *Love in the Time of Cholera* take on a similarly surreal quality.

Another way in which postcolonial fiction may express the plight of the oppressed is in the fragmentation of the narrator/speaker. Cortázar ironizes and marginalizes his speaker/narrators to embody the anguish, the help-lessness, and the gaiety verging on despair that homeless exiles experience. The narrator of Vargas Llosa's *The Storyteller* and the figure of the story-teller himself, Mascarita (alias Saúl Zuratas), are figures living in exile, between two worlds: a world of empty affluence on the one hand, and on the other a primitive world about to be absorbed by the modern, affluent one. The stories that the narrator and the storyteller each relate are them-selves fragmented in time, in genre, and in subject matter. These tech-niques serve primarily to explore the nature and portray the pain of injus-tice. Such features help realize the experience of marginalization, while allowing each work to remain unified by the abiding concern with vocation or love. In this fashion, the qualities of dedication, struggle, integrity, and forgiveness take on a luminousness out of proportion to their surrounding structural or stylistic heterogeneity.

Of course the blending of the two visions of justice—the vision of distributive or retributive justice with the mysterious vision of Yahweh's justice—yields a most complex and powerful effect. One work that exemplifies this blending is Milan Kundera's *The Unbearable Lightness of Being* (1984). A critique of the oppression that followed upon the 1968 "Prague Spring," the novel achieves its purpose through an often almost fantastic analysis of the love that comes to bind the doctor Tomas and his mistress-then-wife Tereza in their passion and love for each other and their homeland. Written when Czechoslovakia was a virtual colony of the Soviet Union, *The Unbearable Lightness of Being* deserves to be classed as a postcolonial novel as much as any novel of South American or South African oppression.

Ill-natured humor, irony, and cynicism are often cited as qualities of Kundera's writing, and these qualities may be seen in this rewriting of the Don Juan story. The Don Juan theme is pervasive but less important than the deep moral questioning that the whole work elicits. Appropriating but also transforming the postmodern fascination with repetition, the narrator explores the implications of human beings living their lives, deciding, and acting, once and for all. Tomas's wanton desire, as much as Tereza's self-hate, come to be interpreted in political and finally moral terms. Clearly, *The Unbearable Lightness of Being* is about a cause—political injustice and oppression—in a specific place and time: Czechoslovakia in the late 1960s and early 1970s. But more importantly, it also dramatizes the love and vocation of its chief characters. It is in love of country that Tomas and Tereza finally transcend their obsessive-compulsive behavior and redefine their sense of vocation and self.

Because of his having supported the uprising, however minimally, Tomas loses the opportunity to practice his vocation: medicine. For a while he becomes a window-washer to earn a living. Because of the uprising Tereza redefines and further develops a newly discovered vocation as photographer. In time, however, because of her own commitment and the oppressive political situation, she loses the opportunity to practice this vocation. As the months go by, both characters are forced to redefine themselves in terms of their love for each other and for their country. Theirs are lives and vocations sacrificed, it seems, for love of a country and a world as it might have been. When Tomas and Tereza die, Tomas's son arranges for the funeral and the gravestone. "The inscription he chose to go under his father's name on the gravestone read: HE WANTED THE KINGDOM OF GOD ON EARTH. He was well aware that his father would not have said it in those words, but he was certain they expressed what his father actually thought. The kingdom of God means justice. Tomas had longed for a world in which justice would reign" (276).

Despite internal evidence that Kundera's ironic text invites moral and religious reading, such an interpretation might seem open to the objection that I am merely "baptizing" a work of secular literature—as Tomas's son's epitaph does his father's motives. I would counter that the degree to which Vargas Llosa, García Márquez, and Kundera acknowledge the mystery of evil, the mystery of love, and the mystery of transcendent goodness with which human beings respond to each of the other two mysteries, marks these works as radically unlike more skeptical (and technological) exercises meant to prove that forces and not individuals effect change and bring about revolution. A respected critic has observed that minimum belief in a personal God characterizes a Christian literary perspective (Bishop 196). Human reason alone cannot explain the world. According to this view, it would not be enough to say that these examples of postcolonial literature show to a greater extent than other works a substantial concern with distributive and retributive justice, or that in their concern for individual human characters they embody the Beatitudes of Matthew's gospel. The fact must be faced that biblical ideas of justice may not be an explicit horizon of the individual novelist's writing.

None of the authors to whom I have referred is overtly theist. Yet whatever their avowed beliefs—or nonbeliefs—their writing acknowledges a surplus of meaning in life that they do not dismiss or deconstruct as part of what a critic like Umberto Eco might call an infinite semiosis (93, 94). For these authors there is something open-ended and mysterious about human life and its hopeful striving after meaning and justice. While these works are not written out of an explicit Christian faith experience, then, all are still within the dim light of a Christian tradition by which they are faintly illuminated. It is a tradition unlike that of the pre-Christian era or pagan era partly because of the mystery of hope for justice and reconciliation to which these works pay homage. What Hans Urs von Balthasar says referring to the almost post-Christian world of Solzhenitsyn's *The Cancer Ward* applies to these works as well: "The landscape of humanity, painted for us in all its fearsome and tragic colours, is lit by a glow of reconciliation which one cannot specifically designate as 'Christian,' but which in an almost inexplicable manner brings this estranged world back to reality. The ideologies behind which men hide fall away like scales, to leave their true faces unmasked . . . . It is precisely this 'anonymous light' of Christianity which lights up all places and all characters, unique, unparalleled, penetrating, which irritates ideologists and stirs them to persecute and fight for its extermination" (*Engagement* 19–20). This tradition reverences language, for it is itself built upon implicit, tacit awareness of the hope embodied in the Word made flesh. For these authors, language is an expressive intimation of hope, a transcendent venture by means of which the characters in these works can sometimes, especially with the poetic resources of language, "shine with a light not of this world" (von Balthasar, *Reader* 115).[3]

We might conclude that an ultimate condition for biblical themes of justice to emerge is the author's openness to mystery in a post-Christian world. That openness can be expressed in a variety of ways. Magic realism is just one mode by which the quasi-miraculous might reenter the world. In the fiction of García Márquez and Cortázar, for instance, we come to believe that revelation, *metanoia* (a fundamental change of mind or character), and the miraculous await us beyond the next door, at the start or the end of each day, in the "chance" meeting with the stranger on the road. García Márquez's discontinuous weaving of life and afterlife intimates what it would be like to transcend time. One can also speak in terms of style and structure "overpowering" narrative. The result is that these works take us out of time as we know it and intimate a sense of the mysterious in everyday life.

The sense of mystery is also enmeshed in Cortázar's discontinuous and surreal juxtapositions. The mystery within which human beings live—alone and struggling to love, desolate yet sustained by a spirit larger than themselves that they acknowledge in unconditional obedience and responsibility—has a genuine religious dimension about it. The larger spirit need not be an explicit, doctrinal acknowledgment of a personal God. Clearly, however, without some kind of transcendent belief the writer runs the risk of falling into gnosticism, or assuming a falsely tragic or stoic resignation. Belief must also be larger than the state, an ideal of humanity, even the "family of man." At the same time, the nature of the mystery is less important than the writer's openness to it and the work's celebration of it. African writer Chinua Achebe notes that such a mystery, one that "celebrates existence," is what unites both the indigenous and postcolonial traditions of literature in his native Nigeria.[4]

In the last analysis, the condition for justice to make its effective claim in a work of fiction is the concretized experience that love is realized in action, not words, in a "lasting lived faithfulness" (von Balthasar, *Reader* 118) that transcends merely human understanding. In other words, for even a novel by a non-Christian to manifest biblical themes of justice, the synthesis must be a love whose nature is itself a mystery. Von Balthasar describes the experience of love in relevant terms: "The brilliance of the living choice from the regions of the divine raises the individual, lost in the anonymity of the species, to the uniqueness of a person. In this ultimate mutual acknowledgment between two lovers, eros is able not merely to offer the initial spark, it can go along the whole way, if only it allows itself to be purified into transfigurations beyond itself" (*Reader* 117). Florentino Ariza, the tremendous lover of García Márquez's *Love in the Time of Cholera,* possesses this kind of love and has the power to share it. Despite an early promiscuous eroticism not entirely unlike Tomas's in *The Unbearable Lightness of Being,* Ariza's faithful love of the aged Fermina Diaz finally raises her, himself, and the entire novel to a level of illumination that reflects something of the radiance of God's justice. United near the end of the novel, Florentino and Fermina Diaz enjoy an almost transcendent experience of such love: "They were together in silence like an old married couple wary of life, beyond the pitfalls of passion, beyond the brutal mockery of hope and the phantoms of disillusion: beyond love. For they had lived together long enough to know that love was always love, anytime and anyplace, but it was more solid the closer it came to death" (345). As Thomas Pynchon notes in his review, "This novel is also revolutionary in daring to suggest that vows of love made under a presumption of immortality—youthful idiocy, to some—may yet be honored, much later in life when we ought to know better, in the face of the undeniable. This is, effectively, to assert the resurrection of the body, today as throughout history an unavoidably revolutionary idea" (47). Love, like belief in resurrection, is revolutionary, especially when, as in much postcolonial fiction, it dares to propose the possibility of justice in an unjust world.

What does this outline of a criticism oriented toward biblical themes of justice yield us? To answer this question it is necessary first to ask: why does this critical practice apply particularly to postcolonial literature? Perhaps part of the reason is that in this literature the forces ranged against justice and humanity are often more obviously manifest than in much of postmodern Western European and American literature. Perhaps it is because in the injustice, deprivation, and oppression of countries like Peru, Czechoslovakia, South Africa, and Colombia, the light of virtue, holiness, and justice shines out with an intensity lacking in more affluent, self-indulgent, and self-absorbed nations. To assert such a priority is not merely to wallow in what West Indian poet Derek Walcott called "barb-wire envy." In the luminousness of justice that shines from such novels, we see a hope for escaping the imprisonment in self. Overcoming solipsism or disabling individualism and nationalism is only possible when, vicariously or actively, we become aware of a different vision, one characterized by communal virtues like justice and love.

Much of Western European and American fiction no longer offers with the same intensity that experience of otherness by means of which the earlier tradition of the novel had succeeded in expanding consciousness, sensibility, and a sense of justice. Despite its emphasis on marginality and diversity, poststructuralist theory has itself inclined and even coerced writers to focus on aberrant forms of marginality, on violence with no point, or on only the harshest forms of retributive justice. The claim that Don DeLillo's *Mao II* (1991) has a moral vision sounds hollow when this fictional chronicle of a disenchanted novelist seeking personal dissolution as a Beirut hostage is measured against the struggles that the works I have discussed describe. Because of just such an idiosyncratic focus, however, much recent fiction has lost what used to be called the generality (Goethe's sense of the German *Allgemeinheit* conveys the idea better) that carries persuasive, ethical force in the great narratives of George Eliot, Dostoyevsky, and Tolstoy.

To renew the spirit and to break out of the aesthetic-analytic ennui, we turn to postcolonial literature for a model of engaged moral sensibility, and there we find presented those authentic experiences that overcome solipsism as they awaken a search for justice. What Ernest William Hocking, in *The Coming World Civilization*, says about political experience applies to literature as well: "National individualism imitates personal individualism; we move beyond it through experience, often at first vicarious and later direct" (qtd. Gelpi 191). Theologian John Langan comments on the achievement of biblical justice in our secular world: "The Christian form of commitment to justice in the human city grows out of hope and faith in a God who both transcends history and is active within it" (178). Langan also quotes Alan Paton, the South African writer, on this hope for the triumph of righteousness: "The might and the power of hope must come, and can only come, from a faith that there is a might and a power that is above all, and that rules all. It is a faith in the Holy Spirit . . . . It is not the power of rulers and parliaments and armies, but the power of the Spirit; and when men and women have believed in such a power, they are able, if it is required of them, to defy rules and parliaments and armies. . . . Our task is to be the instruments of the Holy Spirit, knowing in full faith that his purpose also is the triumph of righteousness" (Langan 178). With W. H. Auden, I believe that "poetry [in the broad sense that includes fiction] makes nothing happen." It can, nevertheless, predispose us to new experiences or new perspectives on perennial problems. It opens our eyes to the existence of events and forms of suffering about which we have been unaware, or unfeeling. To acknowledge the effective claim of a literature that powerfully presents the vision of a world in which greater justice may be possible is an important step toward transforming that vision into practice.[5]

2.

The Kingdom of God on Earth
Ernesto Cardenal's *Salmos*

TERRY DeHAY

The Nicaraguan poet Ernesto Cardenal, a Catholic priest and a political and social activist, served as minister of culture in Nicaragua's Sandinista government after the success of the revolution in 1979. His life and poetry reflect his commitment both to active political reform and to religious contemplation. His poetic search to resolve the apparent opposition between his Catholicism and his Marxism is clearly traced in the language and imagery of his work, which emphasizes the convergence of ideals he sees in the two systems of thought. In accordance with liberation theology, Cardenal believes that Christianity must take a stand to alleviate the suffering and oppression in the world. The clearest poetic statement of his version of liberation theology is in his *Salmos*, a group of poems he wrote while studying in Colombia in the early 1960s.

Cardenal was born in Granada, Nicaragua, in 1925. After studying literature first in Managua and then Mexico City, he spent two years, from 1947 to 1949, as a student at Columbia University in New York City. There he discovered North American poetry and was especially influenced by Ezra Pound. He returned to Nicaragua in 1950, working with the Nicaraguan poet José Coronel Urtecho in translating and compiling an anthology of North American poetry. His involvement in the politics of his country also became concrete at this time, and he participated actively in the "April Rebellion" against Anastasio Somoza in 1954. His early poems, such as *Zero Hour* (1956), already reflect his interest in the history and political turmoil in Central America, and his concern with the political intervention of the United States.

In May, 1957, to the surprise of some, Cardenal entered the Trappist monastery at Gethsemane, Kentucky. While at the monastery, he worked closely with Thomas Merton, the noted priest, philosopher, and poet, and together they planned the establishment of a religious and contemplative community. Cardenal left the monastery in 1959 for personal and health reasons, and continued his studies with the Benedictines in Cuernavaca, Mexico, and at the Seminary of La Ceja near Medellín, Colombia. In 1965, at the age of forty, he was ordained as a priest in Managua.

At that time he and some companions founded, on the island of Solentiname in the middle of Lake Nicaragua, the Christian community that he had first envisioned at Gethsemane. The objective of Cardenal and his companions was to construct the ideal community, without classes or private property (Martínez Andrade 25). Here Cardenal compiled *El evangelio en Solentiname*, a reexamination of the Scriptures by the workers and peasants living in and around the community of Solentiname. This commentary on biblical teachings and how they relate to the lives of the people was as much an investigation of the problems facing Nicaragua under Somoza as it was an attempt to achieve a closer understanding of the Christian faith (Urdanivia Bertarelli 149). In fact, many of the inhabitants of Solentiname at this time began to take an active part in the struggle against the government.

Cardenal's poetry also became increasingly political, directly addressing the injustice in Nicaragua and supporting resistance to Somoza's regime. In 1970, Cardenal visited Cuba as a judge in a poetry competition sponsored by Casa de las Américas. His firsthand experiences in socialist Cuba (described in his book *En Cuba* [1972]) led to his conversion to Marxism, directly influencing the poems written after this visit. Cardenal has referred to the poems written at this time, in particular "Oráculo sobre Managua" and *Canto nacional*, as "Christian-Marxist" (Martínez Andrade 26).

Many members of Solentiname also began to translate their religious convictions into political commitments, becoming active in the FSLN (Frente Sandinista de la Liberación National) and extending their desire for an ideal community into a larger context. The political power of the religious community of Solentiname and the threat of the increasingly international influence of Cardenal's writing were demonstrated when, in

1977, Somoza's National Guard bombed the island, completely destroying the community. At this point Cardenal went into exile in Costa Rica, actively supporting the FSLN until its victory in 1979.

Tocar el cielo, first published in 1981, is a collection of poems written between 1974 and 1980, illustrated with paintings from Solentiname and photographs of Nicaragua. Dedicated to the struggle of the Sandinistas against the government of Somoza, it is what Urdanivia Bertarelli calls "a hymn in praise of the Sandinista revolution and of hope in the reconstruction of Nicaragua as a free country" (149). Many of the poems in the collection reflect Cardenal's growing conviction of the relationship between the love of God and a just society, which he came to understand as the goals of Marxism. He writes in a poem called "Epístola a José Coronel Urtecho":

> They can be good, according to Marx. Some capitalists
> have good hearts. For this reason: the goal is not to change the heart,
>   but rather the system.
>
> Private property—that euphemism.
>   Thieves, it is not rhetoric.
> It is not a figure of speech.
> Charity in the Bible is "sedagah" [justice] [1]

In 1979, after the triumph of the revolution, Cardenal returned to serve as the minister of culture for the new government. In response to concern that the Sandinista government was anti-Catholic, Cardenal has pointed out that the revolution put a priest in the office of minister of culture (*La democratización* 28).

Cardenal's vision of the world appears to presume the existence of a totality of which Catholicism and Marxism are both manifestations. Like many other writers and thinkers, he senses a connection between the historical patterns of the Bible and those of Marxism. He does not see these patterns as conflicting, nor does he seem to see the need for transplanting one system of beliefs for another. Rather, in his poetry he discovers or creates points of convergence. As John Beverley points out in his book *Del 'Lazarillo' al sandinismo*, "Cardenal is *at the same time* a mystic and a communist. His principal preoccupation (which he shares with Liberation Theology) is to create a synthesis of Christian eschatology with a Marxist sense of dialectic contradiction and transformation of history and nature" (136).

Liberation theology reinterprets the Bible and the basic concepts of Christianity in terms of the direct struggle of the people against aggression. The 1968 Medellín proclamation demonstrates the relevance of Vatican II to the political and social realities of Latin America. At Medellín the bishops declared "that the people were oppressed by the 'institutionalized violence' of internal and external colonial structures which, 'seeking unbounded profits, ferment an economic dictatorship and the international imperialism of money'" (Randall 19). These statements gave official sanction to the active involvement of Catholics in political affairs. For the people of Latin America, who are generally very religious, this reinterpretation has an enormous impact. It reconciles the ideological gap between their religious beliefs and the very concrete need for political and social change. As Beverley points out, the hierarchical structure of traditional Christian belief reinforces the political and economic stratification that leads to the oppression of large segments of the population: "God— the world below is weighted forever with the violence of the relationship master-slave" (*Del 'Lazarillo'* 133). Liberation theology rereads the Bible, restructuring the hierarchical relationship between God and the world so that God is fighting alongside men and women to bring an end to oppression. A primitive painter from Solentiname describes this relationship as he represents it in his painting of the crucifix: "I paint Christ as one of us, a man, that is to say a *compañero guerillero* who comes out of the mountains and is taken by the enemy" (Cardenal, *La democratización* 21). In other words, Christ sacrifices himself in the struggle for the liberation of the people. The painting thus described has been reproduced in a number of publications, including Cardenal's *Tocar el cielo*.

Not all proponents of liberation theology or Christian revolutionaries are Marxists. For Ernesto Cardenal, however, there is a clear connection between the two; he asserts, in fact, that he had two conversions in his life, the first to Catholicism and the second to Marxism. He sees an extremely close relationship between the two systems of thought, so close that the study of Christ led him to Marxism and to a commitment to revolution: "I became politicized with the contemplative life. Meditation, exploration, mysticism is what gave me a political radicalization. I arrived at revolution through the gospel. It was not because of reading Marx but because of Christ. It is possible to say that the gospel made me a marxist" (qtd. Forcano 7). Again according to Beverley, Cardenal's reading of the Bible focuses on understanding its message in terms of the teachings of Marxism. As Cardenal states: "The Bible as much as Marxism gives us the assurance to work toward the perfect universe. If not, the universe would not make sense; if not, the Cuban Revolution would not make sense, and we know well that it does. However, to achieve completely what Lenin referred to as the assault on the heavens, it may take, in my opinion, as much time as that which has transpired from Homo Habilis to us" (qtd. Beverley, *Del 'Lazarillo'* 106). For Cardenal, the biblical version of history and the Marxist version of history are not separate or opposing concepts. Instead, they are each evidence of the existence of the inevitable progression of history toward a perfect society, "the Kingdom of God on Earth" (*Canto nacional* 53). He does not need to replace the material of Christianity with that of Marxism, but only to cleanse Christian doctrine from centuries of distortion so that the similarities of the two doctrines become evident, and they can work together to bring about a just society. To this end, the rhetoric of Marxism and that of Christianity are frequently juxtaposed in his poetry. In "La economía de Tahuantinsuyu," a poem from *Homenaje a los Indios Americanos,* Cardenal uses poetic devices to illustrate this relationship between religion and politics:

Religious truth
                and political truth
were for the people the same truth
                (*Nueva* 150)

First illustrating the two truths' separation through the line division, the poet then unites them in the minds of the people. For Cardenal, a symptom of a corrupt society is the lack of a comprehensive moral base with religious and political values on the same plane. As a priest and a revolutionary, Cardenal serves as an example of the possible fusion of these traditionally dialectical forces, a fusion he portrays in his poetry. He strongly emphasizes that in the ideal society (such as that of Tahuantinsuyu, the Quecha name for the Incan emperor) politics and religion are one; in modern society they are in opposition.

In his *Salmos,* Cardenal uses a past poetic model that assumes a direct relationship between the Christian God and the historical world of the speaker. Beginning with the basic form and content of the biblical Psalms, Cardenal reinterprets them from a contemporary perspective to reflect the modern struggle for liberation in Latin America, emphasizing the strength and commitment of the people. The Psalms Cardenal chooses as models generally come from the category referred to by Robert Alter as "Psalms of supplication," which he describes as "a poetic cry of distress to the lord [*sic*] in time of critical need," distinct from the Psalms of praise (*Literary* 247–48). Walter Brueggemann makes a further distinction, dividing the

Psalms into three categories: "psalms of orientation," which evoke the fundamental goodness, coherence, and dependability of God's world; "psalms of disorientation," which express anger and frustration with the world; and "psalms of new orientation," which emphasize the hope implicit in change (19). The focus of Cardenal's *Salmos* is clearly on the disorientation, the anger and frustration in a world marked by "disequilibrium, incoherence, and unrelieved asymmetry" (Brueggemann 51).

Cardenal uses the vision of the world implied by the Psalms of disorientation—that of men and women as oppressed beings in a world dominated by a powerful few, "*los impuros*" (the impure)—as a historical reinforcement for the actual situation in Latin America.[2] Into the referential field established by the biblical model, Cardenal places contemporary language and concrete images to create a modern context for the biblical vision—"I do not worship movie stars"—and a context defined by the political situation in Latin America: "liberate me from the dictator / and from the gangsters' mafia / Their machine guns are summoned against us."[3] In this way, he adds a twentieth-century political interpretation to the spiritual conflict expressed in the Psalms. The supplicant in the original text asks repeatedly for protection from the evil in the world. For Cardenal, this evil is clearly defined as the dictators and all those who exploit the people. In a highly original simile, he describes God's presence as "a Line of Defense / like an air raid shelter" (*Salmo* 30). God's protection is essential, and Cardenal infuses it with a material meaning, directly asking God to take an active, political stand against oppression: "Declare, Lord, war on those who declare war on us / Because you are our ally" (*Salmo* 34).

The *Salmos* belong to the type of poetry that Cardenal refers to as "exteriorist poetry," an expression first used by José Colonel Urtecho, another twentieth-century Nicaraguan poet. It is defined by Cardenal as "objective, narrative, and anecdotal poetry, made with the elements of real life and with concrete things, with proper names, and precise details and exact dates and figures and deeds and statements" (*Poesía* viii). In other words, he writes a poetry that refers directly to the concrete world in which people live. That poetry should communicate is essential to Cardenal; he states, "for me poetry is above all prophecy in the biblical sense of guidance" (*Poesía* viii). Because of his vision of the world and his commitment to change, Cardenal's poetry is highly political and carries a direct statement of his beliefs. As a result, his work has been criticized as overly political and occasional, compromising "pure poetry." Cardenal counters this accusation by asserting that all great poetry, including the Bible, is exteriorist, confronting the real world and real human needs: "It is as ancient as Homer and biblical poetry (in reality, it is that which has constituted the great poetry of all times)" (*Poesía* vii–viii).

In his *Salmos,* Cardenal basically glosses only the first few lines of the original text; the changes he makes define the emphasis of his thought. In *Salmo* 5, for example, his first two lines—"Listen to my words, oh Lord / Hear my sighs"—echo fairly directly the original text: "Give ear to my words, O Lord, / consider my sighing." In the third line, however, he diverges significantly from the original text. Cardenal's speaker states, "Listen to my protest"; the original text reads, "Listen to my cry for help." This change indicates a major shift from the biblical speaker as supplicant to the more exhortative speaker in the *Salmos.* Cardenal emphasizes the "clamor," which in this context represents his call for action. He rejects the more meditative aspects of the Psalms, emphasizing the demand that God assume an active stance alongside men and women against oppression. The direct references he makes to the original text also reflect this imperative:

Awaken
  Rise up in my favor
      My God
        in my defense!

In this sense the biblical model plays a major role, serving as a contrast to underscore Cardenal's message. Although the poems stand independently, their relationship to the original text enhances their meaning.

This enhancement is especially clear in the way Cardenal reinterprets the relationship between the speaker and the hearer. In the biblical text there is an "I" addressing a "thou," or "God." Although the third-person pronoun enters the discourse when the speaker asks protection from "them," the emphasis is on the dialogue between the speaker and his God. This is not true in Cardenal's *Salmos.* The poetic situation, the dialogue between the "I" and "thou," serves basically as a means of defining and criticizing "them." In *Salmo* 57, for example, Cardenal exploits the dichotomy between the pious "I" and the impious "them," using irony to define the situation he sees in today's world, with an emphasis on the power and corruption of "them": "The liberty of which they speak is the freedom of capital / Their 'free world' is free exploitation / Their law is of guns and their order that of the gorilla." This shift away from "I" also places a stronger emphasis on the relationship between "them" and God. If God fails to assist the oppressed, represented by the speaker, then he has chosen sides against the oppressed. In Cardenal's *Salmos*, God cannot stand apart or above, but must accept his responsibility. In fact, the speaker in *Salmo* 43 is not simply asking for protection; he concludes the poem with a demand that God accept responsibility and take action: "Wake up / and help us! / For your own prestige!" (*Salmo* 43). Although the corresponding biblical Psalm 44 has the same theme of the apparent desertion of God in the face of enemies, it ends with a much humbler note: "Rise up, come to our help. / Redeem us for the sake of your steadfast love."

The speaker of Cardenal's *Salmos* also differs from that of the biblical text in that he merges into a larger whole. The biblical Psalms are traditionally thought to have had more than one author and to have been attributed to David at a later date. As king, David becomes the spokesperson for a collective Israel. Cardenal reverses this process to an extent, emphasizing the significance of the poet as the voice of the people. In addition, in accentuating the attitude of supplication and disorientation, Cardenal shifts the more personal tone of the Psalms to a general, political one: "We are the displaced / We are the refugees who do not have papers" (*Salmo* 43).

Pronoun shifts from the biblical source to the revisioned text underscore this process. In many of Cardenal's *Salmos*, a collective but carefully defined "we" replaces the first-person pronoun of the correlative text. *Salmo* 15, for example, like the corresponding Psalm 16, begins and ends with the first-person pronoun; however, unlike Psalm 16, the "I" becomes a "we" in the series of stanzas that make up the body of the poem, identifying the speaker with a larger voice. *Salmo* 34 also alternates between the singular and plural pronouns, in contrast with the corresponding Psalm 35, this time stating directly that the "I" is the poet who speaks for the whole: "I will sing of you in my poems / all my life." Because "we" appears more frequently in Cardenal's poems than in their biblical correlatives, the "I" becomes a spokesperson for a group, for all oppressed people. The speaker, in this case the prophet-poet, is the link between God and the people, between religion and politics: "But, I will be able to speak of you to my brothers / I will praise you in the gathering of our people" (*Salmo* 21). He speaks both for and to God, relaying God's message to the people and delivering their cry for help. For Cardenal, this is a major role of the poet: to create an articulation and unification of purpose.

In doing this, Cardenal's *Salmos* both describe an existing situation and communicate a hope. Although the conditions he describes in *Salmos* and his other poetry are devastating, the message is one of hope and survival.

In *Salmo* 21 ("Why have you abandoned me?"), the speaker describes a multiplicity of horrors from a first-person perspective in the present tense:

> They have brought me naked to the gas chamber
> and divided up my clothes and shoes between them
> I cry out begging for morphine and no one hears me. . . .
>
> I cry in the police station
> on the porch of the garrison
>   in the torture chamber

In spite of the atrocities of the present, the speaker ends with a description of an ideal, inevitable future: "Our people will celebrate a great fiesta /The new people who are going to be born." As though to underscore this hope, the redemption that God promises to the righteous is equated in the *Salmos* with liberation: to be redeemed is to be free from oppression. *Salmo* 18 refers to "Señor / my Liberator," while the corresponding Psalm reads "my / Redeemer" (Ps. 19: 14). Again in *Salmo* 129, Cardenal writes, "But the Lord is the Liberation / the Liberty of Israel," reinterpreting the original "and with him is great power to redeem. / It is he who will redeem Israel / from all its iniquities" (Ps. 130: 7–8). The speaker requests, even demands, redemption not from his own sins, but liberation from the sins of others.

As in *Salmo* 21, the general feeling of the *Salmos* is that the people will inevitably triumph over oppression. In fact, God is defined in relation to the people's struggle: "We will celebrate the anniversary of the Revolution in great plazas / The God who exists is that of the proletariat" (*Salmo* 57). There is no other possibility within this religious-political context; any other god is a false god. And in the context of the *Salmos*, God becomes part of history, no longer separate or independent of the actions of people in history. Rather God receives definition and validation in terms of a relationship with human beings. The abstract, transcendent principles of the Christian God only become "real" and valuable in their historical application, in the way they directly affect people's lives. This concept clearly coincides with the revision of the traditional Christian hierarchy proposed by many liberation theologians, placing God alongside human beings in the struggle to end oppression.

This use of the poetic space to juxtapose political and religious points of view is very evident in Cardenal's longer poems as well. In *Canto nacional*, published in 1973 and dedicated to the Frente Sandinista de Liberación Nacional, Cardenal uses the correspondence he sees between Christianity and Marxism to establish a connection between religion and politics: "A land promised by the Revolution / with things in common / 'as before the fall of our First Parents' " (32). The last line in this text, along with the reference to "the promised land," defines the Nicaraguan revolution, and any revolution which works toward the liberation of the repressed, in the context of the prophecy of the Bible, as an act of redemption (liberation), indicating a return to a better time, to a prelapsarian Eden. In this context, communism is the possibility of creating an earthly Eden: "Communism or the Kingdom of God on earth, which is the same" (*Canto* 53). Cardenal's vision of liberation theology is a blending of religion and politics, an identifying of themes central to both systems of belief. On one level, he uses the relationship between an already established system, Christianity, to demonstrate the legitimacy of another less established one. At the same time, however, on another level Cardenal questions the values of the already accepted religious system, restructuring them in accordance with his own concept of a universally acceptable or "legitimate" value system. The correspondence of Christianity and Marxism is established in relation to a universal system of values, or totality, and both are redefined in its terms. The poetry that presents these redefined concepts is itself a taking apart, literally of line and texts, and figuratively of history and time. This poetic deconstruction of existing ways of interpreting the world opens up these systems of beliefs, revealing equivalences and disrupting any claim of universality for one particular political or religious ideology.

Raymond Williams, in *Marxism and Literature,* defines three different aspects of culture that create "internal dynamic relations" within any system. The most obviously identifiable is the hegemonic, or dominant. But along with the dominant, the "residual" and "emergent" function as part of the dynamic process that is culture. The residual, according to Williams, "has been effectively formed in the past, but it is still active in the cultural process, not only and often not at all as an element of the past, but as an effective element of the present. Thus certain experiences, meanings, and values which cannot be expressed or substantially verified in terms of the dominant culture, are nevertheless lived and practiced on the basis of the residue—cultural as well as social—of some previous social and cultural institution or formation" (122). Williams also distinguishes between the residual that has been incorporated into the hegemony and that which presents an alternative or opposition to the dominant aspects of culture. Williams's example of organized religion presents a convenient analogy to the relationship of liberation theology and the traditional Catholic Church. He states that organized religion, although basically residual, has been effectively incorporated into the hegemony. At the same time, oppositional elements remain active. In terms of liberation theology, these oppositional forces emerge in the vision of the early Christians as revolutionaries, as opposed to the more static, hierarchical belief system that has been incorporated into the dominant culture and tends to support and reproduce the status quo.

The emergent aspects of culture are "new meanings and values, new practices, new relationships and kinds of relationships" that are continually being created (Williams 123). The emergent very often defines itself in opposition to the hegemony as well, although it runs a greater risk of incorporation into the hegemonic culture. The example of the emergent given by Williams is the development of the working class that accompanied the Industrial Revolution in nineteenth-century England. Clearly this new class was incorporated by the hegemony into the dominant ideology and reinterpreted in terms of the dominant values and social patterns. As Williams points out, the incorporation of emergent cultural processes is difficult to detect and combat because it often appears as "recognition, acknowledgement, and thus a form of *acceptance*" (125).

In terms of Williams's distinctions, we can understand Cardenal's poetic synthesis as a means of identifying the present dominant capitalist system as negative, and both the residual and emergent as important alternatives to that system. He is clearly interested in the residual aspects of organized religion that have not been incorporated into the hegemonic culture, especially in terms of liberation theology. Looking to the Old Testament God of the Psalms, Cardenal's poetry revives the God who directly punishes the evil, the oppressor, and comes to the aid of the poor:

> Rise up Lord
>   do not forget the exploited
> Because they believe that they are unpunished
> Thou seest it
>   Because thou seest our prisons
> The persecuted rely on thee
> and the orphaned child entrusts to thee
>   the little orphans of our assassinated
> Burn Lord their secret service
> and their Councils of War
> that their military force cannot be found
>
> Because thou art he who governs for eternal centuries
> and hears the prayers of the humble
>   (*Salmo* 9)

Cardenal uses the basic structure of the *Salmos*, the speaker's direct address to his God, to reexamine and to revise the relationship of God and the people, to restructure the vertical separation of heaven and earth so important to the Church within the dominant culture. The God of Cardenal's *Salmos* is an opponent to the existing system of exploitation, rather than a supporter of the status quo, as God is traditionally defined in terms of the dominant aspects of culture.

Marxism, in turn, can be seen as an emergent political system, especially in the process that many Latin American Marxists have articulated as the creation of the "nuevo hombre/mujer," or the new man/woman. As Cardenal repeatedly emphasizes, the goal of the revolution is to restructure the existing system and to create a new one in which all men and women live free and equal. At the same time, he states in "Por una Cultura de la Paz," "a socialist economy is an economy with religion. I am not interested in an economic liberation of man without the liberation of the whole man" (qtd. White 65–66). Here again, liberation is equivalent to redemption.

The process of Cardenal's poetry does not contrast the two alternatives of Christianity and Marxism, but rather focuses on their similarities. In fact, the identification of the residual elements of culture with the emergent, the poetic juxtaposition of Christian imagery and Marxist images, may be Cardenal's method of protecting them from appropriation by the dominant culture. By revealing the similarities between Christian and Marxist thought, he is able to emphasize what he wishes from each system, creating in their synthesis a new way of understanding and shaping the world. The emergent and the residual have in Cardenal's poetry the same goal: "the kingdom of God on earth." For Cardenal, they are not separate, but rather have similar roots in the universal struggle to attain the Kingdom of God on Earth: "I believe in the kingdom of Heaven. But I believe that this kingdom will be established on earth because Christ taught us to pray for the Kingdom to come to us—not for us to go to it" (White 65).

3

Biblical Justice and the Military Hero in Two Novels of Gabriel García Márquez

Lourdes Elena Morales-Gudmundsson

Mikhail Bakhtin has most eloquently drawn attention to the multiplicity of sociolinguistic elements present and orchestrated in the novel. This is certainly a fundamental acknowledgment to make when studying the novels of Gabriel García Márquez who, like few others, has known how to "dialogue" effectively with the full gamut of human life. This study analyzes the ways in which two García Márquez novels—*No One Writes to the Colonel* and *The Autumn of the Patriarch*—dialogue with the concept of justice as it is present both in the Bible and in Latin American liberation theology.[1] García Márquez's definition of justice, though certainly not purposely Christian, does contain many important elements implicit in the biblical, Judeo-Christian understanding of that concept. The Colombian novelist finds in the Bible ready-made images and symbols that he will use to deconstruct received sociopolitical structures in order to build his case for the application of justice and love to broken human beings. Drawing on many of the fundamental tenets of liberation theology, he consistently breaks down human hypocrisies and uncovers individual and corporate injustice. Employing the biblical concept of justice and selected teachings of liberation theology, I will look at the manner in which García Márquez handles the theme of justice in these two novels and thereby extract his understanding of the concept.

Liberation theology begins with Moses at the burning bush, the point of departure for the story of Israel's deliverance from unjust captivity and the establishment of God's covenant with Israel, which is associated with the exercise of justice and mercy both by God and humanity (Motthabi 6). Liberation theologians also understand Christ's work on earth as one of liberation. Citing Paul, Gustavo Gutiérrez states that Christ frees us so that we may enjoy freedom (Gal. 5:1). Liberation from sin is important as a freeing from an egocentric withdrawal into oneself ("un repliegue egoísta sobre sí mismo"). Sin separates humanity from God, and it is the ultimate cause of all misery, injustice, and oppression in which human beings live (Gutiérrez, *Teología* 66). These facts reveal, furthermore, that behind every unjust structure, there is a personal or collective will responsible for injustice, a will to reject God and one's neighbor. In general, justice, as understood by liberation theology, "comprises not merely the cardinal virtues as inherent in persons, but the comprehensive moral rectitude of society and humankind, expressing itself in social order as opposed to disorder, particularly the radical disorder of the denial of human dignity . . . together with the radical disorder of neglect of the common good" (Clarke 59). In Latin America the fundamental assumption of liberation theology is that the present social order is founded on a principle of injustice: the exploitation of the many by the moneyed few. If the kingdom of God is to be ushered in by Christians, then they must contribute to bringing justice to society.

For liberationists, the axiomatic injustice at the heart of poverty calls for the Christian's highest virtue, love, a concept espoused by Gutiérrez and other Latin American theologians. José Porfirio Miranda argues that perhaps one of the most devastating mistakes of Christianity, under Greek influence, was to differentiate between love and justice. In fact, says Miranda, the Bible calls "justice" what later Christianity called the act of Christian love, "almsgiving" (14). He further points out that in the Magnificat ("He has filled the hungry with good things and sent the rich away empty" [Luke 1:53]), God is partial to the poor, a notion quite distant from the Greek idea of justice's blind impartiality (Miranda 17).

Finally, liberation theology picks up on the eschatological/soteriological as well as apocalyptical dimensions of this process of liberation/salvation in the Judeo-Christian tradition. Liberation at either the individual or the collective level is a type of the ultimate liberation for all who practice justice and mercy on the earth. The final liberation will occur, according to Revelation, with the entrance into the heavenly dispensation, a new heaven and a new earth, where justice and mercy will reign forever and ever. Salvation

as understood in the Bible moves inexorably to a final conflagration of all
that is unjust (Rev. 20:11–15).

García Márquez, always in tune with the realities surrounding him,
enters into dialogue with the Christian concepts of justice as they are present in the Scriptures and in Latin American liberation theology. In his
recently published biography of García Márquez, Bell-Villada points to
the importance of the Bible in the novelist's formation as a thinker and
writer. In a 1982 interview with the biographer, García Márquez said that
he had begun to read the Bible as a teenager and that he was fascinated by
"all the good stories" to be found there. His youthful journalistic work
reveals that he was already experimenting with parodic uses of Biblical
stories and figures as early as 1948 (Bell-Villada 75).

It is evident that García Márquez does not necessarily believe that the
Christian gospel is the answer to social injustice, but neither is he reluctant
to take from the Judeo-Christian system of thought what he can use to give
a more universal character to the struggles of humanity for justice. By his
own admission, García Márquez is interested in the Bible as a primitive
and gutsy text in which "fantastic things" happen (Mendoza 7). But he
also seems interested in the durable structures, symbols, and themes that
this text offers him as he searches for a useful framework for his treatment
of some fundamental issues of human existence. Indeed, García Márquez
seems very interested in what the Bible, as a document of Judeo-Christian
culture, has to say about how the human being relates to the call of the
higher virtues.

In his concern for human rights as the rights of the poor, García Márquez enters the flow of thinking that emanates from liberation theology
every bit as much as from Marxism. Although García Márquez is a man
who has always been politically committed to socialism, Camilo Torres
Restrepo—one of his closest friends and the priest who baptized his son
Rodrigo—was a liberation theologian and eventually a Marxist revolutionary. Certainly García Márquez's combined concern for justice and love—
his persistent search for the important links between them—reveals that
he was not unconscious of how the liberation theologians had already
linked them.

Justice lies at the heart of the basic predicament of *No One Writes the
Colonel*, a short novel whose protagonist is a retired colonel who is still
waiting after many years for his well-deserved veteran's pension check. At
the core of the novel is a biblical-liberationist theme: the plight of a poor
man who seeks justice. Despite his having fought nobly for a worthy cause,

those in a position to deal justly with the colonel have ignored him for years and, as if to add insult to injury, they have been responsible, directly or indirectly, for the death of his only son.

Regina Janes suggests that the original for many of the novelist's beaten old men was his grandfather, Colonel Nicolás Márquez Iguarán, who served under the Liberal General Rafael Uribe Uribe during the War of a Thousand Days (1899–1902) (10). Although Janes considers the War of a Thousand Days to be the ostensible setting for *No One Writes the Colonel*, Stephen Minta places the story somewhere around 1956 when Colombia had suffered through ten or more years of "la violencia," a period (approximately between the years of 1946 and 1966) of interminable wars between Liberals and Conservatives.[2] That the protagonist is a war veteran who is also a survivor of postwar political conflict is evident in the colonel's matter-of-fact observation, as he prepares to attend a funeral, that this is the first death by natural causes in his city for many years. In the story of a retired colonel, García Márquez has found both a typical and specific political-historical situation that breeds injustice in Latin America.

As opposed to the implied violence that surrounds and sporadically affects the decaying backwater town in which he lives, the colonel's life of implacable waiting is the only significant "activity." Waiting, in the novel, is a silent yet spiritually dynamic quest. On the surface, the colonel is simply waiting for a letter and a pension check for his services to his nation. However, two images with biblical resonances exacerbate the frustration and despair of the waiting and suggest some larger implications: the dead son and the fighting cock. The colonel's only treasured possession is a fighting cock that once belonged to his son, who died a martyr's death at the hands of ruthless government henchmen: he was distributing clandestine antigovernment flyers at a cockfight when he was gunned down. The colonel's tenacious insistence on keeping the cock, even when, at the end of the novel, the cock refuses to fight, and even if keeping it means starvation for him and his wife, represents his refusal to give up on justice.

Robin W. Fiddian uncovers some important aspects of the novel by which we may see how themes of caring for one's neighbor and the injustice of poverty are given form. Two of the three Christian elements he finds in the novel are of interest for our discussion: the idea of a corrupt and fallen world and the messiah figure (389). The idea that "the world is corrupted," enunciated early on in *No One Writes to the Colonel* (13), is associated with the hopeless waiting for the "Messiah" (justice in the colonel's particular case and overall collective and individual justice). Fiddian believes that the subsequent reference to the civil war fought in Macondo by Colonel Aureliano Buendía suggests that the defeat of the Liberal cause in the War of a Thousand Days reenacted the fall of the world. Yet the suggestion of continued violence throughout the novel implies that the time in which the colonel is holding his implacable vigil for justice continues to belong to that apocalyptical time in which the world is predominantly corrupt and evil, and thereby ready for deliverance.

The corrupt world motif reappears when the colonel goes to sell the cock to Don Sabas. The reference to the "sky falling" indicates a present apocalypse (45), characterized by indifference to the neighbor and injustice toward the poor. The messiah theme is inevitably linked with the theme of waiting for deliverance from injustice when the colonel expresses his hope that there may be incorrupt elections this year. The doctor who hears him replies: "Don't be so naive, colonel. . . . We're too old now to be waiting for the Messiah" (66). But justice is foremost in the mind of this forgotten military hero, obsessed with the arrival of a letter of exoneration and his pension check, precisely because he is that "neighbor" to whom justice is due. His hope for deliverance from poverty and death and for justice to return to the earth is a hope for the return of the Messiah; waiting for the letter is a type of the other more significant waiting for justice.

Why is this waiting so intensely painful? The answer arises out of the colonel's keen sense of the injustice and his awareness of himself as a victim. This realization is made all the keener by its obvious links to liberation theology's concept of the individual. The individual possesses a kind of authenticating creativity, the freedom of the authentic person, a privilege that ought not be limited to the wealthy and the powerful. The poverty-ridden colonel refuses to succumb to an inevitable destiny. Just as he fought on the battlefield for collective justice, so now the dispossessed military man fights for personal justice, as well as for a larger justice in which his son is implicated. In the end, the colonel's fight for justice takes the form of his refusal to sell the cock in the face of hopeless poverty and cruel government indifference.

As to the meanings that can be attached to the cock, it should be noted that Mario Vargas Llosa was among the first to see the cock as the embodiment of the people's collective hope for change. But, as Minta aptly points out, the long-awaited cockfight (where change was to begin) is anticlimactic: neither the colonel's cock nor the other one want to fight (78). If the cock represents hope for change, the failure to fight reveals the hopelessness and beaten will of the people. However, Fiddian argues persuasively that the cock represents rather the dead son, as messiah, given the other New Testament elements that complement the theme. He suggests that the dead son is an allusion to the hope for a risen messiah (390–92).

The cock reveals the government's treason and so becomes a two-pronged symbol of justice: justice for the colonel and justice for a nation rife with political wars. At the historical level, within the fiction of the novel, the colonel who has fought bravely for a just cause is waiting to receive his just reward. The inherent injustice in futile waiting is exacerbated by the death of his son, another courageous "soldier" in the battle for justice. But García Márquez will go one step further to suggest that one death—the death of the son with all its biblical echoes—can bring collective life in that it keeps hope for justice alive. At the mythic-biblical level, that death is hope-filled, in that it is a vicarious one that must come so that new seed may grow into the sturdy plants of justice. At this level, waiting for the messiah is concomitant with an indestructible hope in the triumph of personal, social, and political justice.

But does García Márquez believe in such a sweeping triumph?[3] The novelist seems to echo the determined optimism both of Scripture and liberation theology. The prophetic literature of the Old and New Testaments attests to an ultimate liberation. Comfort and hope offered to the poor in Isaiah is always given in light of the call to obedience (implying the exercise of love and justice in the present) which in turn brings on the reward, understood as restoration and eternal life. Gutiérrez certainly believed in the abolition of the exploitation of human beings by human beings, and Miranda picks up on the biblical *eschaton* implicit in history by stating that every small effort in favor of justice contributes to the consummation of all things (296). The final, defiant stance of the colonel in the face of crass injustice suggests that the author, too, shares a similar belief in victory for good on the earth.

The Autumn of the Patriarch is the work in which García Márquez most successfully merges biblical images with liberationist themes to expose the fundamental sinfulness at the heart of the human struggle for power that creates human injustice. He works out this multifaceted problem by using familiar biblical figures and motifs to reveal the crass selfishness and pathetic frailties that lead to injustice. The apocalyptic setting for the nefarious career of the dictator protagonist, through his early years of popular idolatry to his demise in utter isolation, is seen from the perspective of "judgment," a view that allows for hope in an otherwise hopeless review of blind brutality. The textual association of the dictator with the biblical antichrist (8) clearly places the events of the novel in a kind of time-prior-to-consummation that precedes the introduction of a new and presumably better era. Here again the author draws on received Christian eschatological notions that serve him well to organize events and employ evocative images to characterize the dictator and his people.

The military figure here is none other than the Latin American general as dictator. García Márquez has said that the dictator is the only mythological figure that Latin America has ever produced (Minta 95). Unwilling to create yet another unilateral monster, like the dictators of other Latin American novelists, García Márquez employs parodic biblical figures and themes to demythologize the dictator. The confrontation of the people with their dictator appeals to a fundamentally liberationist theme: the obligation of political leaders to be the guardians of social justice. The entire book is the story of a people's liberation from their tyrant through the gradual revelation of the true nature, not only of political slavery, but of human selfishness, the antithesis of human love. This revelation is set out in terms of various parodied biblical and Christian motifs that underscore the cosmic dimensions of the battle: the dictator as patriarch, almighty god, and messianic figure is juxtaposed to the dictator as satanic antichrist and apocalyptic beast. The author also plays with the concept of the Trinity to reveal the futile attempts of the dictator to create a kind of triune godhead, under his command, who will rule the world made in his image.

The ultimate meaning of justice is suggested in the very structure of the novel, divided up into chapters introduced repeatedly by the same scene: the people discover the rotting body of the dictator in what remains of his once-luxurious palace. Somehow the horror that seems to cling to every page is mitigated by this persistent reminder that justice will triumph over the ill-gotten glory of humanity, a recurrent theme in García Márquez's novels. More importantly, for our study of justice, the entire book is organized around biblical sea imagery, very closely related in the biblical writings with Satan (as sea monster) and the chaotic dwelling place of evil. The dictator's betrayal of the "royal covenant" with his people is given in terms of biblical images associated with the biblical king-messiah—often portrayed in Scripture as winning victories for the people by slaying the dragon of the deep or quelling the turbulent sea.[4] As a kind of human-satanic antichrist, the dictator-patriarch, on the one hand, takes on the sea as his private property to dispose of as he wills. On the other hand, the satanic antichrist becomes a victim of that sea, a drowning man.

The dictator as godlike figure is everywhere in the novel. According to popular opinion, he can make the world stop at his command or be omnipresent, if he so chooses. It is later discovered that his reputed omnipresence is a ploy to confuse people into thinking that he is a god: he has hired a perfect "other" in the form of Patricio Aragonés, his double. The link with the biblical deity becomes evident in the implied "covenant" with the people that the patriarch-god has not kept. The Old Testament concept of justice is one of liberation from spiritual servitude—"You shall have no other gods before me" (Ex. 20:3)—as well as from sociopolitical injustice and slavery. It is precisely in this relationship to his people that the dictator is seen as having violated a covenant of trust at both the personal and political levels.

The idolatry inherent in his ascent to deity is, ironically, fashioned by those he most disdains. In the early years, when he still believes that the people love him, he basks in the servility with which the men, women, and children of the city leave what they are doing to shout his praises as the royal coach rolls by. He is referred to as the "nameless patriot who sits at the right hand of the Holy Trinity" (16). Later, he is no longer a mere aristocrat, but a veritable god figure. So convinced is he of his godlike status that he is amazed that when he dies (in the person of his double, Patricio Aragonés) the sun rises the next day and life continues as usual (34). Rhonda Buchanan, in a Jungian reading of the novel, sees the dictator as an impotent man hounded by a serious moral and psychological affliction that Jung calls "psychic inflation" (77). In his desperate search to be omnipotent, the patriarch compensates for his inadequacies by identifying with his office—he is the government. His deep-seated sense of personal deficiency, however, leads constantly to anxiety about the loss of power. The turning point in his delusions of grandeur is the disappearance of Manuela Sánchez, the beauty queen who disdains his love. He suddenly feels "older than God" (83), and begins to cultivate the solitude that will alienate him from others and even from himself.

The dictator clearly reveals a very human need for love, but his inability to give it or receive it on anybody's terms but his own is consistently underscored. Martha Canfield describes the dictator here as a pathetic being who establishes a relation of possessive love with the people, a man engaged in an obsessive search for a response to his love, but unable to understand the give and take inherent in the love relationship (1020). The multivoiced narration, which changes back and forth between the voice of the people and that of the other characters, is careful to point out the decay of the dictator in terms of his increasing unwillingness to give love as well as to take it. Hours before his death, he will suddenly assume the arbitrary prerogatives of an angry and vengeful god who invokes his creative powers to quell his fears of death (248), but now there is nobody to follow his commands.

With respect to the dictator's "infidelity" to his people, we are reminded of the liberationist concept of covenant. Assman, for example, sees God's covenant as having "life" and "human life" as its fundamental reason for being. Therefore, God has entrusted human beings with the mission of perpetuating, enriching, and protecting life (10). In the novel, the covenant relationship of the patriarch to the poor is violated in his unwillingness to see his neighbor as a true "other" rather than as a mere extension of his inordinate ego. The closest he comes to a sense of the other is when he allows room in his life for his favorites—Patricio Aragonés, Rodrigo de Aguilar, Leticia Nazareno, and finally the ruthless José Ignacio Sáenz de la Barra—all of them, as it turns out, mere Jungian shadow archetypes or moral reflections of the egocentric personality of the dictator (Buchanan 77) and eminently expendable. Indeed, he ignores the poor's right to think for themselves and refuses to acknowledge their inalienable autonomy. He has succeeded, like the exploiters of whom liberationists so insistently complain, in separating ethics from politics and social life, so that he is free to manipulate the people for his purposes.

The messianic figure is the most eloquent allusion to liberation in the novel. The biblical Messiah comes to save the poor and enslaved from their oppressors. In the novel, the patriarch as an inversion of the biblical Messiah appears in the context of the structural violence that characterizes his domain of power. Liberationists understand "structural violence" to mean a social order that by necessity allows the few to receive the fruits of the work of the many, an "order" that ironically guarantees political disorder on the one hand, and powerlessness of the victims on the other. Violence, not freedom, is the mechanism used to maintain the status quo and effect change (García 27).

Liberationist analysis shows how the most effective way for oppressors to achieve a semblance of social order is to make the poor accept the present state of affairs as natural. The slow process of "desengaño" or disillusionment, the realization that their myth is being dismantled before their eyes, is set against the people's credulity and their acceptance of the status quo dictated by their betrayer. The dictator's messianic character is in fact attributed to him by the people, at first, and later by his adulators, who cooperate with him in rewriting and recreating reality as well as history for the people. The biblical patriarch ostensibly elicits admiration and suggests heroic pioneering on behalf of the people. But the messianic role of liberation and justice is consistently countermanded by the dictator's self-serving attempts to set up a comfortable trinity consisting of himself as a kind of God the Father and Son rolled into one, his mother, Bendición Alvarado, as a kind of Virgin Mary (she is believed to have conceived him without the intervention of man [47]), and his political favorites who carry out his commands, as a kind of Holy Spirit.

Unable to have his almighty will done on earth, the patriarch turns to a kind of matriarchal idolatry that serves as a means of private "salvation." There are clear echoes of the Virgin Mary in the "immaculate" mother figure to whom the dictator confesses his joys and woes (48–53) and whom he invokes to strengthen him in his isolated battle to retain power: "he passed by the windows with a heavy heart crying out mother of mine Bendición Alvarado illuminate me with your wisest lights . . ." (247). But this mother worship is yet another outgrowth of his self-serving exercise of what he understands love to mean. The savior role and its concomitant ushering in of a just world are undermined consistently by the dictator's incapacity to understand how love saves.

Perhaps one of the easiest associations to make between the dictator and Christian concepts is that of the antichrist. The Christian understanding of this figure originates in Saint Paul's references to "that man of sin" who must come before Christ's return to earth at the end of time. Although the concept is not always clearly delineated, there is a connection between apocalypse and antichrist in all Catholic Christian thinking. Siemens has already studied the antichrist figure as García Márquez employs it in this novel (113–21), but it is important to remember that in Christian thought the antichrist is a satanic formulation. García Márquez attempts not only to depict the dictator in the role of an optimally evil man (like the antichrist), but to project the dictator's character and actions onto the larger setting of the satanic or evil forces that ever fight against good on this earth. To achieve this larger connection in the mind of the reader, García Márquez depicts the dictator in exaggeratedly grotesque lines. What emerges is a larger-than-life caricature who takes on the cosmically evil qualities of a Satan figure, even as he assumes the pathetic doom of a defeated antichrist.

On the one hand, we are given the physical and "spiritual" dimensions of the dictator through the "official" elementary school textbooks—a kind of beneficent giant who loves children and birds and whose secret potion heals lepers and the lame. He is a miraculous being "who had the virtue of being able to anticipate the designs of nature, who could guess a person's thought by one look in the eyes, and who had the secret of a salt with the virtue of curing lepers' sores and making cripples walk" (46). Those same textbooks tell how he is the product of an immaculate conception, his mother discovering his "messianic destiny" in a dream (47). However, as the reader is introduced to the truly weak, pathetically clownish, and endemically evil nature of the patriarch, the ironic messianic/redemptive imagery gives way to animalistic and diabolic associations. The relentless references to the man as a slow-moving, heavy-footed, elephant-like beast place him squarely in the animal realm and, more importantly, in the metaphoric lineage with such biblical monsters as Behemoth, a ferocious-looking but mild-mannered land beast somewhat like the hippopotamus or the prehistoric mastodon. However, the dictator is more obviously associated with another of the biblical monsters, namely Leviathan, a kind of twistingly sinister sea monster (Isa. 27:1). When John refers to Satan as a dragon in Revelation, he is drawing on this Old Testament association between the sea, the sea monsters, and Satan, who will be destroyed at the end of the world (cf. Ps. 74:13–15).

That we are meant to associate the dictator with Leviathan is evident in the patriarch's insignia: a dragon. Furthermore, the dictator's cold-blooded reptilelike eyes (154), which blink while still open (124), draw on the reptilian imagery (in this case, the reptile is an iguana) that so often is associated with the biblical devil. The indifference with which he assassinates army generals and children alike (115) and his penchant for vengeance (238) underscore the unfeeling, satanic nature of this military prince of implacable injustice.

We have already seen how the satanic is often associated with the sea in biblical literature. The conflict Yahweh of the Old Testament and the Christ of the New wage with the satanic adversary is a common thread that runs through the entire Bible into later Christian theology. In that context, the appearance of the dragon in the sea is a common combat image. The powerful and comprehensive way García Márquez uses the sea motif reveals a more than casual understanding of its biblical form and function. As in its biblical context, the sea/waters imagery in the novel is associated with the eventual triumph of justice over the powers of evil.

The sea imagery is set out like the two faces of a coin: the sea as the arena of confusion (the biblical dwelling place of Satan, cf. Ps. 104:2–9) and the sea as masses of peoples (Dan. 7:2–7, 16–17; Rev. 13:1). García

Márquez uses the confusion model to structure *The Autumn of the Patriarch*. Like a monstrous satanic creature, the dictator exercises his power in the midst of a seemingly endless confusion of people who are treated like marketable wares. His indulgence in egocentric acts of aggression against the people places the dictator in direct line with biblical associations between evil and the sea. The author seems aware of the biblical sea, with all of its implications of evil and peoples and salvation, when he lets his protagonist die the victim of a drowning.

As we begin the novel, the nature of the dictator's death slowly becomes evident to us. We are first told that it was commonly believed that the dictator's demise would coincide with a number of cataclysmic events: "on the day of his death the mud from the swamps would go back upriver to its source, that it would rain blood, that hens would lay pentagonal eggs, and the silence and darkness would cover the universe once more because he was the end of creation" (125). Prophecy here, however, is equivalent only to mere superstition. In the end, the dictator dies in spite of prophecies and quite differently from the dramatic way it was commonly predicted he would die.

What, then, is the significance of his death by drowning, a kind of death emphasized by the repeated description of the corpse opening each chapter? The visual image is that of a cadaver tossed on a lonely shore where we are allowed to stand and look out over the dark, chaotic waters in which the narrators and their dictator have lived out their life. The dictator's habitation of the sinister deep is hinted at early on when we are told what happens when he takes his siesta. A wave washes over the city and the nation when he sleeps the sleep of a "solitary drowned man" floating "face down on the lunar waters of his dreams" (9–10). After his death, the people find that his body "was sprouting tiny lichens and parasitic animals from the depths of the sea" (6). Later, as they prepare the body for burial, they will have to scrape off with fish scalers the "deep-sea shark suckers" from the body (166). The characterization of the dead dictator as a parasite-infested waste product of the sea clearly points to his role as insidious destroyer whose apocalypse has arrived so that the reign of justice can now begin.

The biblical imagery of the sea as peoples or nations is related to the last and worst offense of the dictator: the sale of the sea to foreign interests. Throughout the story, the patriarch is depicted as having a special love for the Caribbean sea that his palace overlooks—a precarious love, as it turns out, similar to the "love" he has for his people. Again, this love is revealed as self-serving in that when he must give it up to preserve his power, it, too, is expendable. The sea, just as his people, can be sold for a price. This trafficking in masses of people through the sale of the sea is rich with apocalyptic overtones, in that it constitutes the supreme act of injustice.

The absence of the sea has echoes of the other meaning of the biblical sea. After the general desolation of the earth and the destruction of the dragon or Satan, John finally sees in a vision a new earth, and he observes that "there was no longer any sea" (Rev. 21 : 1). The betrayal of his people by the dictator-antichrist-Satan reaches its climax in this supreme act of utter egotism. At this point, the sea ceases to be the dictator's dominion and becomes his executioner. Those same people whom he would so easily betray will take their sweetest revenge on their dictator by outliving him and taking up life after his "eternal" reign. This pivotal victory is at the core of a book that reveals García Márquez's faith in the eventual triumph of love and justice.

In both *No One Writes to the Colonel* and *The Autumn of the Patriarch* the Colombian novelist uses various biblical and liberationist concepts to build his own theology of justice. He has chosen the military man as the focus of these stories of injustice because the latter's privileged position within Spanish-American society allows for a more comprehensive understanding of what is heroic and demonic in Latin American society as it relates to the underlying theme of justice.

On one hand, in the *Colonel*, the liberationist idea of rediscovering the biblical neighbor complements the focus on the injustice of poverty, and both concepts are set in the context of apocalypse, a time of supreme wickedness that culminates a long period of waiting and precedes deliverance. The colonel's determination to have justice is firmly rooted in his faith in the essential dignity of the individual and the possibility of transforming society. The affinity with Latin American liberationists is also seen in the blame placed on negligent political leaders who ignore those whom they have been called to serve. On the other hand, to depict the universal implications of human injustice, García Márquez employs the biblical Christ/Son figure and the cock to capture the deep betrayal inherent in injustice in general and in the particular injustice being perpetrated on the poverty-stricken war hero. The persistence of injustice contrasts with the colonel's uncompromising faith in the eventual triumph of justice; the cock as symbol of the indomitable human spirit makes waiting for the cause of the messianic, sacrificed son bearable and even heroic.

In both novels, García Márquez sets forth liberationist ideas and ideals through a reworking of biblical motifs with the ultimate purpose of communicating his own understanding of justice. There is a clear underlying optimism in both novels, but they are laid out in less-than-rose-colored terms. The evil at the core of political-military power denies the colonel justice; the evil at the core of the dictator denies justice to an entire nation. In both novels, the struggle for justice is not limited to the political arena—it launches into the moral and spiritual realms of human selfishness that are set against the exercise of human love. The dialogue with biblical images and liberationist themes is the indispensable means by which the author first understands the parameters of the problem, then sets it out for the reader's consideration: How can human love grow in a context of blatant injustice, even if it has been accepted as the status quo? In the end, García Márquez clings to his faith in the victory of good over evil, love over selfishness, while still recognizing the wretchedness of the human heart.

4.

Mask and Mirror
Isabel Allende's Mechanism for Justice in *The House of the Spirits*

Claudia Marie Kovach

No one brings suit justly,
  no one goes to law honestly;
They rely on empty pleas, they speak lies,
  conceiving mischief and begetting iniquity.   (Isa. 59:4)

The prophet Isaiah thus envisions how the lack of truth, righteousness, and integrity in relationships brings the divisiveness of sin into the world. Injustice splinters the wholeness of creation, causing a disintegration of personal and interpersonal integrity. Novelist Isabel Allende echoes this cry when she tells an interviewer: "I feel terribly angry at the world. I think that the world is a crazy place, very unjust and unfair and violent, and I'm angry at that. I want to change the rules, change the world" (Douglas Foster 46). Such a changing of the world requires, in religious terminology, a conversion, a method of promoting reconciliation. But reconciliation must begin with oneself, and Allende seems to realize this requirement. Suffering isolation from family and country after going into exile as a result of a military takeover, Allende felt the need to recapture her inner being. She turned to writing, that very significant social practice embraced by those seeking to express both the spiritual and social requirements of integrity and justice. Her own spiritual goals upon writing her first novel, *The House of the Spirits* (which began as a personal letter to her dying grandfather still back in Chile), centered on a recovery of identity, a recon-struction of self, a fostering of emotional, psychological, and spiritual in-tegrity.[1] By recovering and recounting her memories Allende gained the kind of wholeness that ontological liberationists cite as a first step toward the attainment of economic and social justice.

Although usually associated more readily with the current Latin Ameri-can aesthetic of magic realism and with secular political fiction rather than with theological perspectives, Allende says that *The House of the Spirits* achieved a spiritual goal: "I felt that my roots had been recovered and that during that patient exercise of daily writing I had also recovered my own soul" ("Writing" 43). Allende's statement implies her sensitivity to that in-sight found in Isaiah that connects social justice with personal integrity. An inner sense of worth and wholeness that comes from connection to and rec-ognition of family and culture remains a basic prerequisite for achieving social justice. What Allende achieved in her own life by writing the novel is reflected in the novel as well, for it illuminates how reconciliation and mediation, particularly within the self, work together as necessary precur-sors to achieving biblical justice. Moreover, Allende's novel highlights through the women characters a particularly feminist focus that reflects biblical feminists' concern for recovering human integrity within the fe-male person and by means of female intercession.

The first step to understanding the mechanism Allende uses in *The House of the Spirits* to set up a prophetic vision of female integrity and justice is to look at how the novel presents the role of memories. Achieving personal integrity in the face of experiences and social structures that have served to shatter, oppress, or repress identity cannot be accomplished by simple im-perative. Integration requires an exploration of possibilities, a trying-on of alternatives, a viewing and reviewing of experiences. Continual reinte-gration by means of seeing memories from all angles, in both masked and mirrored ways, allows—as we shall see—for the reconciliation of self. This process establishes in *The House of the Spirits* a framework for conver-sion, a literal "turning toward," an instance of what Kierkegaard described as the ancient ideal of "recollection": "just as they [the Greeks] taught that all knowledge is a recollection, so will modern philosophy teach that the whole of life is a repetition" (381). The life that Allende "re-peats" and "re-collects" throughout the novel by means of the women characters is her own and that of her family and country. Yet the novel points as well toward the possibilities of reconciliation inherent in all humanity; it speaks out for the conversion of oppressive social structures.

By writing, Allende breaks the oppression of her own silence and implicitly joins in the Latin American movement of *concientizacion*. This process of recovering the lost, of remembering what has been neglected, of reconstructing what has been left out, of reclaiming a forfeited heritage, is at the heart of a revolutionary liberation theology. This process of self-liberation "aims at breaking through the pervasive 'culture of silence,' that defines the oppressed condition, by an inner resurrection of soul that transforms a person from an object of conditions which determine his reality and consciousness to a subject of his own history and destiny" (Ruether 178). Perhaps more importantly, this movement prompts people to question the dominant power structure that forms the basis of their whole inherited tradition. The women of Allende's novel both individually and together shatter the silence that sustains and contributes to oppression; they discover the power of repeated memories; they forge a new personal and cultural consciousness positing a chain of connection, love, and reconciliation. Forms of repetition in their lives help lead to self-liberation and to reconciliation beyond the self.

This radical recovery and reconstruction is at the center of Elisabeth Schüssler Fiorenza's ground-breaking *In Memory of Her*, a work that uses a combination of New Testament historiography and theology to define a "discipleship of equals": "Feminist biblical spirituality must be incarnated in a historical movement of women struggling for liberation. It must be lived in prophetic commitment, compassionate solidarity, consistent resistance, affirmative celebration, and in grassroots organizations of the *ekklesia of women*" (349). This stance promotes unity and reconciliation; it provides a formula for justice that arises from relationships supported by repeated memories. Indeed, the very essence of solidarity for Fiorenza resides in the reclaiming of the lost: "to insist that women's history is an integral part of early Christian historiography [implies] the search for roots, for solidarity with our foresisters, and finally for the memory of their sufferings, struggles, and powers as women" (xix–xx). Remembering this erased "her" takes the form of recollection, both as a kind of religious contemplation and as a recalling to mind of the temporarily forgotten. Solidarity is achieved by means of a recitation of memories, a repetition of the historical details that women share.

Such unity underpins the biblical call for justice, an appeal that centers on good and proper relationships—with God, with nature, and with other human beings. The personal, God-centered ideal seeks conversion, personal integrity, and self-discovery, what John S. Dunne calls "self-appropriation"; [2] reverence for nature asks for responsible and ongoing stewardship of creation; social commitment reaches out beyond the self and penetrates both the macrocosm of political institutions and the microcosm of family life. [3] Yet of all the relationships highlighted by Scripture, the first—personal peace and reconciliation with God (always for the Christian a product of the inner working of God's grace in one's life)—is perhaps the most important since it inspires attachment to the other two. As a result, the process of self-appropriation, the constant, repeated becoming of what one is, remains a prerequisite for this ideal and ultimately allows integration of all relationships into an harmonious whole, creating an experience of the *shalom* ideal described by Nicholas Wolterstorff. [4] The act of self-discovery is a crucial step that leads to justice.

Primarily by means of the women characters of *The House of the Spirits*, Allende reconstitutes the biblical feminists' formula of solidarity by means of various kinds of repetition to achieve self-appropriation and *shalom*. The image of the mask (the irrational, the unconscious, the soul) and the image of the mirror (the rational, the conscious, the self) provide a mechanism for tracing the inner integrative conversion necessary for this rather complex but ideal form of justice. Allende's method is to create and recreate the images and themes of mirror and mask in a way that brings together the double-sided coin that unites the rational and the irrational, the objective and the subjective, the analytic and the intuitive. Repetition in its mirrored state and repetition in its masked form become for Allende a mechanism for complete reconciliation and justice.

The House of the Spirits reveals a world rife with injustice and peopled with individuals who lack the righteous integrity needed for such reconciliation. A family chronicle tracing several generations, the novel presents a concatenation of conflicting patriarchies that serve merely to spawn a chain of hatred and revenge. Personally, characters in the novel experience social alienation, spiritual perplexity, and psychological instability. Socially, the work depicts mistreatment of women, the abuse of tenant farmers, and the squalor of the city shantytowns. Politically, injustice reigns in the excesses of the conservative right, the extremes of the left-wing socialist reformers, and the violence of the deposing military dictatorship. Institutional religion stands as an oppressive purveyor of guilt and fear and a self-serving supporter of the status quo. Even nature adds its share of terror, destruction, and pain with the devastations of earthquakes and plagues.

Much of Allende's view of the world stems, of course, from her experience of injustice in her native Latin America. Exiled for sixteen years in

Venezuela after the assassination in 1973 of her uncle, the former Chilean president Salvador Allende Gossens, Allende draws deeply upon her family history and the political upheaval in modern Chile. Yet she sides with Isaiah and the Psalmists who recognize the potential for divine and human justice, the hope for ultimate reconciliation for the faithful people of God: "Zion shall be redeemed by justice, and those in her who repent, by righteousness. But rebels and sinners shall be destroyed together, and those who forsake the LORD shall be consumed."[5] Allende's hope is evidenced by her novelistic choices: she does not depict in *The House of the Spirits* merely an unjust, unfair, violent world. Like Isaiah, she denounces evil but also proclaims the potential for unity and equality; like the Psalmist, she demonstrates the possibilities for love in the world.

In recovering her own memories, Allende mirrors her own experiences and magically weaves a world in which women preserve their memories in various artistic forms, simultaneously breaking the silence of oppression and achieving solidarity. Clara's notebooks give witness to life; Blanca recounts the magic stories from her uncle Marcos's enchanted trunks; Alba cherishes the past in her own writing, succeeds in getting her grandfather to write his memories, and retrieves her grandmother's notebooks. Likewise, Rosa's fantastically embroidered tablecloth, Blanca's creches of imaginary animals, and Alba's amazing frescoes record the "wishes, memories, sorrows, and joys" of their lives (270). In every case, the recall of memories involves a constant and inexhaustible recurrence or repetition of shared actions, events, feelings that begin to carry out the program for community and remembering that Fiorenza advocates. Even the narrative structure of the novel itself reflects the goal of iterating personal memories in a way that mirrors the connection of the characters. The combination of Clara's notebooks (which span the whole period of her life), Alba's notes and experiences, and Esteban's reminiscences forges the essence of the three major personalities of the novel; the narration that shifts among these memories reflects these characters' close emotional and physical interrelation. Indeed, Clara's notebooks are organized according to events, not chronologically, to emphasize that the process of remembering in life often makes exact dates secondary to powerfully remembered personal experiences, events that can only be mirrored experientially rather than categorized systematically. Such repetition serves as a mirror of life and adds to the viewing and reviewing of self that eventually aids in the working out of conversion, redemption, reconciliation, and understanding. Repeated memories function as a mirror to bring into the open what is needed to realize emotional and spiritual integrity.

Another aspect of repetition appears in the image of the mask in which the action of concealing also serves, in a surreptitious way, to promote integration of the self and the soul. Early in the novel Nana tries to cure Clara's muteness by scaring her with innumerable costumes—much as one would try to cure a case of hiccups. In another instance where a type of healing is required, Férula is described as wearing an idol's mask when she returns from her agitated, detailed confession of what she witnessed as she peered through the partially opened door to Clara and Esteban's bedroom. Later, when she dies alone, having been expelled from the Trueba home by the wrathful Esteban, Férula is discovered decked out, masked, in finery found on the garbage dump. This masquerade shrouds her tortured soul yet speaks to the nature of the desires that her life of denial caused her to reject. Alba, too, knows the secret of the mask as she learns from her uncle Nicolas how to "conquer pain and other weaknesses of the flesh" (273) by calling to mind countless examples of frightening, even macabre situations, or by inflicting physical pain so that she can learn to relax and let it pass through her. As a result, much later she does survive her ordeal of torture by masking reality and immersing herself in the task of retelling her story. In addition, the various establishments in which we meet the prostitute Transito Soto provide costumes that mask the truth of the situation and provide illusion for those for whom reality is unthinkable. The mask satisfies the inherent need for subconscious healing through the rehearsal of hidden, secret feelings. Only after the experience of such personal healing can the greater goal of reconciliation with the world and others successfully take place.

The narrative structure of the novel also adds another layer of mask. It contains an amalgam of first-person and third-person narratives, with Alba as the main compiler. The resulting shifts from the first person to the third, reflecting as well the "appropriation" of each person by each of the three narrators, keep the reader continually off balance in regard to point of view. The reader is made to experience at first hand a masking of voice, an (at least) intermittent veiling of person and reality. Moreover, the culling of event rather than chronology from Clara's notebooks may mirror many people's experience of life, but it also serves to incorporate a translucency that hides as much as it reveals. Reading the novel, then, becomes an experience of being transported into the sometimes hazy world of memories, the place where dreams, reminiscences, facts, guesses, wishes, and regrets intermingle.

Besides providing repeated thematic images, the juxtaposition of mask and mirror within the novel's narrative strategies begins to show how, in Jungian terms, the tensions between the irrational and the rational are evoked. Jung explains how elements sometimes found in dreams are not derived from the dreamer's personal experience but appear to be "aboriginal, innate, and inherited shapes of the human mind." Such irrational pieces, these "archetypes," are part of the so-called "collective unconscious," "the biological, prehistoric, and unconscious development of the mind in archaic man, whose psyche was still close to that of the animal" (*Man* 67). As human beings we all share this collective heritage, manifested in ritual, dream, and literature (Frye 105). Feminist archetypal critics note how repeated rituals, especially their modern manifestations in the form of novels, aid in the process of recovery and healing: "The novel performs the same role in women's lives as do the Eleusinian, dying-god, and witchcraft rituals—a restoration through remembering, crucial to our survival" (A. Pratt 176). Allende's juxtaposition of irrational mask and rational mirror in her novel serves to move her characters to these deeper levels of conscious and unconscious experience. As Allende also knows, recovering the lost requires the exercise of memory and the result is a reintegration of self that leads to personal integrity and the possibility of justice in the world. Creative expression, as in Allende's own exercise of it in *The House of the Spirits* and in the various examples of it in the lives of the female characters in the novel, provides an ideal landscape for repeating memories in their masked and mirrored forms in order to work out issues of identity and integrity.

Although, roughly speaking, the mask in *The House of the Spirits* symbolizes irrational myth and the mirror evokes rational, objective reality, the interrelationship of these elements is complex. Jung holds that the artist is peculiarly attuned to the unconscious, which manifests itself in visions within the imagination. Unlike Freud, however, Jung believed that such visions were not personal but transcended the artist's experience ("Psychology" 175–88). Allende's mirror tends to repeat personal visions; her mask simultaneously rehearses mythical forms. Together, mask and mirror move the self and soul to a higher level of understanding so that justice may result. Accordingly, Aniela Jaffé explains the archetype that blends myth and reality as the psychological phenomenon, occurring equally with artists and medieval alchemists, of finding in objects a "secret soul," a "mysterious animation," a "spirit in the matter" (254–55).

This archetypal interplay of mask and mirror, of irrational and rational, also derives in part from the action of magic realism in the novel, which illustrates Jaffé's discussion of the "secret soul" in objects. The source of much of current Latin American literary enchantment, magic realism can be traced to Europe during the period between the two world wars. Menton describes the movement as "longing for order, stability, reality, tranquility, and naive optimism" despite political, economic, and social tumult (59). It is not difficult to envision a similar psychological situation in Allende's Latin America where violent dictatorships, outrageous inflation, and unconscionable poverty are common. Because the goal of magic realism is to discover "the magic quality of everyday life and things" (Menton 52), it contains both an ordered, stable, objective, representational treatment (mirror) and a mosaic-like, ghostly, mythological, visionary, playful presentation (mask). The first evokes the rational side of repetition, which consciously mirrors reality in an analytic, lineal, objective, abstract way. The second shows a masked, unconscious side of repetition that draws upon the intuitive, concrete, subjective truth. Allende's narrative technique of magic realism thus negotiates both mask and mirror, embodying a holistic vision of the world. It allows the individual conversion of character evident in the archetypal elements to begin the important move to the wider realm of social responsibility.

The distinctions between the two types of repetition that make up such mediation—irrational masking and rational mirroring—are not always clear; however, with Allende's characters this vagueness becomes a virtue. Seen from another perspective, one might say that such repetitions are capable of drawing upon both sides of the brain. Indeed, findings in recent neuroscience indicate the importance of a linguistic theory that includes a consideration of language's dual tracks, roughly analogous to the action of the mask (right brain) and the mirror (left brain). As Brownstein notes, "it is likely that minds whose principal functions are managerial operate out of categorical imperatives, out of more heavily left-lateralized strategies, while the survival of women and other colonized people depends upon bilateral strategies, upon minds adept at negotiating difference" (5–6). Allende's women seem to have this ability, and in *The House of the Spirits* this aesthetic forms a basis for the mediating mechanisms that allow justice through reconciliation.

Furthermore, to achieve reconciliation, neither mask nor mirror alone will suffice to mediate the discrepancies injustice propagates. The female approach in Allende's novel, especially that of the four women spanning generations, seems somehow to merge the two to create a kind of magical mediation—repetition with a difference. Accordingly, the novel gives insight into the mechanism of creative conversion and reconciliation; even the very names of the women repeat with a difference. Clara, Blanca, and Alba have names that indicate similar meaning: clarity of light, whiteness, brightness of dawn. The purity of the rose is hinted at in the name of Rosa.[6] But for Allende's women, mediation requires an embrace of both the pain and the joy, the ugliness and the beauty, the evil and the good. Only then can an integrated wholeness serve as a reasonable expectation of justice.

Rosa, the first mediator in the female sodality of Allende's novel, embodies the contradictory elements necessary for this kind of integrity. Her name is indicative of clearness and purity, yet does it imply a red or white rose? Paradoxically, this ambiguity acts to unite rather than to separate the elements of reality and myth, the apparent and the hidden, the concrete and the abstract. For Rosa surprisingly holds a beauty that "struck fear in their hearts" (24), an apparent contradiction that does much to explain her unique nature. Concrete beauty, which should please and attract, instead causes the opposite emotions of dread and intimidation. Both immediate family and potential suitors recognize this special quality of Rosa, and it marks her as an unforgettable being who in her very essence transcends the ordinary. She herself exists on a level beyond what most people experience and thus points to the possibility of another reality. Opinions and beliefs do not separate people in such a world where both mask and mirror are integrated. The possibility of justice thus exists in an environment where one can accept, in spite of the pain or insecurity they might bring, the shock and despair as well as the joy and the surprise of disparate elements.

Besides indicating paradox, both red and white images are important in symbolizing Rosa's mediating function. The red rose of martyrdom, of blood, adumbrates Rosa's early death and the guiding symbolism of her spiritual, saintly mediating presence throughout the generations of the del Valle and the Trueba families. Indeed, Rosa's perfection seems reflective as well of the stainless, matchless Blessed Virgin Mary, the "Rose of Sharon," the "rose without thorn," the mediatrix par excellence. Her simultaneous oneness with nature and otherworldliness even in death comes with a "scent of roses" (26) as Nana, unsuspecting, brings her a morning breakfast tray. As Esteban Trueba stands watch over her coffin, he sees the beautiful "green fountain of her hair" (37), an indication of her ephemeral nature, a magically real symbol of how her fair skin made her not only appear delicate, sickly, a somewhat unreal creature from the sea (half woman, half mermaid), but also signaled—as Nívea's premonition foretells—that Rosa was "a heavenly being, that she was not destined to last very long in the vulgar traffic of this world" (6). Her death from accidental poisoning, rather than from frailness of constitution, is then another example of how expectations formed by the outer reality can be usurped by the play of forces beyond one's control. Rosa's impact on her family, especially the female members, comes in large part from this striking amalgamation of mask and mirror, of the unexpected and the expected, of the hidden and the revealed.

Rosa as mediator serves as the first touchstone in the family, especially as a basis for the process of self-appropriation that presupposes an ability to be reconciled with the Almighty. C. H. Dodd reviews "the problem of reconciling the immanence and the transcendence of God, which has its roots in primitive tension between the 'otherness' and the familiarity of the Divine." He describes the mediating use of angels, the Law, and "poetical or philosophical constructions in which the immanent Divine . . . conceived as the Wisdom, or the Spirit, or the Word, of the transcendent God and these aspects of God are given a quasi-personal existence." Dodd sees these attempts at mediation as abstract, with the concrete manifestation emerging in the New Testament incarnation of the Word as Jesus Himself (208–09). Rosa mediates in a similar way by her ability to unite ephemeral otherworldliness with a very real sensual attractiveness. As angelic mediator, she can thus unite abstract and concrete, human and divine. Furthermore, she becomes a Christ-like symbol of mediation, a kind of scapegoat, in her death by innocently taking the poison intended for her father by his political enemies. But Severo del Valle's conscience is not cleansed by her death. On the contrary, he was "incapable of thinking that his daughter had died instead of him. He crumpled to the floor, moaning that he was the guilty one because of his ambition and bluster" (29). She is a scapegoat, but an inadequate one. She can save her father from death (the action of the mirror), but she cannot redeem his conscience (the play of the mask). Rosa the Beautiful, the pure, becomes by her death enshrined in everyone's memory as the cause of the "shadow of suspended vengeance" (32).

With these limitations, then, how does Rosa succeed as a mediator? Additional insights into mediating mechanisms can come from a look at René Girard's anthropological forays into the circumstances of mimetic desire as the mainspring of all human disorder and order. For Girard, identity or loss of difference stemming from the desire for identity can cause the disintegration of community structure: "The scapegoat victim provides an outlet for violence by unifying the entire community against him" (104). Rosa operates instead in a more Christ-like capacity. Rather than forging community identity, Rosa unifies despite her inadequacy to relieve her father's suffering because identity is replaced by integrity. Instead of dissolving difference, Rosa embodies difference, the conflicting and competing elements of mask and mirror. The unification of community is thus not an artificial imposition of structure but a natural acceptance of heterogeneity. Christ's call to embrace one's enemies demands the embodiment of difference, the incongruency that Rosa represents in the family memory. She is the first in a line of women in *The House of the Spirits* who integrate mask and mirror in their lives symbolically and concretely. She displays her weaving of the rational and the irrational by embroidering "the largest tablecloth in the world" on which could be found concretely "a paradise of impossible creatures" (6). An awareness of the destructive violence found within the desire for identity described by Girard should argue afresh for this alternative process, this integration of mask and mirror that Allende's women use to forge justice. With Rosa as the mediating scapegoat, the first step is taken in a self-appropriation, an action of becoming that includes both the dark, masked side and the reflective, mirrored part of experience. It is a process that unites positively rather than negatively and takes several generations to complete.

In a magical, spiritual way Rosa even becomes in death the mediator between her former fiancé, Esteban Trueba, and her sister Clara. Described by Esteban as "an apparition" that entered his life "like a distracted angel who stole my soul as she went by" (22), Rosa is his first love and remains with him in dream and fantasy. It is memory of her, in fact, that leads him to seek a wife in the del Valle household: "He had gone to see the del Valle family to inquire if they might still have an unmarried daughter, because after so many years of absence and barbarism, he knew of nowhere else to begin to keep his promise to his mother of giving her legitimate grandchildren, and he concluded that if Severo and Nívea had accepted him as a prospective son-in-law in the days of Rosa the Beautiful, there was no reason they should refuse him, especially now that he was a rich man" (87). After Clara's death Esteban builds "the most fitting, the most luxurious mausoleum in the world . . . with statues made with angel wings" and plans to lie there one day between Clara and Rosa, thus finding support in life and death from the pair of sisters he loved so well and so long.

But Clara functions even more than Rosa as the mainstay of the family. Clara's clairvoyance often makes it seem that she too "lived in another world" (98). Her reality is a "kaleidoscope of jumbled mirrors" (82). Again, mediation occurs in a jumbled mosaic of the rational and the irrational, of the conscious and the unconscious, of the mirrored and the masked. By virtue of her clairvoyance, Clara has a special connection with nature. She is therefore quite sensitive to the contrasts between the life in the city and the life at Tres Marías, the Trueba ancestral homestead where Esteban had made "progressive" improvements for which he prided himself. From the first, Clara recognizes the situation at Tres Marías to constitute "her mission in life": "She was not impressed by the brick houses, the school, and the abundant food, because her ability to see what was invisible immediately detected the workers' resentment, fear, and distrust; and the almost imperceptible noise that quieted them whenever she turned her head enabled her to guess certain things about her husband's character and past" (105). She devotes herself to teaching the inhabitants of Tres Marías the basics of hygiene, literacy, and women's liberation. Only when she once again becomes pregnant does she revert to her "visionary tasks, speaking with apparitions and spending hours writing in her notebooks" (112). By the act of writing, communicating her memories, she retains the mirror within the mask of the supernatural and secures a true mingling of the concrete and the abstract.

Clara's ability to combine mask and mirror becomes most apparent during her periods of silence in which she communicates only through writing. Once when fatigued with advanced pregnancy and long travel between Tres Marías and the city, Clara announces: "I think I'm going to elevate." "Not here," her husband replies, unsure whether mask or mirror would be presenting itself. He was "[t]errified at the idea of Clara flying over the heads of the passengers along the track. But she wasn't talking about physical levitation; she meant she wanted to rise to a level that would allow her to leave behind the discomfort and heaviness of pregnancy and the deep fatigue that had begun to seep into her bones. She entered one of her long periods of silence—I think it lasted several months—during which she used her little slate, as she had in her days of muteness. This time I wasn't worried . . . since I had come to understand that silence was my wife's last refuge, not a mental illness as Dr. Cuevas said it was" (113). Whether masking her physical discomfort as in this pregnancy, or masking her emotional pain as in her childhood response to Rosa's death, Clara still continues to mirror, to externalize her inner self through writing.

Despite her psychological distance during much of her time with her family, Clara nevertheless serves as a mediating force throughout the generations. Her self-appropriation takes Rosa's to the next stage of unifying the self and the soul, transforming her experiences of both mirror and mask into a source for communication. As a result, despite her apparent otherworldliness Clara can show compassion to the poor, a clear example of personal integrity that leads to justice. In fact, she includes an important "active" element to both sides of her personality in her compassionate helping of the peasants at Tres Marías and, when again in the spiritual realm, in writing her memories. Clara intuitively seems to know that when Genesis describes how "God created man in his own image" (1:27) the message is that human beings have an innate ability to reach out and find God in others. As a result, Clara's trip to the hacienda becomes an outreach as she improves both the physical and spiritual plight of the farm workers and contends with the results of earthquake and plague. Similarly, the active, concrete exercise of writing in her notebooks serves the purpose of externalizing her memories. She thus reaches out to her family through the chronicling of tangible events.

Even after Clara's death her notebooks, "which gave witness to life" (128), give her granddaughter Alba the courage to transcend her ordeal at the hands of Colonel García. These notebooks also inspire Alba to convince her grandfather, the tough-skinned, violent *patrón* who started the chain of hatred and revenge, to write the story, the memories of their lives. Clara thus mediates primarily by uniting the mirror of memories and the mask of the visionary within the medium of her notebooks.

In the case of Clara's daughter Blanca, mediation takes place as a human defiance of social class in the quest for love and as a mystical connection to nature in her creative work in clay. The first form of mediation draws upon the mirror of concrete, uncompromised passion; the second appears within the mask of artistic self-expression. Indeed, when Blanca—this intended "white" one—is born, she shocks everyone with her hairy darkness and is described as appearing at birth as an "armadillo" (101). Her double personality emerged even as a child: "She was considered timid and morose. Only in the country, her skin tanned by the sun and her belly full of ripe fruit, running through the fields with Pedro Tercero, was she smiling and happy. Her mother said that that was the real Blanca, and that the other one, the one back in the city, was a Blanca in hibernation. . . . she showed

not the slightest inclination for her mother's spiritualism or her father's fits
of rage. The family jokingly said that she was the only normal person for
many generations, and it was true she was a miracle of equilibrium and
serenity" (143). Emblematic of the secret, hidden soul behind the evident,
mirrored self, Blanca—despite her surface differences from other family
members—retains in her artistic creations of imaginary animals the visionary ability of the beautiful Rosa who embroidered fantastic tablecloths and
of Clara the Clairvoyant. She is especially important in the process of self-
appropriation occurring in Allende's family of women because she mirrors
the biblical message of reconciling love on all three levels of religious experience. Significantly, Blanca is first introduced to the process of pottery
and the use of clay by Old Pedro García, her lover's grandfather, when he
wishes to help her keep her hands busy and her mind off of her migraine
headaches. Later, she shares this therapeutic gift of nature with mongoloid
children, bringing them joy by teaching them how to mold the clay. Most
importantly, through the power of human love, she transcends distinctions
of class, essential to attaining justice in the world. Her devoted love for
Pedro García Tercero, who was not of her own social class, adds the human
side of Fiorenza's "*praxis of agape*" (323) to the iterative yet incremental
process of self-appropriation throughout the generations of women.

Alba, Blanca's daughter from her liaison, similarly contains the double
action of self and soul. Her name, in fact, containing within it the idea of
"white" and "dawn," also embraces the mediating connection that makes
distinct definition unattainable, for it is impossible to determine exactly
when night is completed and daybreak has arrived. In Spanish, the word
can also mean "alb," the full-length white linen vestment with long sleeves
that is gathered at the waist with a cincture and worn by a priest at Mass.
Alba's mediating function is certainly priestlike in her ability to bring con-
solation to the tortured soul of her wrathful, vengeful, bitter old grandfather; indeed, she has always been the only one who could brighten the aging
patriarch's life. Her visible legacy from her great-aunt Rosa, the first mediator, comes as distinctive "algae tones in her hair" (331), a reality that
cannot help but influence Esteban's feelings. Despite Alba's illegitimacy
and the fact that her father is Esteban's bitter enemy, she becomes for Esteban "the only person I would ever have close to me the rest of my life"
(202). Wearing metonymically the masked vestments (hidden concrete outside garments) of the reconciler, Alba is likewise in the novel described as
showing her mirrored soul (revealed abstract inside reality) when her transforming vision in the basement comes from a veritable "kaleidoscope of

the mirror" (331). Attributes of mask and mirror, inside and outside, abstract and concrete, soul and self, are finally merged in this woman who is able to transcend the hatred of several generations by piecing together the memories of many events, first in the torture chamber without paper or pen and later with the help of her grandfather Esteban's remembrances and of her grandmother Clara's notebooks. Because Alba has appropriated not only her own life experiences but also the souls of her women forebears, she forges community and can say that "now I seek my hatred and cannot seem to find it. I feel its flame going out as I come to understand the existence of Colonel García and the others like him, as I understand my grandfather and piece things together from Clara's notebooks, my mother's letters, the ledgers of Tres Marías, and the many other documents spread before me on the table" (432). Alba realizes that not only through the repetition of life events through writing, thereby communicating the events, experiences, and "mission" (432) of a person, a family, indeed of all human beings, but also through the repetition of the inner soul (which stage by stage brings one to be what one truly is) can the inimical, masked, dark side of the soul and clear-sighted self-integrity converge. This elimination of anger makes possible reconciliation and justice.

Alba's self-appropriation includes the appropriation of the qualities of her great-aunt Rosa, her grandmother Clara, and her mother Blanca, as well as her own experiences. She more than anyone else learns how to heed the biblical call for justice through a reconciliation with other people. Through her period of torture Alba mirrors the scapegoat experience of Rosa, but survives. At this level, Alba can finally dissolve the guilt, violence, and hate that Rosa's death could only augment in the family. Consequently, she can say: "It would be very difficult for me to avenge all those who should be avenged, because my revenge would be just another part of the same inexorable rite" (432). She can indeed become an instrument of mediation by appropriating—a repetitive process—both the masked evils that terrorize her soul and the mirrored integrity of existence: "I want to think that my task is life and that my mission is not to prolong hatred but simply to fill these pages while I wait for Miguel, while I bury my grandfather, whose body lies beside me in this room, while I wait for better times to come, while I carry this child in my womb, the daughter of so many rapes or perhaps of Miguel, but above all, my own daughter" (432). Alba thus recognizes the process of appropriation in the generations of the past and the future. Her integration includes the all-important task of communicating her memories and those of her family.

The reconciliation begun by Allende's women results from their being able somehow to see the integrated whole in its masked/mirrored manifestations of reality: distorted, gruesome, secret, magic, hidden. The process of writing, that is, mirroring, bearing "witness to life" (432), allows an acceptance of responsibility for life, provides reverence for life, and finally brings reconciliation of all disruptive, excessive emotions. Justice ultimately comes from a blurring of the details that cause hate, revenge, jealousy. In engendering peace and forgiveness, acceptance of both mask and mirror recreates an integrated wholeness and regenerates that integrity in the world as justice.

Fiorenza notes that through the praxis of agape the women disciples of Jesus could exemplify true discipleship, a discipleship that indicts hate and the death-dealing powers of the world. This "discipleship of equals," one of service and love, is "continually recreated" (334), for "[t]he true spiritual person is according to Paul one who walks in the Spirit, she who brings about this new world and family of God over and against the resistance and pull of all oppressive powers of this world's enslaving patriarchal structures" (346). In *The House of the Spirits* Allende recreates in a way that integrates the totality for which justice strives. Her women recognize (intuitively if not cognitively) that in the end a personal experience of conversion (a literal "turning toward") is the key to true peace and justice. They learn that they must transcend suffering on the personal level before they can hope to apply this skill, sensitivity, and knowledge to the level of politics and society. In this sense and in the literal sense that she inhabits the world of her family memories—the spiritual reality of Rosa, Clara, and Blanca—Alba can be said to "walk in the Spirit" (346). Her acts of gathering and communicating her memories in the form of the story preserving her "roots" (430) reflect the identical process Allende herself goes through in writing *The House of the Spirits* and make her a kind of prophet promoting justice on the deepest levels. Fiorenza reminds us that the Gospel requires *ekklesia*, "a dynamic reality of Christian community. It is not a local or static term, it is not even a religious expression; it means the *actual* gathering of people" (345). Can a work of fiction provide such a gathering? As it witnesses to an exploration of possibilities, a process of self-appropriation, a concrete reconstitution of memories, it can move toward Fiorenza's requirement of commitment, accountability, and solidarity in community that she finds to be "the hallmarks of our calling and struggle" (346).

The concept of social class, especially, becomes insignificant in this feminine process of mosaic mediation reflecting a kaleidoscopic reality that engenders true reconciliation, a conversion that "converges" mask and mirror. Ironically, Esteban García does not realize that the woman he is torturing is his own cousin, through not only the *patrón* but also through the son of his grandmother's brother. Likewise, Alba's ignorance of the paternity of her unborn daughter—the result of multiple rapes—loses importance. Thus no longer do guilt, hate, or revenge control the interplay of relationships that knit human beings and their creator. Instead, redemption comes to Zion through a kaleidoscopic mirroring, a re-imagining and re-creation of integrity and justice.

5

Deciphering the Wounds
The Politics of Torture and Julio Cortázar's Literature of Embodiment

Lois Parkinson Zamora

"You have seen how difficult it is to decipher the script with one's eyes; but our man deciphers it with his wounds."

Franz Kafka, "In the Penal Colony"

That's not a man in pain
        but a *Brazilian Phone*—
It won't be making any outgoing calls.

That's not a woman sprawling on the floor
But *an old-fashioned dance*,
        like the tango.

Pull up a chair with a knotted rope.
let's have a *tea party with toast*
        and *hors d'oeuvres*.

Let's take a seat
        on the *parrot's perch*.
Let's rock to *the motorola* with headphones.

Do you want to bathe
        in the porcelain tub?
Do you want to sing to *the little hare*?

Let's stroll over to the *guest room*
Let's take a bus ride
        to *the San Juanica bridge*.

Forget the ovens and smokestacks.

Forget *the rack and screw,*
        the tiger's cage.
We're celebrating a *birthday party*
        in your honor.
We're lighting candles on your favorite cake.
We're taking you to *a parade*
        on a sandy beach.
You're going down in a *submarine.*
        Edward Hirsch, "A Short Lexicon of Torture in the Eighties" (16–17)

I am concerned with acts of political torture and with literature that resists and impugns those acts by embodying them in language. My discussion will focus on two short stories by the Argentine writer Julio Cortázar (1914–1984) that indict human rights abuses in Latin America. Over the past two decades, torture has been a widespread political tool in Latin America, as it has been in many parts of the world. My purpose here is not to document those practices, or the United States government's complicity with them in many areas; Amnesty International's book *Torture in the Eighties* (1984) provides documentation enough, and there are many other sources as well.[1] I want, rather, to discuss the mechanisms by which writers embody in language the outrage of intentionally inflicted pain, and the crucial importance of their doing so. I will refer centrally to Elaine Scarry's exploration of this subject, *The Body in Pain: The Making and Unmaking of the World* (1985). Scarry's far-reaching study will aid me to outline a critical approach to literary works that engage the concept of embodiment to oppose political injustice. By addressing the ways in which Cortázar's stories translate the silence of pain into reverberating denunciations of the most extreme forms of political abuse, I hope to serve the overarching purpose of this collection of essays.

As is perhaps already clear, my use of the term *embodiment* in the context of stories about political torture will have to be less metaphorical, more starkly referential, than it ordinarily is in literary critical discussions. I do not intend to use it loosely, as when we say that a fictional character or setting "embodies" an idea or belief or set of values. Instead, I will be using the term phenomenologically, to suggest the ways in which the "lived body" (to use the French phenomenologist Maurice Merleau-Ponty's term) takes an active part in conferring meanings upon the world, and the ways in which literature projects that participation. The term *embodiment* here indicates an awareness of the physical body's presence in the world, as a condition of consciousness and community. For Cortázar, the "body politic" is an extension of the "lived body" and implies as well an ontological dimension of existence—let us call it a "cosmic body." Cortázar's sense of embodiment depends both on a phenomenological understanding of being and on a materialism that views language not as the origin of meaning but as the product of material phenomena, capable of referring to (and influencing) material phenomena. The body, language, and the phenomenal world are inextricably associated: the voice is an extension of the body; language is shaped by and also shapes the world; unspeakable acts can and must be spoken. In his late short stories dealing with political violence, Cortázar strives to make material the immaterial pain of the victim, to shape the physical matter of history with language, and to assign it significance.

I will take my argument one step further. Despite my awareness that Cortázar was, as he put it, "a man without religious convictions,"[2] I want to relate his project of literary embodiment, in which flesh is made word, to the Christian concept of incarnation, in which word is made flesh. To the extent that Cortázar's stories are about betrayal and bodily torture and the painful process of overcoming these acts, they may be considered in terms of the Christian story of embodiment. As Christ's physical being is construed as encompassing both immanence and transcendence, so Cortázar's phenomenologically conceived "lived body" also incorporates immanence and transcendence. I will argue that Cortázar's exploration of the relation between physical suffering and ontological significance links his late fiction to biblical concepts of being and justice.

Julio Cortázar's commitment to liberal reform in Latin America is well known, as is his concern for the renovating capacities of art and the artist in this political process. He analyzes these capacities in his critical essays on literature and the visual and performing arts, and he dramatizes these capacities in much of his fiction. The protagonists of his best-known short stories and novels, from the late 1940s through the 1960s, are artists—either accomplished or aspiring. In these early works, Cortázar examines the complex dynamic that occurs when an artist confronts the constraints of the self, society, or the system. Cortázar's early works often reflect as well the artist's struggle against the limitations of form and convention in his or her artistic medium, whether photography, music, or words: art must challenge not only social limitations but aesthetic ones as well in order to fulfill its imperative as art. In his later fiction, Cortázar's definition of revolutionary artistic expression came to insist upon revolutionary political action as well. Cortázar came to view liberation not only as a psychological and expressive problem but also as a material one. Like William Blake, Walt Whitman, Monique Wittig, and contemporary theorists such as Luce Irigaray, Cortázar construes the body as the primary locus of liberation. In his last collections of short fiction, we see an elemental struggle for political liberation being played out upon the human body.

"Press Clippings," published in *"We Love Glenda So Much" and Other Stories*, is perhaps Cortázar's most explicit dramatization of the response and responsibility of the artist when confronted with political torture. The story refers to the political situation in Argentina. Like Cortázar, the first-person narrator is an Argentine writer living in Paris, who, like Cortázar, writes essays on the visual and performing arts that are intended as literary extensions of the artwork or the performance under consideration.[3] So the narrator seems to be a surrogate for Cortázar himself. There is, however, an important departure from the autobiographical parallel: the narrator is a woman. This comes as a surprise to the reader. The narrative is in the first person, so we have no external description of her. Because of the autobiographical details given us, we naturally assume that we are listening to a male voice, and we are not given contrary information until after our erroneous assumption has had ample time to establish itself. The gender of this narrator is, then, foregrounded by its structural positioning. I will return to what I take to be the significance of this positioning in a moment.

The story begins with the narrator's description of a meeting at the Paris apartment of a friend, another Argentine artist, a sculptor who has asked her to prepare a text for an exhibition catalogue of his sculptures. The intent of his sculptures is revolutionary in the narrator's (and Cortázar's) terms, for, we are told, it challenges the very root of political injustice— the brutality inherent in human nature. His sculptures are described as "a series of small pieces whose theme was the violence in all the political and geographical latitudes that man inhabits as a man/wolf" (*Glenda* 82). Furthermore, the narrator finds the sculptor's formal aesthetic appropriate to his theme: "there wasn't anything systematic or too explicative in the sculptor's work, that each piece had something of an enigma about it and that sometimes one had to look for a long time to understand the modality that violence assumed there" (82). The violence in question is political torture, "that last form in which violence takes the place of the horror of immobility and isolation" (82). The sculptures do not specifically depict tortured bodies, but, rather, recreate in their abstract and enigmatic forms the paralyzing horror of the practice itself. The narrator expresses her hope that she herself can manage to replicate in her essay the act of embodiment so effectively accomplished by the sculptor.

This interaction of form and content quickly increases in complexity and intensity. As the two artists discuss their art, the narrator produces a newspaper clipping that describes in terrible detail a number of incidents of torture and murder in Argentina. They read of mass graves, disappearances, beatings, and "hands cut off her body and placed in a jar that carried the number 24" (a phrase that repeats itself obsessively in the narrator's mind). The utter reality of this grotesque newspaper report irrupts into their discussion, forcing them to question their own artistic involvement and the efficacy of any and every artistic response to acts of torture. Perhaps the simple fact of their physical distance from the victims' suffering makes them not the victims' allies but the torturers' accomplices. Perhaps material objects can never represent (and hence alleviate) the immateriality of physical pain. Perhaps art is hopelessly external to the internal pain it attempts to describe and thus is necessarily a trivialization of that pain. Cortázar's narrator also questions whether the artist who embodies torture risks responding (however unwittingly and unwillingly) to degraded motives. In societies in which the media are in love with violence, the artist may be pandering to his or her audience's fascination with violence, succumbing to the seductions of the marketplace. These questions plague the narrator, as they did Cortázar, and as they must the reader and the critic—all of us securely situated beyond the actual physical pain that we attempt to embody. But the narrator reassures herself and concludes that her sculptor friend has effectively avoided the error of fetishizing the suffering body, has avoided making it into a spectacle.

When the writer leaves the sculptor's apartment to return home that evening, yet another element is added to the obstacles facing the narrator's project of literary embodiment. If until this point the focus of narrative attention has been on how the art object embodies and indicts brutality, our attention is now directed to the artist's personal involvement in the reality of torture. On the way home, the narrator is accidentally drawn into a gruesome domestic scene of physical abuse, first as a witness, then as an accomplice. She intervenes to rescue a battered woman from her husband and then helps the woman take revenge in kind. After a hallucinatory scene in which she experiences herself as both a victim of torture and as a torturer, she escapes from the impoverished dwelling and stumbles home. Her recognition of her own capacity to condone and participate in torture is part of the horror of her experience. The next day the narrator writes the story of the night before, which, we are told, will serve as the text for the sculptor's exhibition catalogue. It is also the story that we have just finished reading.

I want now to consider the phenomenological and physical issues raised in Cortázar's story. The difficulty of articulating pain is primary. Elaine Scarry's essential book on this subject, *The Body in Pain*, begins by making the point that "physical pain is exceptional in the whole fabric of psychic, somatic, and perceptional states for being the only one that has no object . . . in the external world" (161). Whereas sight, hearing, touch, hunger, and desire connect to objects outside the boundaries of the body, pain alone does not refer to any world outside of itself. But this phenomenal absence can be reversed. The body in pain can and must be projected into visibility or audibility, or it will simply remain invisible, mute, and in pain. The embodiment of pain in images or gestures or words is crucial because a clear relationship exists between expressing pain and eliminating pain, whether in medical situations or political ones. Scarry argues that "the act of verbally expressing pain is a necessary prelude to the collective task of diminishing pain . . . the human voice must aspire to become a precise reflection of material reality" (9). The terrible irony of this necessity is that the worse the individual's pain, the less able he or she is to describe or create expressive embodiments of that pain. The claims of the body will override the claims of the world and ultimately destroy consciousness. This is an irony upon which the torturer depends: the female victim in Cortázar's story emits only "gagged shrieks," and the narrator speaks of the "silence where something seemed to vibrate and tremble with an ultrasonic sound" (*Glenda* 92). The narrator knows that it is she who must objectify the pain of the victim, because the victim herself has been reduced to the level of an animal, to prelinguistic cries and whispers. She also knows that pain may be appropriated by language to serve the ends of debased forms of power, as it always is in situations of torture.

Scarry explains the torturer's inversion of the process of embodiment: "If the felt-attributes of pain are (through one means of verbal objectification or another) lifted into the visible world, *and if the referent for these now objectified attributes is understood to be the human body*, then the sentient fact of the person's suffering will become knowable to a second person. It is also possible, however, for the felt-attributes of pain to be lifted into the visible world but now attached to *a referent other than the human body*. That is, the felt-characteristics of pain . . . can be appropriated away from the body and presented as attributes of something else" (13). Whereas Cortázar's narrator aims to embody the victim's pain by expressing it in ways that reflect back upon the reality of the body in pain and thereby begin to alleviate the pain, the torturer misappropriates that pain to reflect his own power. (I use "he" to refer to the torturer in accordance with evidence that the practice of political torture is overwhelmingly the province of males, and despite the narrator's recognition of her own capacity to inflict pain.) As the victim's pain causes the world to shrink, the torturer's world grows, magnified by the pain it is able to inflict and justify. The practice of political torture frequently arises during periods of political and cultural instability when, Scarry notes, "the sheer material factualness of the human body will be borrowed to lend [the unstable regime] the aura of 'realness' and 'certainty'" (14). The obliteration of the victim's world confirms the world of the torturer; bodily pain is translated into disembodied political power. So "Press Clippings" oscillates between the physical reality of torture and the linguistic processes by which pain is embodied in expressive form—by both artist and torturer. The artist uses language to express the victim's pain, whereas the torturer uses language as an instrument to increase his own power. One embodiment aspires to alleviate pain, the other to falsify and exploit it.

The torturer's falsifications perversely mirror the artist's expressive efforts. Interrogations become "trials," torture chambers "hospital rooms," torturers "doctors." The linguistic conventions of torture repeatedly revolve around the institutions of medicine and law, that is, the institutional elaborations of the body and the state. Like the poem that serves as epigraph to this essay, "Press Clippings" and other of Cortázar's late stories uncover these false equations. In "Second Time," in *A Change of Light,* arrest and torture are "procedures," the sites of such activities "offices," and the people summoned to these offices "patients," presumably sitting in doctors' waiting rooms. "Encounter within a Red Circle" in *A Change of Light* (1980); "Nightmares," "Satarsa," and "Night School" in *Deshoras* (1983); and "Graffiti," "Moebius Strip," and the title story in *We Love Glenda So Much* (1980) also use the torturer's euphemisms to show how the victim's pain is falsely embodied by the torturer to assure his own political power. These stories point as well to the fact that the torturer's distortions move with horrifying authority outside the torture chamber itself. The ubiquity of their recurrent forms—the trial, the doctor's office, the wholly false judicial economy of crime and punishment—and their acceptance as explanatory justifications for widespread political practice suggest that even people standing safely beyond the torturer's reach are highly susceptible to his deformations. Scarry argues, and Cortázar dramatizes, the ease with which the referentiality of language breaks down in such situations: "as physical pain destroys the mental content and language of the person in pain, so it also tends to appropriate and destroy the conceptualization abilities and language of persons who only observe the pain" (Scarry 279). That Cortázar situates his narrator first outside the torture chamber, then draws her inside, calls our attention doubly to the expressive problem of the observer. Cortázar, living in Paris, knew this problem to be his own.

The metatextual nature of Cortázar's story—it is, after all, a text about a text about abstract sculpture that embodies physical pain—might also seem a falsification, a structure that distances it from the pain it seeks to express, as his narrator has earlier feared. This is not, however, its effect. On the contrary, it is precisely the story's metatextual structure that gives form to the problem of expressing pain, as well as to the pain itself, and thus reaffirms the narrator's project of embodiment. The conclusion of the story makes clear that Cortázar wishes not only to embody pain and indict the politics of torture but also to point to the expressive difficulties confronting the artist who attempts to do so.

The story ends with a second clipping. It is from *France-Soir*, and it describes the scene of domestic torture witnessed by the narrator. It does not, however, mention her participation in the incident, nor is it reported to have happened in Paris, but rather in Marseille. The sculptor, after reading the article in *France-Soir*, assumes that his friend's text is based on the article, rather than on her own experience. In a note to her, he indicates his sense that she has fictionalized her own involvement for dramatic and literary effect—in other words, that she too has appropriated pain for her own purposes. Horrified, she begins to doubt her own experience of the night before and rushes to the street where she believes the events to have taken place. There she encounters a child whom she believes to be the daughter of the abused woman, but she cannot be sure. Did she imagine the incident or experience it? The reader is obliged to accept this final indeterminacy along with the narrator. We are given no resolution to the troubled relation between torture and its artistic embodiment, between the said, the not-said, the not-sayable. Cortázar's epigraph acknowledges these ambiguities. Referring to the two press reports of torture in Argentina and Marseille (or is it Paris?), the epigraph reads, "Although I don't think it's really necessary to say so, the first clipping is real and the second one imaginary" (81).

I said that I would return to the fact that the narrator of this story is a woman. Clearly Cortázar structures his story to emphasize the female identity of his narrator. The narrator's solidarity with the female victim of torture, her immediate intervention on behalf of the woman, her unspoken alliance with her against her male torturer—all of this would seem to depend upon the narrator's empathetic understanding (as a woman) of women's physical vulnerability to abusive male power. So Cortázar addresses sexual as well as governmental injustice, repositioning the sexual with respect to the political and focusing attention on the gendered body. Because control of one's own body is basic to feminist critique, it is tempting to conclude that Cortázar's narrative repositioning corresponds specifically to feminist concerns. I do not, however, take this to be the case. The narrator recognizes her political power (and its potential perversion) in her complicity with the violence of the torturer, even as she intercedes to free his victim. This complicated relation to both male torturer and female victim suggests that Cortázar wishes to avoid simplifications about gender and torture. He *is* concerned with gender, but with the negation of gender, that is, with physical abuses that undo distinctions, annihilate differences. Cortázar dramatizes—and this is my point—that the very function of torture is to dis-integrate the body, to deprive it of its identifying marks, among the most essential of which are those of sexual identity. The struggle for physical reintegration against the torturer's power of dis-integration constitutes the political center of this story. It is a center that encompasses gender but is not contained by it.

Cortázar's narrator and her press clippings describe situations in which the body can no longer "make sense" of the world, literally and figuratively: it can no longer create an embodiment of sentience that signifies. For Cortázar, this draining of the self, language, and the world ultimately goes beyond politics to ontology, to questions of being. He is acutely aware that to contemplate torture, to embody and resist it in writing, requires of the writer an act of almost religious respect, because it requires that one confront what it means to be human. Cortázar knew that he was writing not only about the human body but also about the human spirit. I must, then, qualify the statement that I made at the outset: Cortázar's late work insists not only upon the necessary relation of politics and art, but also upon their relation to spiritual realities. Cortázar refused to separate the physical body and its extension, the political body, from their ontological context. He dismissed binary systems that divide mind and body, spirit and matter, subject and object, self and other, ideal and real. For him, these were not oppositions but continuities of the "lived body," a concept given philosophical expression by Maurice Merleau-Ponty.[4] By tracing the outlines of Merleau-Ponty's theory, I will bring into sharper focus Cortázar's literary practice of embodiment.

From Merleau-Ponty's first major work, *Phenomenology of Perception*, published in 1945, to his last, uncompleted work, *The Visible and the Invisible*, published posthumously in 1968, the philosopher elaborated his theory of the lived body. He developed this term as part of his resistance to inherited binarisms: he rejects the external, objectified sense of the body used in the sciences and the Cartesian sense of consciousness as wholly interior and separate from body. For Merleau-Ponty, human beings are born into a world that already possesses meaning. In order for the infant to establish its identity in the world, it must see itself from the outside, as a body like the other bodies around it, as well as an image projected by consciousness into the world. This body image is both object and subject, sensible and sentient, seeing and seen. As an image, it is object; as a self, it is subject. Merleau-Ponty writes in "Body as Expression and Speech," a central chapter in *Phenomenology of Perception:* "I am my body, at least wholly to the extent that I possess experience, and yet at the same time my body is as it were a 'natural' subject, a provisional sketch of my total being. Thus experience of one's own body runs counter to the reflective procedure which detaches subject and object from each other, and which gives us only the thought about the body, or the body as an idea, and not the experience of the body or the body in reality" (198–99). So Merleau-Ponty refused the separation of mind and body, or of ideas and phenomena: "The problem of the world, and, to begin with, that of one's own body, consists in the fact that *it is all there*" (198).

Merleau-Ponty's lived body, then, does not mediate between consciousness and the world, but encompasses both. It is both inside and outside, the site where thought originates and where it discovers its external symbols or embodiments. It is capable of both corporeal reflex and conscious reflection, and language is conceived as its product and extension. "My body," writes Merleau-Ponty, "reverberates to all sounds, vibrates to all colours and provides words with their primordial significance through the way in which it receives them" (*Phenomenology* 212). Being is the "intertwining" of body, language, world. "Sensation is literally a form of communion" (212).

Given this conviction, it is not surprising that Merleau-Ponty is centrally concerned with perception, how the body situates itself in the world, how it is created by and also creates the world. As his sensuous language and interacting images imply, he conceives of perception as more than merely the impingement of the outside world on the senses: "It is the momentum which carries us beyond subjectivity which gives us our place in the world prior to any science and any verification through a kind of 'faith' or 'primary opinion' " (343).

The French word *sens* (meaning both "sense" and "direction," as *sentido* does in Spanish) is important in understanding Merleau-Ponty's fundamental relation of embodiment and sense perception as a reversible movement between interiority and the world. He writes, "The disclosure of an immanent or incipient significance in the living body extends . . . to the whole sensible world, and our gaze, prompted by the experience of our own body, will discover in all other 'objects' the miracle of expression" (197). Merleau-Ponty describes the interaction between the lived body and the world as a "magical relation, this pact between [objects] and me according to which I lend them my body in order that they inscribe upon it and give me their resemblance, this fold, this central cavity of the visible which is my vision" (*Visible* 146). The sentient body directs itself toward the world, confers meaning on the world, and is also conferred with meaning by the world.

This last essential point is fully explored by Merleau-Ponty in "Eye and Mind" (1961) and in *The Visible and the Invisible*. In this final work, he is concerned less with the movement of interiority through *sens* to the world than with the movement from the perceived world to ontological understanding. Always struggling to avoid the binary structures encoded in Western thought and language, he eschews the terms *spirit, mind,* and *soul,* because they automatically suggest an opposition to *body*. Instead, he coins the term *non-sens* to describe that which is not accessible to the senses (*sens*), an immaterial realm of being that is nonetheless conditioned by sentience.

This back and forth movement between *sens* and *non-sens,* between the physical and metaphysical, Merleau-Ponty termed *reversibility*. Daniel Frank Chamberlain explains, "Reversibility rebounds back along the process of perception in the depth of a 'non-sense' core of being. The rebound does not begin with a first-hand experience of the world, although it does presuppose this experience. It begins in knowing, in thought, in what is described by the full semantic value of the term *reflection*" (34). In defining this process, Merleau-Ponty raises a final question:

> What is that central vision that joins the scattered visions, that unique touch that governs the whole tactile life of my body as a unity, that *I think* that must be able to accompany all our experiences. We are proceeding toward the center, we are seeking to comprehend how there is a center, what the unity consists of . . . . [E]ven when a particular vision turns out to be illusory . . . I remain certain that in looking closer I would have had the true vision, and that in any case, whether it be this one or another, *there is a true vision*. The flesh (of the world or my own) is not contingency, chaos, but a texture that returns to itself and conforms to itself. (*Visible* 145–46)

Meaning arises from the body's existence in/to the world (*être-au-monde*), reflects back upon an immaterial "center" of thought, moves toward a "true vision."

Merleau-Ponty's conception of the lived body parallels Cortázar's repeated rejection of what he considers the Western dichotomizing of subject and object. Cortázar often recurs to spatial metaphors to express his phenomenological sense of intersubjectivity. In an interview, he speaks of the "porosity" of body and world, the "permeability" of self and other.[5] In his novel *Hopscotch* (1963), Cortázar uses the spatial metaphors of "constellation," "crystallization," and "*figura*" (figure) to describe the artistic process whereby fragmentary phenomena may coalesce into an *imago mundi*. A verbal or visual or musical "figure" suggests a complex interaction of matter and mind, of experience and imagination, of visible and invisible. Morelli, the novelist in *Hopscotch*, insists upon the use of the word *figura* rather than *imagen* (image), saying that he aspires to write a novel that "conforms to the condition of a *figure* . . . a work which may seem alien or antagonistic to the time and history surrounding them, and which nonetheless includes it, explains it, and in the last analysis orients it towards a transcendence within whose limits man is waiting" (489).

The word *figura*, like its French and English cognates, refers in two directions—to language ("figures of speech") and to the body. In French, *figure* carries the primary significance of "face" as it does, though secondarily, in Spanish; in English, the word originally referred only to the exterior form, the contours and physical features of human beings and animals. Morelli's preference for *figura* implies an analogy between human form and figures of speech, and suggests an understanding of language as an extension of the body, as reflecting the form and features of physical bodies. Words are situated phenomenologically, that is, in a phenomenal realm that is experienced physically. Cortázar's literary language—his *figuras*—"face" reality, bring together the experience of sense and sensation, thought and feeling, psychology and physiology. His aesthetics of the *figura* is consonant with Merleau-Ponty's philosophy of the reversibility of *sens* and *non-sens:* both signal the intertwining of body, world, and expression. Meaning, and with it language and literary expression, is not solely mental but proceeds from the living body to the whole sensible world. Meaning is physical; the physical has meaning.

Cortázar's phenomenological aesthetic is particularly resonant in his stories about torture. Because pain lacks an object in the world, its effective embodiment most obviously depends upon a reflexive movement between *sens* and *non-sens*, body and non-body. The embodiment of physical pain must be two-directional: it must move outward to operate in and on the world and also reflect back upon the immaterial "center" of being. This is the reflexive process that Cortázar dramatizes: by its operations, the onto-logical draining of the world by pain may be resisted and reversed, and the self and world remade.

To relate Cortázar's practice of literary embodiment to the Christian concept of incarnation, I return to Scarry's *The Body in Pain*. In her dis-cussion of the Bible, Scarry extends her theory of the relations between pain and power to consider the relations between the body and belief. She argues convincingly that in both Hebrew and Christian canons, the human body provides an essential form of verification of God's existence. In the Old Testament, belief in the disembodied voice of God is contingent upon human embodiment, specifically upon what Scarry calls scenes of bodily alteration—scenes of begetting and injury. Whether in the accounts of the creation of humanity and in the physical increase of God's people, or in accounts of physical wounds and human sacrifice, Scarry argues that the Hebrews constructed and substantiated God's spiritual authority by alter-ations in human bodies. She points out that in historical times of disbelief and doubt among the Hebrews, their texts predictably describe scenes of bodily hurt (wounds, human sacrifices, physical punishments), because the materiality and immediacy of the human body in pain served to reconfirm for a doubting people the immateriality and timelessness of their God. The urgency of the Old Testament injunction against graven images can be understood in these terms: for the ancient Hebrews, their God's power depended upon his disembodiment, which distinguishes him utterly from them, his embodied creatures. God's power and authority are in part based on the fact that people have bodies and God has no body. It is above all this structure that is revised in the New Testament.

The Christian incarnation of God in a human body is a profound revi-sion indeed. Scarry writes, "In the Old Testament scenes of hurt, Jehovah enters sentience by producing pain; Jesus instead enters sentience by healing and, even more important, by himself becoming the object of touch, the object of vision, the direct object of hearing" (214). In a fascinating elabo-ration of this point, Scarry shows that Christ's life is a retelling of "the largest framing events of the Pentateuch—first, creation; second, exile; third, rescue—*but a retelling from the point of view of sentience*. The same framing story is told but now it is God himself, not man, who is described as created, exiled, and rescued: hence human sentience is deeply legiti-mized by its having become God's sentience as well" (217).

The emphasis in the Gospels upon Christ's physical presence among his followers and his own physical suffering hardly needs belaboring. Scarry looks at many instances of Christianity's "revised form of verification," which repeatedly involve incidents of touching, seeing, and hearing of and by the physical Christ. The story of Doubting Thomas, who must touch Christ's wounds to know that he is God, epitomizes this radical revision of the relations of body and belief in Christianity. As this relation is revised in Christianity so, Scarry writes, is the relation between pain and power. "[Pain and power] are no longer manifestations of each other: one person's pain is not the sign of another's power. The greatness of human vulnerability is not the greatness of divine invulnerability. They are unrelated and therefore can occur together; God is both omnipotent and in pain" (214). It is perfectly appropriate that the instrument of Christ's bodily torture and death should have become the central symbol of this revision. Cortázar engages this Christian drama of embodiment in a second story about political torture, "Apocalypse in Solentiname."

Cortázar was not a Christian, but he had a profound understanding of the significance of the cross. His political and literary commitment to the suffering and disenfranchised peoples in Latin America led him to associate himself closely with liberation theologians, in particular the Nicaraguan priest and poet Ernesto Cardenal. In "Apocalypse in Solentiname," the author honors Cardenal and Solentiname, his Christian community in Nicaragua.[6] Cortázar's narrator (another author surrogate, but this time a man), describes his visit to Solentiname, where he is particularly struck by the beauty of the naive paintings that members of the community have created, "some signed and others not, but all so beautiful, once more the first vision of the world, the clean look of a person who describes what's around him like a song of praise: midget cows in poppy fields, the sugarmaking shed with people coming out like ants, the horse with green eyes against a background of cane fields, *a baptism in a church that doesn't believe in perspective* and climbs up or falls down on top of itself, the lake with little boats like shoes and in the background an enormous fish laughing with turquoise teeth" (*Change* 121–22, emphasis added). So impressed is Cortázar's narrator with the profound simplicity of these paintings that he takes slides of them to enjoy and share with his wife and friends when he returns to his home in Paris.[7]

I quote this passage at length because I think the sensuousness of Cortázar's description of the paintings, and his metaphoric language of praise, baptism, and vision, are designed to suggest a Christianity that is not so much a nexus of ideas as a concrete participation in a body—the "body of Christ" as Scarry describes it—and the Christian community that this phrase implies. Cortázar describes an artistic perspective that is not organized by abstract concepts of subjective consciousness or autonomous ego, as is Renaissance perspective, but by the sentient experience of a circumambient world of lived bodies. Cortázar's descriptions recall Merleau-Ponty's statement, quoted above: "My body reverberates to all sounds, vibrates to all colours and provides words with their primordial significance through the way in which it receives them." The paintings convey Cortázar's sense of the primary connectedness of these human beings to the world by fragile and transitory bodies. We are reminded that the root of the word *religion, relig(are)*, means to tie, fasten, connect.

Visual images have, since the Middle Ages, provided strong formulations of Christ's physical body and, by extension, the significance of human physical existence.[8] Nowhere in Latin America does religious art turn away from the bodily marks of Christ's suffering, nor does it detract from the physicality of his passion by emphasizing solely its mystical (hence, disembodied) meaning. Holy Week celebrations throughout Latin America are more elaborate on, and the celebrants more moved by, the elaborate ritual remembrance of the events of Maundy Thursday and Good Friday than by the events of Easter Sunday. The blood, wounds, and instruments of torture (not only Christ's but the martyred saints') are often dwelt upon in hyperrealistic and—it may seem to North Americans and Europeans—hyperbolic detail. North Americans unaccustomed to Latin American religious art may feel uncomfortable with what seems a grisly physicality (though two recent films, *The Last Temptation of Christ* and *Jesus of Montreal*, have graphically reminded moviegoers of the violence of Christ's physical torture, of the human suffering of his death by crucifixion). Cortázar's story describes a traditional community's belief in a Christ whose body has not been spiritualized beyond physical suffering, whose incarnation is still a matter of flesh and blood. Much Latin American religious art reflects this strong personal identification with Christ's human condition, that is, with his suffering.

In European art we must go back to a time before the end of the sixteenth century, before the Renaissance separation of mind from body was fully established—to Andrea Mantegna's *Dead Christ* (ca. 1466) or Matthias Grünewald's Isenheim altarpiece (1510) or Hans Holbein the Younger's *Christ in the Tomb* (1521)—to find equally vivid depictions of Christ's physical (mortal) status. Though Michelangelo's *Pietà* (ca. 1499) is from this same period, his depiction of Christ has already integrated Renaissance

ideas as Mantegna's, Grünewald's, and Holbein's have not. In Michelangelo's *Pietà*, the arm of the dead Christ is shown with engorged veins,
a physiological impossibility after the heart has stopped; and his Christ's
hands gesture as if alive. It was not that Michelangelo did not know anatomy, but that (unlike Mantegna, Grünewald, Holbein, and the Latin
American religious art to which I have referred) he did not wish to portray
the crucified Christ as a cadaver. Instead of emphasizing Christ's human
nature, which suffered physical death, Michelangelo chose to emphasize
Christ's divine nature, which does not suffer death. The genius of his *Pietà*
is not in question, nor is our strong sense of the simultaneous presence of
human death and divine life in Michelangelo's Christ. My point is that the
proportions and emphases and ways of embodying Christ's simultaneous humanity and divinity vary greatly, and that modern European depictions of
Christ (following Michelangelo) tend to etherealize Christ as Latin American depictions generally do not. This is surely part of what Cortázar's narrator means when he describes one of the Solentiname paintings as "a baptism in a church that doesn't believe in perspective."

This visual tradition in Latin America of depicting Christ's flesh-and-
blood suffering and death remains strong. It is arguable that the strength
of this tradition is the result of a continuing history of physical pressures
and limitations (disease, hunger, inadequate shelter, the unending exertion
of physical labor) less widely experienced in more industrialized regions of
the world, and also the result of ongoing abuses of political power, the most
extreme of which are dramatized by Cortázar. Christ's physical suffering
continues to lay essential claim on the popular imagination, as Cortázar
depicts it in Solentiname, because many believers can immediately empa-
thize and identify with such suffering. But Cortázar's point is more subtle.
He does not, after all, describe paintings of Christ's passion but paintings
that celebrate the sentience (and sensuousness) of daily physical existence in
its ordinary physical surroundings. For the people whom Cortázar honors
in this story, the validation of human sentience through the incarnation of
Christ is as clearly visible in their representations of daily life in Solentiname as it is in their representation of biblical scenes. Cortázar's phenomenological understanding of the lived body coincides with the Christian understanding of the residents of Solentiname in refusing the absolute
distinction between physical and spiritual life, between religious art and
the art of the everyday.

The community's identification with Christ's betrayal and death is clearly
more than a spiritual matter. Cortázar's narrator attends a Mass, and the

Scripture reading for the day is about Jesus' arrest in the garden of Gethsemane, "a theme that the people of Solentiname treated as if they were talking about themselves, about the threat of being pounced on at night or in broad daylight, that life of permanent uncertainty on the islands and on the mainland and in all of Nicaragua and, yes, almost all of Latin America, a life surrounded by fear and death, life in Guatemala and life in El Salvador, life in Argentina and Bolivia, life in Chile and Santo Domingo, life in Paraguay, life in Brazil and Colombia" (*Change* 122). Though Cortázar's story does not describe them, the Solentiname paintings that do depict biblical events portray them as occurring *in* Solentiname: Christ's suffering includes the political injustices in Nicaragua.

When Cortázar's narrator returns home to Paris and projects his slides of the Solentiname paintings, he does not see bucolic scenes but scenes of torture and killing that foreshadow the destruction of Solentiname by the then-Nicaraguan dictator, Anastasio Somoza. The narrator looks at the screen and sees a man shot down on a corner in Buenos Aires; he looks at another slide and sees an execution in a jungle clearing, then a car exploding "in a city that could have been Buenos Aires or Sao Paulo," and then "waves of bloody faces and parts of bodies and women running and children on a Bolivian or Guatemalan hillside" (126). He turns off the projector and leaves the room. His friend enters as he leaves, projects the slides once again, but sees none of the nightmarish transformations that he has witnessed. Her viewing does not, however, cancel his. For the narrator (and the reader), the Christian validation of human sentience that the paintings represent has been subverted. Bodies are broken and destroyed by the disembodying power of totalitarian politics.

It would seem, then, that in this story the emptying of the world by pain is *not* reversed, that Cortázar describes the failure of embodiment rather than its accomplishment. Whereas the narrator of "Press Clippings" at least writes her text, this narrator is left in stunned silence by the violence he has witnessed. In fact, both stories end in doubt and frustration; both emphasize the vicariousness of the artist's intervention; both suggest that the pain inflicted by the torture will forever exceed the capacity of language to express it or reverse it. Furthermore, as Cortázar's stories make clear, all accounts of torture contain an implicit but nonetheless unbreachable disjunction between subject and audience, between the person who has been tortured and those who have not.[9] This experiential gulf inevitably creates a complex of paradoxical responses to narratives of torture: guilt, sympathy, embarrassment, the wish to comfort, the wish to silence. The listener or reader may abhor the recounted atrocities and still feel responsible for them, feel guilty for having been comfortable in a world where torture exists, for not having intervened, however impossible intervention might have been. Both of Cortázar's narrators recognize the inescapability of their role of voyeurs—repelled, fascinated, distanced by their good luck and their guilt from the scenes of torture they witness and read about. In short, both narrators sympathize with the victims of torture, and both also recognize their complicity with the torturer. There is, it seems, no innocent relation to the practice of political torture. It is this recognition that causes their own violent physical reactions during the course of their narratives.

The narrators' fear that their texts reiterate (condone rather than impugn, exacerbate rather than mitigate) the torturer's inscriptions may be considered in terms of the fundamental connection, proposed by Michel de Certeau, between the body and all texts. De Certeau argues that law is the original instance of this connection, that there is no written law that has not first been inscribed upon the body: "Every law has a hold on the body. The very idea of an individual that can be isolated from the group was established along with the necessity, in penal justice, of having a body that could be marked by punishment, and in matrimonial law, of having a body that could be marked with a price in transactions among collectivities. From birth to mourning after death, law 'takes hold of' bodies in order to make them its text . . . . Every power, including the power of law, is written first of all on the backs of its subjects" (139, 140). The body suffers inscription into the symbolic order by means of what de Certeau calls "incarnate writing." Written texts refer to the body, are metaphors for the body, and in time of crisis, may revert back to bodies: de Certeau refers to historical situations when "paper is no longer enough for the law, and it writes itself again on the bodies themselves" (140). This statement echoes Scarry's argument about bodies and belief in the biblical texts and extends it to all written texts: "Every printed text repeats this ambivalent experience of the body written by the law of the other" (de Certeau 140).

Though "incarnate writing" may be only a distant metaphor in the case of most texts, it is immediately applicable to Cortázar's stories. His narrators' sense of their complicity with the torturers corresponds to the intuition, specified by de Certeau, that *all* texts are corporeally based. Such an intuition, de Certeau argues, is "aroused when reading touches the body at the points where the scars of the unknown text have long been imprinted" (141). This is the experience of Cortázar's narrators and our own experience as readers of these stories. Their narrative power results not only from their specific political content but also from their general recognition of the foundational and always fragile relation between skin and parchment, between bodies and books.

Thus, the issue of literary embodiment is always problematic, most especially when it is the pain of torture that the writer attempts to embody. Cortázar would seem to conclude that rarely, if ever, can the artist achieve his or her aim of embodying and reversing such pain. That both of Cortázar's narrators are closely identified with Cortázar himself increases our sense of this author's feelings of inadequacy when confronted with political torture and murder. But this identification also increases our sense of Cortázar's personal commitment; these stories *do*, after all, manage to say some part of the unsayable, to give voice to human suffering, to speak of unspeakable injustices. That Cortázar's narrators do not, cannot, fully express the pain of others does not invalidate their efforts, nor does it invalidate the power of Cortázar's stories—which can, of course, be distinguished from the dramatized doubts and indeterminacies of their narrators.

Cortázar is joined by a number of Latin American writers who have recently contributed to what I call *la literatura de denuncia*.[10] Barbara Harlow's formulation, "literature of resistance," usefully encodes the oppositional nature of such works, but I prefer the term "literature of denunciation" because it foregrounds the expressive struggle as well as the political resistance in stories like Cortázar's. This struggle to hear the story and to tell it must be an integral part of literary embodiments of torture if they are to communicate the full horror of this form of injustice. Writers of denunciatory literature acknowledge the problematic relation (recalled by de Certeau) between bodies and books; they encode what Merleau-Ponty describes as the "transition from the mute world to the speaking world"; they open "the horizon of the nameable and of the sayable" (*Visible* 154). Their work enacts the ordinary phenomenological process of embodiment on an extraordinary, indeed, a primal level. They make the phenomenological reversibility between body and world their subject, their cause.

Some of the works by Latin American writers of *la literatura de denuncia* indict regimes that have now been displaced, the torturers tried, and justice reinstituted. Despite localized changes for the better, totalitarian political practice continues, in Latin American and elsewhere. These writers are well aware of this fact, and offer the stories and novels as gestures of hope, acts of intervention. In this sense, their writings are apocalyptic literature in the biblical tradition of apocalypticism, for they share the belief that old worlds can be supplanted by new ones, that current injustices can be remedied. They reiterate the hope of the twenty-first chapter of Revelation, literally expressed in the title of Osvaldo Soriano's book *No habra mas penas ni olvido* (*There Shall be no more Pain or Forgetting*): "And there shall be no more death, neither sorrow, nor crying, neither shall there be any more pain: for the former things are passed away" (21:4). In fact, Cortázar's "Return to Solentiname," published six years after "Apocalypse in Solentiname," seems to justify this hope.

In 1983, three and a half years after the Sandinista victory in Nicaragua, Cortázar returned to the island commune of Solentiname. A collection of his journalistic writings produced during this final visit was published nine days after the author's death, in February 1984. Entitled *Nicaraguan Sketches*, it begins by reprinting the earlier story of apocalyptic violence in Solentiname, and appends his coda to that story, "Return to Solentiname." If "Apocalypse in Solentiname" presents Cortázar's relation to this community dramatically, "Return to Solentiname" presents it journalistically. Here Cortázar speaks directly to the reader.

In less than four pages, "Return to Solentiname" describes the vestiges left by Somoza's destruction of the commune and its subsequent rebuilding: "Signs of the Somocista vandalism were still visible: the burnt out craft workshop, the ransacked houses—yet everything is being rebuilt, white and sweet as in those brightly detailed paintings the world now knows. The church was left untouched, and the delectable childlike decorations on the wall still shine with all the colors of the local fish, hens, thatched huts, alligators and little airplanes (*Sketches* 112). The church's meaning is inseparable from the phenomena that surround it, inseparable from their colors, forms, *figuras*. Cortázar assures his readers that "the beauty of the wise and innocent popular art will flourish again." As he walks alone in a meadow, he remembers his first visit to Solentiname, and "the beginning of a communion, of a pact then dark and secret." In this phrase, Cortázar encompasses Merleau-Ponty's lived body ("sensation is literally a form of communion") and the Christian belief in Christ's body as communion, as symbol and repository of human truth.[11]

6.

Charles Eastman, Nicholas Black Elk, and the Construction of Religious Identity

Bradley J. Monsma

My eyes were opened intelligently to the greatness of Christian civilization, the ideal civilization, as it unfolded itself before my eyes. I saw it as the development of every natural resource; the broad brotherhood of mankind; the blending of all languages and the gathering of all races under one religious faith.

Charles Eastman (*Deep Woods* 57)

We have been told that Jesus the Christ was crucified, but that he shall come again at the Last Judgment, the end of this world or cycle. This I understand and know that it is true, but the white man should know that for the red people too, it was the will of *Waken-Tanka*, the Great Spirit, that an animal turn itself into a two legged person in order to bring the most holy pipe to His people.

Nicholas Black Elk (*Sacred Pipe* xx)

Both of these statements by native Americans testify to a faith in Christianity, yet neither the faiths nor the Christianities are the same. To Charles Eastman, Christianity is a "development," an improvement over what it replaces, and is tied to his faith in civilization. Eastman includes both Christianity and civilization in the linear discourse of progress. Nicholas Black Elk, on the other hand, places his Christian beliefs alongside of, and as equal to, his belief in the sacred pipe. Moreover, the two faiths begin to mingle—he describes the biblical Last Judgment in the cyclical discourse of his Lakota tradition. Both Eastman (1858–1939) and Black Elk (1863–1950) lived through the traumatic transition of the Sioux people to reservation life, a time when individuals could choose to "adhere to the old ways, to reject them for new ways, to find some kind of communal and personal reconciliation of the two—or simply to live out one's days" (Krupat, *For Those Who Come After* 115). Neither man resigned himself to a life of avoidance; rather, each produced texts that document active, and at first markedly divergent, spiritual searches. Charles Eastman attempts to assimilate Euro-American culture, to adopt the religion of the colonizer along with the cultural values and ideologies of the colonizer. Black Elk, who also practices Christianity, does so in a way that allows him to remain Lakota and to explore possibilities for identity that include both Christian and Lakota beliefs. While Eastman's struggles finally lead him toward a position not far from Black Elk's, the contrasting strategies of the two men lend historical insight into the problematic nature of negotiating personal and communal identities in the wake of colonization.

From the Deep Woods to Civilization, the 1916 autobiography of Charles Alexander Eastman (Ohiyesa), is at first remarkable for its irrepressible optimism. Eastman sees his transition from a traditional childhood among the Santee Sioux to his position as a professional in white society as embodying all of the possibilities for the survival of native peoples in the United States. Eastman's personal identity becomes the model for his vision of tribal identity. He sees himself as evidence for the ability of a race to be assimilated; he views himself as a testament to the white world of the adaptability of the red man. As he was able to assimilate the white world, so should all other native Americans. Yet the autobiography also represents the tension between Eastman's choice of Christianity and white civilization and the Sioux identity that for much of his life he attempts to deny.

In the autobiography Eastman tells the story of being taught the traditional skills of a warrior by his uncle, who would later fight Custer at the Little Big Horn. The young Ohiyesa dreams of avenging his father, whom the boy's family had presumed to be hanged as one of thirty-eight blamed for an uprising. But the father miraculously returns as a converted Christian and explains to Ohiyesa what he has learned about the white world: "Above all, they have their Great Teacher, whom they call Jesus, and he taught them to pass on their wisdom and knowledge to all other races. It is true that they have subdued and taught many peoples, and our own must eventually bow to this law; the sooner we accept their mode of life and follow their teaching, the better it will be for us all" (*Deep Woods* 8). This statement, recalled through Eastman's adult beliefs, presents the process of conquest as both inevitable and instituted by Christianity. To accept the Christian religion is to become civilized. To become civilized and a Christian is to relinquish Sioux identity. After praying to the "Great Mystery," the boy decides to follow with determination the path out of the deep woods toward civilization.

Eventually Eastman attended the Santee Normal Training School where he learned to read and write English and accepted Christianity. The Santee School reinforced the connection between Christianity and civilization by teaching Eastman "to reverence New England, and especially its metropolis, as the home of culture and art, of morality and Christianity" (*Deep Woods* 70). After leaving Santee, Eastman enrolled at Dartmouth College and Boston University to study medicine, and he continued to study Christian philosophy so as to be of service to his people as both doctor and missionary.[1]

Upon completion of his studies Eastman reported to his first job at the Pine Ridge Agency in South Dakota in 1890 during the rise of the Ghost Dance, which was a religious response to the hopelessness and desperation caused by the conditions of life on the reservation. The teachings of the Paiute messiah Wovoka combined traditional plains religion with the idea of the Christian apocalypse to create a vision of all plains tribes being removed to another world where the buffalo had gone and where the people could live in the old ways. Eastman, yet unaware of the reservation conditions that made the teachings of Wovoka attractive to the Lakota, found himself caught in the middle of a tense situation and urged the Lakota leaders to be loyal to the government of the United States. Soon he would be counting frozen bodies at Wounded Knee.

The fervor of the Ghost Dance caused government officials to become increasingly nervous. The Lakota camps surrounding Pine Ridge also grew apprehensive when Sitting Bull, whom whites mistakenly believed to be the force behind the Ghost Dance, was shot by the army and Indian agents sent to arrest him. A number of camps, including Si Tanka's (Big Foot's) Miniconjou band, decided to move onto the reservation for their own safety. However, on the way, Si Tanka's group met some half-frozen members of Sitting Bull's camp who told of atrocities committed by the soldiers. Si Tanka's people then decided to flee into the badlands, and soldiers were sent to detain them. Perhaps because of some confusion during the disarming of the band, the soldiers opened fire so intensely that some of their own men on either side of the Indians were killed. The Wounded Knee massacre was the last event in the Indian Wars, which had begun in the plains toward the end of the Civil War and has since come to represent the whole history of injustice done to native peoples in the United States. At the time, Wounded Knee signalled to whites the opening of more land for ranching and of the Black Hills for mining. For the Lakota it meant the inevitability of reservation life.

The massacre at Wounded Knee served to reinforce Eastman's conviction that joining the modern white world was the only hope for native Americans. Eastman's belief was rooted in the social Darwinist ideas that were steadily gaining in popularity during the time he had been at Dartmouth (Brumble 147–64). Social Darwinism along with Protestantism formed Eastman's vision of his own life and the survival of tribal people in the United States. Eastman came to believe that tribalism and traditional beliefs necessarily doomed Indians to fall behind in the struggle for the fittest to survive. Thus he could write in the epigraph to his first book, *Indian Boyhood* (1902), that the Indian "possessed not only a superb physique but a remarkable mind. But the Indian no longer exists as a natural and free man. Those remnants which now dwell upon the reservations present only a sort of tableau—a fictitious copy of the past." Eastman's aspirations for "the Indian" help to explain the soft-toned, warm portrait of the Sioux in *Indian Boyhood*. Hertha Dawn Wong points out that Eastman shows awareness of his audience by using descriptions and images of typical "noble savages" to counter white expectations of bloodthirsty killers (144). Eastman's representations are calculated to gain the respect and admiration of white readers who wield power in the society to which he seeks the admittance of all tribal people.

It is because Eastman believes the Indian to be the "highest type of pagan and uncivilized man" that he holds so much hope that all native Americans would be able to abandon tribal life and adopt the modern world as he had. With the rational support of social Darwinism, Eastman, in spite of his good intentions and optimism, ends up supporting the notion of the vanishing American, which had long served the ideology of conquest for white America, from the Puritans who saw Indians as either devils to be destroyed or members of the lost tribes of Israel to be converted, to later writers, artists, and anthropologists who romanticized the passing of the tribes. In his writing, Eastman constructs his own self-image to mirror the values of the Anglo-Saxon American self-image. In one sense, Eastman correctly perceives the threat of tribalism to the dominant culture's emphasis on cultural assimilation and individualism. But because he wishes to become part of that dominant culture, Eastman represses his tribal identity. As a native American living within white civilization, which can see only the opposition of savagism to civilization, Eastman chooses the only option left by a society that depends on the death of the Indian to form its own identity and justify its own progress.[2]

Eastman portrays himself in *From the Deep Woods to Civilization* as a highly principled man who is willing to persevere through adversity in order to realize his vision of what was best for the Sioux at Pine Ridge. Since he assumes that native peoples would die and disappear unless they adopted modern white ways, he can write that he was "of course wholly in sympathy with the policy of education for the Indian children" in spite of viewing painful scenes at the government boarding schools of children being separated forcibly from their parents (82). Later in life Eastman used his position as a Washington lobbyist to support the Dawes Severalty Act, which allotted tribal lands to individuals in the hope of encouraging them to become farmers and participate in the American way of competitive individualism. Eastman writes, "we must quit the forest trail for the breaking-plow, since pastoral life was the next thing for the Indian. I renounced finally my bow and arrows for the spade and the pen; I took off my soft moccasins and put on the heavy and clumsy but durable shoes" (57–58). In reality, much of the land involved in the Dawes Act quickly turned over to white hands because the Indians were either starving and in need of quick cash or uneducated in white commerce and the value of private property in white terms.

But Eastman's social Darwinist vision of the death of tribalism is complicated by his Christianity. His faith, as much as his desire to achieve status in the white world, motivates Eastman's return to his people to be of service to them as a doctor and a missionary. This same Christian ethic provides the vocabulary with which he criticizes ongoing injustices he learns to see on the reservation. Throughout the second half of *From the Deep Woods to Civilization,* Eastman expresses his fury at the reservation conditions, which result from the trail of broken treaties, officials at the Bureau of Indian Affairs who cheat the Lakota out of full payment for land, and self-serving politicians in Washington. Furthermore, Eastman also begins to question Christianity as represented by white civilization. After describing the tragedy at Wounded Knee he writes, "All this was a severe ordeal for one who had so lately put all his faith in the Christian love and lofty ideals of the white men." Yet Eastman follows this by stating, "I passed no hasty judgment" (114). Eastman's commitment to white civilization is so deep that not even the critique of white culture that arises from his Christian concept of justice can shake his belief that hope for the Indian rested with modernity. Toward the end of the book of his life, after telling of his frustrations with the white world, Eastman maintains, "even in deep jungles God's own sunlight penetrates, and I stand before my own people as an advocate of civilization" (194–95). While Eastman separates the ideals of Christianity from the culture that failed to live up to those ideals, he cannot separate his own moral vision from the more subtle ideology of white culture.

The tensions caused by the union in Eastman's thought of tribal memories, Christianity, and the ideology of colonization and progress become most evident in Eastman's narrative attempts to repress these tensions. When Eastman plays his role of missionary, for example, he insists on bringing with his religious message a call for native Americans to adopt the trappings of white culture. Eastman's contact with native Americans who were resisting cultural domination by exerting their tribal sovereignty and maintaining cultural values presents him with a visible critique of his assumption that tribalism (and individuals who identify with a tribe) must die out. It is at this point that the consequences of his union of the progressive discourse of social Darwinism with the discourse of Christianity has its most serious consequences.

Eastman writes of how he often met with groups of men from a number of tribes "to set before them in simple language the life and character of the Man Jesus" (*Deep Woods* 142). Eastman is somewhat surprised that not all of those he meets accept his perception of the contradiction between Lakota religion/culture and Christianity/civilization. One old "battle scarred warrior," for instance, listens to Eastman's message, then states, "Why, we have followed this law you speak of for untold ages!" (142). Another attends Eastman's Bible study for a whole week before he says: "I have come to the conclusion that this Jesus was an Indian. He was opposed to material acquirement and to great possession. He was inclined toward peace. He was as unpractical as any Indian and he set no price upon his labor of love. These are not the principles upon which the white man has founded his civilization. It is strange that he could not rise to these simple principles which were commonly observed among our people" (143). Both men appropriate Eastman's Christian discourse and place it in a new context. Such irony coming from traditionals, whom he calls "children of nature," (183) leaves Eastman literally speechless: "These words put the spell of uncomfortable silence upon our company" (143). In essence, the voices of these traditionals and their understanding of Christianity present to Eastman his own frustration with white culture, but these voices omitted the commitment to "racial progress" he could not abandon. Although Eastman perceived similarities between native American religions and Christianity elsewhere in his writing, he continued to advocate Anglo-Protestant versions of Christianity as an advance over Indians' "primitive" spiritual expressions.

Eastman tells of a similar incident in which local churches in Iowa invite him to speak to a Sac and Fox band which had absolutely rejected "civilization and Christianity." After listening to Eastman's speech emphasizing education for the children and the acceptance of white religion, the chief expressed his dissatisfaction with the inability of whites to live up to their own ideals. He tells Eastman, "As for us . . . we shall still follow the old trail. If you should live long and some day the Great Spirit shall permit you to visit us again, you will find us still Indians, eating with wooden spoons out of bowls of wood" (*Deep Woods* 149). Again, Eastman has little to say in response. From Eastman's point of view these incidents primarily indicate the hypocrisy of a nation that calls itself Christian. Yet what lies just beyond Eastman's understanding is the fact that while his Christian discourse is united with the ideology of "civilization," it cannot articulate its truths meaningfully to the victims of colonization.

Late in his life, after work as a writer, youth camp director, and Bureau of Indian Affairs official on various reservations, Eastman grows less concerned with separating the "deep woods" and the "civilized" parts of his identity. Ironically, it is while doing the colonizing work of persuading tribes to give up sacred objects to museums that Eastman begins to reacquaint himself with his childhood life. Traveling among the Ojibwa, for whose traditional ways he cannot help but express admiration, Eastman lets "the sweet roving instinct of the wild" take hold of him (175). He warmly describes the landscape, the people's stories, the gathering of wild rice, the techniques for catching a loon, and his adventure of getting stranded on an island. Eastman's renewed contact with the way of life he had turned away from helps to reestablish connections with his past and the sense of internal wholeness much of the narrative attempts to repress.

While Eastman strives at first to adopt one culture fully so as to mitigate the difficulties of being part of two cultures, Black Elk attempts to further understand and define the space between cultures. It is important to note that while Eastman finally represents a move toward modernity, Black Elk should not be seen as representing simply Eastman's opposite—the reac-

tionary returning to an order that had existed previously. Rather Black
Elk, like Eastman, was part of two cultures. While Eastman's written
eloquence ends at the point of confrontation between cultures, Black Elk
speaks from the contested space between cultures, languages, and religions
to create new possibilities for individual and group identity. Thus he begins
to fulfill his vision of the sacred hoop uniting and preserving his people.
And by envisioning a future for his people as a people, Black Elk suggests
a form of justice that Eastman cannot admit.

"Behold, a sacred voice is calling you; / All over the sky a sacred voice is
calling" (*Black Elk Speaks* 19). In 1931 Black Elk recalled for John G.
Neihardt the voices and visions that first came to him when he was five
years old and prepared him for the great vision four years later that forms
the center of *Black Elk Speaks*. Black Elk envisions "a world of intercon-
nected, renewing life forms in overlapping images" in which appear elders, the Grandfathers, who change back and forth into stallions, and who
represent the cardinal directions, the seasons, the earth, and the sky (Lincoln 89). They speak to him and give him gifts: from the west—autumn—
a wooden cup filled with water and the sky representing the power to renew,
and a bow representing the power to destroy; from the north—winter—a
healing herb and a feather from the white giant's wing; from the east—the
spring—a medicine pipe; and from the south—the summer—the sacred
hoop and flowering staff. One Grandfather tells him, "Behold, the living
center of the nation I shall give you, and with it many you shall save"
(*Black Elk Speaks* 28). Black Elk looks and sees beneath the branches "the
circled villages of people and every living thing with roots or legs or
wings, and all were happy" (28). Taking the red stick, Black Elk plants it
at the center of the nation's hoop where it grows into a cottonwood. The
people shout, "Here we shall raise our children and be as little chickens
under the mother sheo's [the prairie chicken's] wing" (34). A voice says,
"Behold the circle of the nation's hoop, for it is holy, being endless, and
thus all powers shall be one power in the people without end" (35). But
Black Elk learns that the people must endure four ascents, four generations, in which the nation is starving and scattered and the sacred hoop is
dying. However, after the fourth ascent, Black Elk views the "whole hoop
of the world" and says, "the sacred hoop of my people was one of many
hoops that made one circle . . . and in the center grew one mighty flowering
tree . . . . And I saw that it was holy" (43).

The rest of *Black Elk Speaks* tells of Black Elk's lifelong struggle to
interpret his vision and to respond correctly to it. The book ends with what

is probably its most well-known passage. Black Elk recalls the horror at Wounded Knee and says:

> And I can see that something else died there in the bloody mud, and was buried in the blizzard. A people's dream died there. It was a beautiful dream.
>
> And I, to whom so great a vision was given in my youth, —you see me now a pitiful old man who has done nothing, for the nation's hoop is broken and scattered. There is no center any longer, and the sacred tree is dead.
>
> (270)

Despite its poetic quality and power, this ending serves to obscure part of Black Elk's intention, and it calls into question the role of John Neihardt in the writing of *Black Elk Speaks*. In the preface to the book, Neihardt claims that the relationship between himself and Black Elk was not the typical one between ethnographer and informant. Rather, Black Elk recognized Neihardt's mystical tendencies and came to view Neihardt as a son who would carry on the power of the vision. In a conversation Neihardt had toward the end of his life, he said of the book, "The beginning and the ending are mine; they are what he would have said if he had been able" (McCluskey 238). He also refers to his work as a transformation, not a translation, meant to be understood by the white world. Neihardt never lost the faith, based upon his special relationship with Black Elk, that he had represented Black Elk truthfully. Nevertheless, Neihardt's statements indicate that *Black Elk Speaks*, especially the emphasis privileged by its pessimistic ending, is as much Neihardt's interpretation as his representation.

While few scholars question Neihardt's integrity, many point out that *Black Elk Speaks* was nonetheless shaped in part by Neihardt's ideological assumptions.[3] Clyde Holler, for instance, argues from the basis of the transcripts of Neihardt's talks with Black Elk that Neihardt de-emphasized Black Elk's stated intention of revitalizing Lakota traditions and fulfilling his vision by allowing Neihardt to tell it to the world ("Lakota Religion"). Rather than simply mourning his failure to act on the vision, Black Elk acts to fulfill it. However, Neihardt's emphasis on the symbolism of Wounded Knee as the end of an era serves up a message counter to Black Elk's—that Lakota culture and religious traditions (and the sacred hoop) were dead. Neihardt's assumptions are in this respect similar to Charles Eastman's. Both adopt the ideology prominent in America at the time; neither sees the future of native traditions. Precisely for this reason it is important to distinguish Black Elk's voice from John Neihardt's. The little that remains of Black Elk's regenerative purpose is in the postscript where Neihardt presents the picture of Black Elk standing on Harvey Peak praying to the Grandfathers, "It may be that some little root of the sacred tree still lives" (*Black Elk Speaks* 274).

Neihardt's shaping of the narrative has further consequences in obscuring Black Elk's identity. Perhaps Neihardt's desire to have *Black Elk Speaks* represent an "authentic" Lakota past that was disappearing rather than a living tradition in transition caused him to neglect any reference to the fact that Black Elk had been a Christian for twenty-seven years by the time he met with Neihardt. For Neihardt, authenticity implied homogeneity, thus precluding Black Elk's complex interreligious identity. *The Sacred Pipe* (1947), written from Joseph Epes Brown's conversations with Black Elk long after Neihardt's, is somewhat more explicit than *Black Elk Speaks* concerning Black Elk's Christianity. Nevertheless, Brown's frequent footnotes comparing the words of Black Elk to Christianity and other religions from around the world in order to demonstrate the "universality and orthodoxy of the Siouan religion" (*Sacred Pipe* xii) leave the impression that the connections are merely coincidental, the result of a primitive mind in touch with elemental truths.

Research into Black Elk's life has helped to reveal what Neihardt and Brown hide—that Black Elk, in addition to practicing Lakota ceremonies and healing rituals, also practiced Christianity. In *The Sixth Grandfather,* which makes available the transcripts from which Neihardt worked, Raymond DeMallie has enabled scholars to better understand the depth of Black Elk's involvement with Christianity. DeMallie documents Black Elk's interest in Christianity as early as his trip to Europe with Buffalo Bill's Wild West Show in 1888 (10). DeMallie speculates that Black Elk's loss of spiritual power while in Europe led him toward Christianity (11). But even when Black Elk returned to the plains and regained his spiritual power, he remained interested in Christianity. Eventually, he associated entirely with Roman Catholic institutions at a time when United States government forces were attempting to destroy all sources of Lakota tribal unity, organization, and leadership. Black Elk served as a catechist, holding prayer services when the Jesuits were detained by weather. He also was godfather to fifteen people and traveled as a missionary to other plains tribes. His Christian faith was well known among native Americans, and his letters indicate that he was dedicated to his work and sincere in his belief (DeMallie 17–22). But rather than give up his Lakota identity, Black Elk used his association with Catholicism to enhance his stature as a Lakota.

DeMallie suggests that by "holding to Christian doctrine, he practiced the virtue of charity to its fullest. On the other hand, he was able at the same time to fulfill the traditional role of a Lakota leader, poor himself but ever generous to his people" (23). Thus, in DeMallie's view, Black Elk negotiated the shift of Lakota leadership from political to religious spheres.

While some scholars who acknowledge Black Elk's Christianity maintain that he kept it separate from or used it as a cover for Lakota religion, Clyde Holler views Black Elk as a self-conscious theologian working to integrate the two faiths ("Black Elk"). By resisting the either/or choice urged by the missionaries, Black Elk was able to assert the continued relevance of Lakota religion in the context of constant contact with Christianity.

Holler explains, for instance, how Black Elk's interpretation of the Sun Dance in *The Sacred Pipe* shifts the purpose of self-sacrifice from personal power and glory to the renewal of the people and spiritual revitalization, Lakota values more easily reconciled with his Christian beliefs. Black Elk also de-emphasizes militaristic aspects of the Sun Dance, changing the traditional buffalo skin tied around the dancers' wrists to rabbit skin symbolizing endurance and humility. In addition to serving Black Elk's theological concerns, such changes respond to difficult times where the buffalo, on which the Sioux had depended completely, were scarce.

Furthermore, even while Black Elk asserts the relevance of Lakota religion in *The Sacred Pipe,* he shows his understanding that both the Lakota and Christians worship the same God. "[T]his is my prayer," says Black Elk to Brown, "that through our sacred pipe, and through this book in which I shall explain what our pipe really is . . . peace may come to those peoples who can understand . . . . Then they will realize that we Indians know the One true God, and that we pray to Him continually" (xx). Also, Black Elk teaches a lesson from the young willows used to construct the sweat lodge in which the sun dancers are purified: "for in the fall their leaves die and return to the earth, but in the spring they come to life again. So, too, men die but live again in the real world of Waken-Tanka, where there is nothing but the spirits of all things" (31–32). In its emphasis on a fall and subsequent spiritual redemption to life, Black Elk's use of Lakota symbolism is consistent with the central narrative of orthodox Christianity. Such examples highlight the fact that at the time he spoke with Joseph Epes Brown, Black Elk was able to intermingle successfully elements of both faiths.

Black Elk's response to spiritual domination is hardly unique. The melding of religions has taken place wherever Christianity has come into contact with native traditions. And when this occurs it always confounds the expectations of cultural and religious homogeneity imposed on native American traditions by white culture, represented here by John Neihardt, Joseph Epes Brown, and those who have hailed the words of Black Elk as "authentic" representations of uniquely Lakota religion and culture. Even these well-intentioned efforts to preserve what was assumed to be passing away and to separate the traditional from the Christian have the effect of imposing an uncharacteristic stasis on native religion.

It is not difficult to see how the creation of alternative choices for religious identity that maintain cultural continuity threaten the ideology of the dominant culture, which expects the imminent death of all things tribal. But in addition such alternatives challenge the religious orthodoxy on both sides that would prefer to distinguish the boundaries between religions more clearly so as to enforce rigid choices or to claim individuals for one side or the other.

When Black Elk is hailed (by Vine Deloria, Jr., in the introduction to *Black Elk Speaks,* for example) as a catalyst and inspiration for subsequent generations of native Americans to learn about their tribal roots, it is often deemed necessary to emphasize his faithful recording of Lakota culture and to minimize the role of Christianity and the complexity of Black Elk's religious identity. While Black Elk's words have surely provided historical knowledge and spiritual wisdom for many, underestimating his accomplishment only serves to lessen its potential. By combining the two traditions, Black Elk suggests enduring solutions to the problems of survival and continuance. Black Elk's strategy prevents a dominant culture from controlling, through its imposition of opposition, the image with which a people can represent themselves, and thus prevents the dominant culture from winning the final colonial battle.

Charles Eastman, who learns to see only white culture's divisions, becomes trapped into choosing between those divisions. It does not occur to Eastman that it is possible to wear moccasins and still use a pen to write of his faith in Jesus Christ. Black Elk, instead of adopting white religion in the manner of Eastman, appropriates it and makes it his own. For Black Elk this is not capitulation to white culture. Neither is it complete opposition to white culture, a choice in which part of his identity would still have depended upon the white world. Rather Black Elk chooses one way to remain independent and to survive.

When Charles Eastman arrived at the Pine Ridge Agency in 1890, he was greeted by "Captain Sword," the head of the Indian police force, who explained the Ghost Dance religion to Eastman and warned him of possible trouble (*Deep Woods* 82–84). In an article on this Oglala mediator, George Sword, Elaine A. Jahner makes it clear that Sword was remarkable for more than his minor role in Eastman's drama. Sword was a literate Lakota who composed original and unique mythic texts that resemble oral Lakota stories. Jahner points out that the Bible was translated into Lakota by 1880, and also that sections of Sword's texts unmistakably resemble Genesis. What Jahner argues concerning Sword is similar to what I have suggested about Black Elk: "Sword's exceptional (and bicultural) imagination created tales that comment on ways in which traditional values and beliefs could continue to function in a reservation and a Christian environment" (171). Sword's stories serve "as a narrative that is finally both Lakota and Christian" (176), and they allow "Christian Lakota to see that one way does not have to cancel out the other" (177).

Toward the end of her discussion of Sword, Jahner points out the political importance of Sword's work in ways that suggest how the historical examples of Charles Eastman's and Nicholas Black Elk's religious negotiations inform contemporary political struggles. Jahner writes that Sword's narratives "show the possibility of a sovereign ethos that avoids the colonial mentality and that motivates people to keep alive the political sovereignty guaranteed them by treaties. Political sovereignty is founded in historical continuity" (178). More concretely, a tribal nation's success in legal struggles over land claims, water rights, tribal jurisdictions, and religious freedoms often depends in part upon its ability to demonstrate the continuance of tribal organization, custom, and religion. While Jahner maintains that narratives like Sword's help people "perceive continuity amidst the changes" (178), blended religious identities like Black Elk's and Sword's are easily labeled as unauthentic within legal discourses where questions of sovereignty and freedom are often decided. The syncretistic religion which might represent continuity and survival within a tribal context becomes, within a legal context, evidence of inauthenticity and assimilation.

In his account of the 1976 Mashpee land claims trial, James Clifford writes that "[a]n adversary system of justice, the need to make a clear case to counterbalance an opposing one, discourages opinions of a 'yes, but,' 'it depends on how you look at it' kind" (321). In order for the Massachusetts tribe to reclaim land lost during the nineteenth century, it had to establish that it was indeed a tribe that could claim a continuous tribal history. The claim undoubtedly involved complex internal tribal politics, relationships between native and non-native Americans in the town of Mashpee, as well as a long (one might say typically colonial) history of cultural exchange and intermarriage between Indian, black, and white residents of the community. But most important for this discussion, religion was also a frequent subject of inquiry. A number of Mashpee involved with the trial claimed tribal identity and also attended the local Baptist church. As one woman testifies, "'They [Indian beliefs] are very dear to me, and I respect them. But I also respect God through my Christian belief. And to me God and the Great Spirit are the same'" (Clifford 287).

The woman's statement echoes the traditional men quoted by Charles Eastman, and her practical strategy resembles Black Elk's and George Sword's. But instead of recognizing in such statements evidence of cultural continuity amidst change, the court took religious amalgamation as evidence of discontinuity, a strike against the necessary claims of unbroken ties to pure origins. The court failed to understand that the religious mixture among the Mashpee has historically been politically unifying as well as spiritually nourishing, results similar to Jahner's claims about George Sword's appropriation of Christianity. Clifford writes that "even the partial [historical] record makes it clear that Christianity in Mashpee . . . was a site of local power and of resistance to outsiders. At recurring intervals, it was a focus of openly Indian, or 'tribal,' power" (305).

In the end, the Mashpee trial jury, with the testimony concerning religion as part of the evidence, ruled that the people living in Mashpee had not existed continuously as a tribal nation and thus were not entitled to land claims. Though religious identity was not the centerpiece of the trial, political efficacy would suggest that native American groups making legal claims for rights reach back through histories of colonial oppression to emphasize traditions that seem pure in their precontact origins. Legal contexts might not be the best place to recall the powerful, syncretic responses to oppression developed by Black Elk, Sword, and others.

But even if legal discourses discount the authenticity of heterogenous religious identities, the choices made by Black Elk and those like him suggest powerful alternatives for individuals and communities who must continue to find meaning in the contested spiritual space between cultures and religions. The circumventions of oppressive power represented by Black Elk and others have indeed shown "a way beyond the silence that descends when all language seems to have been shifted to another interpretive realm" (Jahner 178). That certain hearts have hardened and ears closed does not mean that Black Elk and others have not spoken compellingly for many.

7.

We Wretched of the Earth
The Search for a Language of Justice

JOHN C. HAWLEY, S.J.

"In the beginning was the Word," writes John—God's revealing utterance that "was made flesh and lived among us." This incarnational character of the Word, this "living among us," has demanded of Christians in each age a reinterpretation of its original and ongoing meaning. If the protean nature of God's self-expression has seen a continuing "translation" in each age, though, it is becoming increasingly evident among church members that a similar task is also required in each ethnic milieu. The "us" among whom the Word lives is made up of many communities of discourse, and a logocentric theology like Christianity must take special interest in the self-expressive nature of the ongoing local struggles for a forum. Implicated in the colonization of much of the world and the imposition of Western languages, the Church, as a matter of justice, now finds itself examining the role of language in any people's self-definition and consequent worship of God.

The shape of Christendom is changing, and the pace of that change is accelerating. The "Third Church," as Walbert Bühlmann has dubbed Christendom in the emergent nations, will soon set the agenda for the century to come. In 1900 there were 392 million Christians in Western developed countries (Europe and North America), and 67 million in southern countries (Asia, Africa, Oceania, and South America); 85 percent of Christians were in the First and Second Church, 15 percent in the Third

Church. By 1965 there were 637 million Christians in Western developed countries and 370 million in southern countries; 63 percent were in the First and Second Church, 37 percent were in the third. Current estimates suggest that by the year 2000 there will be 796 million Christians in Western developed countries and 1.118 billion in southern countries. Forty-two percent will be in the First and Second Church; 58 percent will be in the Third Church. This change is even more striking in the Roman Catholic Church, 70 percent of whose members will live in the developing countries in the year 2000 (Bühlmann 20).

As the makeup of the church has changed, so has consideration of its role. A new recognition has emerged that the Roman Catholic Church should stand independent from the political intentions of colonizers; the 1953 decree of the bishops of Madagascar, for example, explicitly acknowledged that self-government was a natural right (Bühlmann 43). As recently as October 1991, Pope John Paul II told Fernando Collor de Mello, President of Brazil, that "the objectives of the church in its purely religious and spiritual mission and those of the state pertaining to the common good are certainly different. But they coincide in one point: humanity and the well-being of the country." This common objective involved, he said, the modernization of work conditions, the creation of jobs, a halt to "the violence that has already taken so many lives," and the provision of financial and other services for million of peasants (Cowell, "Pope Challenges" A4). Then addressing Indians of the southern rim of the Amazon basin, he announced that "the Pope has not come, like the bandits of the past and the prospectors of today, to search for gold," and he asked their forgiveness for the "weakness and defects" of some missionaries during centuries of evangelism (Cowell, "Pope Asks" A3).

The search for a national voice among the constituents of this new Christendom is clearly evident in their writers, but that search must first choose the language most appropriate to its expression. In her recent novel *Jasmine,* Indian novelist Bharati Mukherjee has her Punjabi narrator ironically observe that her new American husband "comes from a place where the language you speak is what you are" (8). If he were a native American, the irony would be complete. She, also, is not English, so their language does not fully define who they are. This is crucial because, as the Russian philosopher Mikhail Bakhtin argues, our engagement in language does, in fact, shape our self-definition.

Consideration of this dilemma often takes on a religious cast among the writers themselves. Most postcolonial novelists who write in English, or whose works have been translated into English, have been baptized. They attended religious schools and, for better or for worse, have been shaped by that experience. Their novels, poetry, and essays increasingly call not only for restitution—of their precolonial identity, of their postcolonial voice— but frequently do so specifically in terms of a biblical call for justice. With a lacerating irony, this struggle for justice among peoples upon whom the Gospel was sometimes cruelly imposed draws its strength from the Bible's example of Yahweh's enduring righteousness, the prophets' call to fidelity, and the significance of the individual in the eyes of God.

"In his conversation with Saint Bernard in Paradise," writes Bakhtin, "Dante suggests that our body shall be resurrected not for its own sake, but for the sake of those who love us—those who knew and loved our one-and-only countenance" (*Art* 57). This "one-and-only" incarnated specificity fascinates Bakhtin—but not as it might have fascinated a Sartrean, as the inescapable prison of our individual isolation. Bakhtin's analysis of the human condition, instead, transforms existentialist isolation.

His notion of dialogism, the idea that "we call forth, and are ourselves summoned by, the words of others, which we make our own . . . through borders we build around them" (xliv), is by now relatively well-known. This notion, perhaps, approaches a "door" in the Sartrean prison; the implications are made even more apparent in Bakhtin's earliest writings, dating from 1919 to 1924, in which "there are no things in themselves, no possibility of an actual object understood as an it-itself; [and] thus, the dialogic subject, existing only in a world of consciousness, is free to perceive others not as a constraint, but as a possibility: others are neither hell nor heaven, but the necessary condition for both" (xxxviii). Social interaction demands a porous margin of subjectivity—neither a complete submission to the other, nor a solid wall of difference.

Briefly put, in the Bakhtinian world there is an inescapable "otherness," but our very sense of our distinct self is dependent upon an interaction with the other. I look at someone else and see things about him or her that that individual is dependent upon me to "see": the backdrop, the facial expression, the gestalt. Bakhtin's emphasis in his discussion of this phenomenon is not on the conquest of one by the other, but on the simultaneity of their identification: "the resulting simultaneity is not a private *either/or*, but an inclusive *also/and*" (xxiii). Identity, for Bakhtin and his followers—the identity of a nation and certainly the identity of an individual—is, therefore, an activity rather than a thought. It is an ongoing "mythmaking," in the view of another theoretician (Mariátegui 187–88), which expresses itself as a conversation. No healthy individual wishes to be subsumed by the other: each admits his or her status of foreigner, even in the face of the beloved.

These theories about language and identity take a sharper focus in writers whose language is historically tied to forces that controlled and suppressed the "otherness" of subject peoples. The Senegalese novelist Cheikh Hamidou Kane, first educated in a Koranic school and eventually at the Sorbonne, notes in *Ambiguous Adventure* that he was "personally conquered" by the French through their imposition of their language: "their alphabet. With it, they struck the first hard blow at the country of the Diallobé. I remained for a long time under the spell of those signs and those sounds which constitute the structure and the music of their language" (159). The true power of the French, he claims, "lay not in the cannons of the first morning, but rather in what followed the cannons," the language and culture that were imposed (49).

José María Arguedas and Ngũgĩ wa Thiong'o also speak for this increasingly vocal world, with its prophetic judgment upon the colonizers and its salvific witness to the interdependence of Christian peoples. Ngũgĩ puts it succinctly: "The oppressor nation uses language as a means of entrenching itself in the oppressed nation. The weapon of language is added to that of the Bible and the sword in pursuit of what David Livingstone, in the case of nineteenth-century imperialism, called 'Christianity plus 5 percent' " (*Moving* 31). Writers such as Arguedas and Ngũgĩ represent a pattern repeated throughout the postcolonial world: the Bible, implicitly identified in their writings with the oppressor, nonetheless offers a paradigmatic justification and strategy for liberation.

José María Arguedas was born in a remote Andean village in 1911 and died in Lima, by his own hand, fifty-eight years later. His mother had died when he was three, and his father, a lawyer, remarried when the boy was six. Arguedas did not get along with his stepmother and spent most of his time with the Quechua servants. When he was thirteen he was sent away to school, but his fascination with the world of the servants seems to have shaped his entire life: he later became an anthropologist, a musicologist, an ethnographer, a linguist specializing in Quechua, a poet, novelist, and translator of indigenous myths. He made what liberation theologians call a preferential "option for the poor" (Boff 416), aligning himself with them in a struggle against his own class.

Unless one is a Quechua, the Spanish language is by now identified as the natural language for all the former Incan lands. For Arguedas, however, it embodied the heritage of cultural domination of the Indians by the colonizers. In 1958, accepting the Inca Garcilaso de la Vega prize, he proclaimed, "I have not become acculturated" (Columbus 23). As we have noted, Arguedas was not, in fact, Quechua: he only desperately wished he were and was suggesting as much in his acceptance speech. His novels are written principally in Spanish, but employ Quechua regularly, implicitly asserting the ongoing presence in Peru of these people and their heritage. Of course, despite his claim in accepting the award, Arguedas did have the rather conspicuous trappings of apparent acculturation to the colonizing powers: a doctorate from the University of San Marcos in Lima, for example, where he served as head of the anthropology department at the time of his death. But his suicide suggests an internal division that plagued his life and his stories, a division that he saw no way to heal. It tore him apart, but he also recognized in this angry polarity a power that might be channeled into a salvific dialogue for himself and his Peruvian society, if *both* learned the other's language.

Like many writers in the postcolonial world, Arguedas grew increasingly uncomfortable with his own alienation from the poor that was one consequence of his mastery of the "master's" language. His was, in the words of one critic, a "mythological consciousness," which developed in three stages. The first was a "pre-historic, generative" stage, in which as a child he learned Quechua, the language of the Incas, a language in which "the circumambient situation affects the meaning of root words"—a language, therefore, with "far greater contextual immediacy than either Spanish or English" (Columbus 22). The second stage of his developing mythological consciousness, the agonistic and abstract phase, is symbolized by his formal education and the world represented by the Spanish language. In this experience, writes Claudette Columbus, "the lexical, the lettered, the systematized tried to sever Arguedas from his roots, from the people of his heart, from his place in a community, from his personal past" (23). The third stage of his development in mythological consciousness came in his mature years of fiction writing; here, "the individual accepts a basic helplessness as the condition of openness to others and to the world" (24). Closed, defensive, and self-protective systems are abandoned in favor of an ongoing development of the ancient stories. As if referring to this stage, Arguedas writes that "within the isolating and oppressive walls, the Quechua pueblo (considerably arcaisized and defending itself by dissimulation) *continues* conceiving ideas, creating songs and myths" ("Palabras" 431).

In an entry in his last diary Arguedas saw himself as living between two ages: "The one that closes is the one of the whip and impotent hatred, funereal uprisings of fear of an oppressive god; and the one that opens is the cycle of light and liberating force . . . the liberating God, that God which reconciles and reintegrates" (qtd. Trigo 29). Will it be, he wondered, a humanistic atheism, as in Feuerbach, or can it also be the liberation of Christianity, incorporating its reintegration into the original condition as a servant of humanity? In the light of his suicide, it would seem that Arguedas was not optimistic in his own response to these questions. With our growing recognition of the disparity between the First and the Third worlds, we are not surprised by Arguedas's despair. Considering what we have noted regarding the third phase of mythological consciousness, the transcendent liberation he envisioned would demand a rejection of self-sufficiency, of rationalism, of the sort of individual who creates himself or herself and who "knows" and dominates: it would demand, in short, a rejection of the colonizing mind. Arguedas did not see this happening.

Far removed from Peru, the experience of Ngũgĩ wa Thiong'o nonetheless echoes the mixture of anger, hope, and fear so evident in Arguedas. It also embodies a rejection of the western European model of human, and specifically Christian, expression. Ngũgĩ grew up in Kenya and vividly recalls the stories in Gikuyu that he heard while working in the fields as a child—the same language he spoke at home. This corresponds with Arguedas' first stage of mythological consciousness, the "pre-historic and generative" stage. He began his schooling in the village of Kamaandura; at first this missionary-run school conducted classes in Gikuyu, but after 1952 the colonial regime demanded that all education be in English. This was Ngũgĩ's equivalent of Arguedas' second stage of mythological consciousness. As Ngũgĩ remembers it, "language and literature were taking us further and further from ourselves to other selves, from our world to other worlds" (*Decolonising* 12). English became an enforcement officer especially in the lives of the imaginative and eloquent. If they wished to write, they had to play by the rules set down by the missionaries and the colonial administrators who controlled the publishing houses. The Literature Bureau in Rhodesia would only publish novels that had religious or sociological themes free from politics: "Stories of characters who move from the darkness of the pre-colonial past to the light of the christian present, yes. But any discussion of or any sign of dissatisfaction with colonialism. No!" (*Decolonising* 70).

In Ngũgĩ's opinion, the rise of universities in Africa in the 1950s brought another form of colonialization. The best writers, a Chinua Achebe, Wole Soyinka, or Kofi Awoonor, ended up producing "the Afro-European novel" instead of writing their own people's literature. This sort of Europeanized writing squandered the tightly controlled access to non-governmental and non–religiously aligned publishers and evaded the bold social criticism present in the very novels such authors were imitating. Thus, writes Ngũgĩ, "the African novel was further impoverished by the very means of its possible liberation" (*Decolonising* 70). The earlier control was bad, but so was this false new freedom. Recognizing his own complicity in this scheme, Ngũgĩ includes himself in the list of co-opted authors. Since 1977, however, he generally writes and publishes first in Gikuyu, seeing his own people as his principal audience, and then has the book or essay translated and published in English. This immersion in the language of his roots symbolizes Ngũgĩ's movement into the third stage of mythological consciousness, a recognition of self-empowerment through the very means of apparent alienation.

Some have criticized Ngũgĩ's decision to write in Gikuyu as an unnecessarily political response to his religious and literary training, but his defenders maintain that the colonized have little choice these days but to foreground a choice that all writers in fact make. Terry Eagleton argues that all literary theories are politically grounded. In his view, far more suspect than Ngũgĩ's confrontational stance are those disingenuous theories, supposedly apolitical, that "offer as a supposedly 'technical', 'self-evident', 'scientific' or 'universal' truth doctrines which with a little reflection can be seen to relate to and reinforce the particular interests of particular groups of people at particular times" (195).

The same might be said of theories of missiology and ecclesiology, as revisionist church historians have demonstrated in their analyses of the complex role their spokesmen and spokeswomen have played in colonial cultures. And, as the political insight that informs Eagleton's own vision draws much of its strength from Marxist analysis, so do those contemporary theologies that associate themselves with processes of liberation. For a Christian literary critic, and perhaps for others, the intersection of these disciplines provides a lively source for a discussion of fiction that is explicitly moral in its tone and marginalized in its voice, fiction like that of Arguedas and Ngũgĩ.

Both the literary theory Eagleton describes and the theology informing my analysis here share what Pedro Arrupe calls "an attention to economic factors, to property structures, to economic interests which motivate this or that group"; both share a "sensitivity to the exploitation that victimizes entire classes, attention to the role of class struggle in history . . . [and] attention to ideologies which can camouflage vested interests and even injustice" (308). Whatever may be true of Marxist literary analysis, however, it must be noted that truly Christian liberation theology does not attribute an exclusive character to historical materialism nor to an economic framework for reality. The notion of class struggle, seen as the inevitable vehicle for historical evolution in Marxism, is here tempered by the broader framework of biblical prophecy and the call to conversion. The Latin American bishops, writing in 1979, note that there is an inspiration for liberation that is contained in the Bible. Relying on strict Marxist analysis dangerously leads, in their view, to "the total politicization of Christian existence, the disintegration of the language of faith into that of the social sciences, and the draining away of the transcendental dimension of Christian salvation" (Puebla 245). Like native peoples in the face of a colonizing power, the bishops are here objecting to the usurpation of their voice, their "language" of faith.

As Gustavo Gutiérrez, the best known of these theologians notes, liberation theology "implies a firm, Gospel-oriented witness to God's love and, as a concrete expression of that love, a firm commitment to those who are most oppressed and dispossessed" ("Criticism" 419).[1] It means "not becoming accustomed to seeing the newspapers filled day after day with pictures of mutilated corpses, of mass graves, of innocent people mowed down. . . . It means maintaining a permanent attitude of shock and rejection in the face of . . . indignities" (420). "Our task," he writes elsewhere, "is to find the words" (On Job 102).[2]

If a sense of ultimate hope and a belief in the transcendent distinguish liberation theology from strict Marxist analysis, therefore, the sense of urgency and the emphasis on praxis, or action, distinguishes it from other theologies. These theologians do not see liberation as a topic to be studied, but as an event in which to engage. As Leonardo Boff notes, liberation theology "examines the concrete practice of the oppressed, their progress and their allies; it asks about the participation of individual Christians, base communities and sectors of the church in the overall liberation process. . . . it is necessary to participate as an active member in a particular movement, a base community, a center for the defense of human rights, or a trade union. This immersion in the world of the poor and oppressed gives theological discourse a passionate edge, an occasional mordancy, a holy wrath— and a sense of the practical" (416–17). Such theologians are making a case for the retrieval of the theological language of the preexilic prophets, and they are meeting with opposition from those who now speak the colonizer's language of stability and control.

There is, of course, a common "language" of myths and symbols in these various cultures. As Ngũgĩ himself notes, "I use the Bible quite a lot, or biblical sayings, not because I share in any belief in the Bible, or in the sanctity of the Bible. It's just simply as a common body of knowledge I can share with my audience, and the same is true when I'm writing in Gikuyu language" (Wilkinson 130). Still, what is generally missing in any confrontation between language groups, however metaphorically we may wish to apply the term "language," is an acceptance of the truth that is tied to the language itself. Perhaps the words that are effective in one culture are specific to it and can never fully be translated. In Ngũgĩ's *The River Between,* for instance, "Gikuyu myth and Judaic Old Testament touch, and in the touching the established order of each is threatened. . . . Opposing tribal religion and cosmic structure is Christianity—equally as biased, equally as ordered, and equally as necessitated by the psychological dispositions of the people who espouse it" (Howard 100). Yet Ngũgĩ describes himself as having been "deeply Christian" when writing this novel, as though he sensed that a hidden language of faith needed to be unearthed from the arbitrary historical encrustations. He describes the writing of the book: "In school I was concerned with trying to remove the central Christian doctrine from the dress of western culture, and seeing how this might be grafted on to the central beliefs of our people. 'The River Between' was concerned with this process" (E. Wright 97).

A parallel struggle shapes the works of Arguedas. Anyone familiar with the Catholic Church as represented in his *Deep Rivers* will see little social concern in that institution. Arguedas, in fact, depicts the Church as a great enslaving instrument. The indictment the novelist brings against the Spanish overseers is brought with even greater force against the policing function undertaken by the Church: the rector imagines his paternalistic words to be a necessary caution for his flock. However well-meaning he considers himself to be, he clearly embodies for the reader a pacifying role that maintains colonial power. As Pedro Trigo, the novelist's best critic, has noted, "the urgency for liberation impregnates all Arguedas's work" (37, my trans.) and there *is* liberation in the novel. This conclusion is demonstrated in detail by Gutiérrez (*Entre* 75–78). But the distinction Arguedas makes is important: it is a liberation that is brought to the Church from forces arising in, and defining, the indigenous peoples. This act of liberation in Arguedas, though not made to appear explicitly Christian, shares with liberation theologians an emphasis upon the local, even "base," community as essential to and even coterminal with one's individual "salvation." Arguedas holds out less hope for transcendence than liberation theologians, however, embodying whatever little there may be in characters who have been driven crazy by their immediate circumstances.

A literary critic with an interest in liberation theology would implicitly address Arguedas's and Ngũgĩ's challenges to institutionalized religion and explicitly foreground a shared search for transcendence by stipulating the commonality of a human "metalanguage," possibly a literary equivalent to natural law, while still embracing the irreducibility of localized languages. The positing of a "metalanguage" would be an act of faith in the value of an ecology of heteroglossia, an option for explicit recognition and valorization of the other's language as *forever* Other. It would demand the patience to withhold a self-comforting digestion of the inexplicable and inexpressible in the Other. It would conduct its criticism almost with the reverence implied in Martin Buber's suggestive phrase "I and Thou." It would allow and even encourage difference, and resist the need to categorize or canonize.

The paradox that becomes increasingly evident in the closing days of the twentieth century, however, is that the linguae francae that have helped establish a global village have historically implied the subjugation of one community by the other. The result, which is increasingly resisted, is the obliteration of difference. And this is especially true in the realm of language. As Ngũgĩ notes, "a specific culture is not transmitted through language in its universality but in its particularity as the language of a specific community with a specific history." In the context of this discussion, this insight is particularly significant because, again in Ngũgĩ's words, "language carries culture, and culture carries . . . the entire body of values by which we come to perceive ourselves and our place in the world (*Decolonising* 15 – 16). This specificity amounts to the "otherness" that polarizes individuals and communities, with a resultant devalorization of one by the other.

Like Arguedas, Ngũgĩ identifies the poor as the seedbed of the cultural specificity and language, the site of implicit defiance of the imposed order: "What prevented our languages from being completely swallowed up by English and other oppressor languages," he writes, "was that the rural and urban masses, who had refused to surrender completely in the political and economic spheres, also continued to breathe life into our languages and thus helped to keep alive the histories and cultures they carried. The masses of Africa would often derive the strength needed in their economic and political struggles from those very languages. Thus the peoples of the Third World had refused to surrender their souls to English, French, or Portuguese" (*Moving* 35).

As Arguedas and Ngũgĩ exemplify, and as the critic Simon During has noted, "in both literature and politics the post-colonial drive towards identity centres around language, partly because in postmodernity identity is barely available elsewhere" (During, "Postmodernism" 43). The unfortunate historical pattern, as Ngũgĩ points out, has been the denigration of the local language and the elevation of the colonizer's (*Moving* 32). And today the global village obliterates difference: all is consumed, relativized, homogenized. Resistance to the ease of communication in the language of the former colonizer, on the other hand, as with Ngũgĩ, is a political recognition that something (or someone) is lost in the translation.

As any liberation theologian would emphasize, and as Mikhail Bakhtin recognized, the human condition is such that we are in this boat together. And we are called upon to row. That is to say, there is an ethical component to this interactional philosophy of personal and national identity. In his earliest published essay, for example, Bakhtin asks, "What guarantees the inner connection of the constituent elements of a person? Only the unity of answerability. I have to answer with my own life for what I have experienced and understood in art, so that everything I have experienced and understood would not remain ineffectual in my life" (*Art* 1–2).

And what would an effectual understanding of literature possibly demand for the contemporary, postcolonial, postmodern Christian? "Answerability" seems a suggestive response. In the context of the essays in this volume it is a wonderful term, because it implies the prior question—a question posed by others, by other cultures, by others' needs as "they" stand before "us" and babble in an intransigently foreign tongue. It suggests a demand, as well, lest the question be left hanging in the air. As communal as such a critic believes the human situation *ultimately* to be, honesty and justice require that those in traditionally colonizing countries stand up for the wonder of an "invading," alien word: one that disrupts; one that makes new.[3]

8

The Dialogical Imagination
of Chinua Achebe

Susan VanZanten Gallagher

No discussion of postcolonial literature would be complete without consideration of the work of the Nigerian author, essayist, and politician Chinua Achebe. *Things Fall Apart,* first published in 1958, can in one sense be seen as the first postcolonial novel. It was certainly the first widely distributed book written by an indigenous author that examined the effects of colonialism from the point of view of the colonized. Today, *Things Fall Apart* is probably the most frequently read postcolonial novel; continually in print throughout the English-speaking world, it has also been translated into over thirty languages. An estimated three million copies have been sold, and it is regularly adopted as a textbook in a variety of university, college, high school, and even elementary-school courses (Lindfors, *Approaches* ix). Achebe is often acclaimed as "the father of the African novel" (Innes 19), and Simon Gikandi asserts, "For many students and scholars of African culture, the inaugural moment of modern African literature was the publication . . . of [his] *Things Fall Apart*" (1).

At the heart of all of Achebe's work lies the troubling relationship between colonizer and colonized, between African and European traditions. Thematically, his novels repeatedly consider the tensions aroused by this collision of cultures; similarly, as a writer, Achebe has had to struggle with a complex inheritance of indigenous and European languages, literary forms, and definitions of art. A crucial and often primary part of that

struggle involves Christianity—its different manifestations in the colonizers and its strong impact on Igbo society. In Achebe's work, we find a
probing treatment of the notion of justice and the postcolonial situation; as
that treatment emerges in his themes, characters, and language, Achebe
demonstrates the kind of dialogical imagination that, according to Mikhail
Bakhtin, characterizes the most artistically and morally profound works of
fiction. Furthermore, reading Achebe's work can be in itself an act of Bakhtinian dialogue for the Western critic committed to the biblical notion of
justice.

Bakhtin's dialogical theory has become popular in critical circles even
though there are several different understandings of that theory. This confusion stems, in part, from the unusual history of Bakhtin's publications
and academic career, the sketchy documentary and textual evidence, and the
chronology of his "discovery" by Anglo-American critics.[1] In my discussion I will draw on the view, cogently and convincingly argued by Gary
Saul Morson and Caryl Emerson, that one of Bakhtin's central concerns was
ethical behavior and that a critical emphasis on Bakhtin's idea of carnival
is distorted. Those who embrace the carnivalesque, deconstructive Bakhtin
understand him as celebrating an infinite semantic and ethical openness, but
others, myself included, understand dialogue as an unending, "unfinalizable" process that makes room for ethical actions and that recognizes that
truth and a provisional unity do exist.

"Real dialogism," write Morson and Emerson, "will incarnate a world
whose unity is essentially one of multiple voices, whose conversations never
reach finality and cannot be transcribed in monological form. The unity of
the world will then appear as it really is: polyphonic" (61). Morson and
Emerson are reluctant to call Bakhtin a relativist, for they claim that rela-
tivists both agree that moral duties are a matter of rules and deny that
nonarbitrary rules can exist (26–27). In "Toward a Philosophy of the
Act," Bakhtin condemns the view that "denies the autonomy of truth and
tries to make truth something relative and conditional. . . . In our view,
the autonomy of truth, its methodological purity and self-definedness are
completely preserved; precisely on condition of its purity can it be responsibly participatory in existence; truth that is relative from within itself is
not necessary to the event of existence. The signifying power of truth is
sufficient unto itself, it is absolute and eternal."[2]

It is admittedly difficult to reconcile such pronouncements with Bakhtin's
embrace of unfinalizable dialogue. Arnold Krupat attempts to do so by
suggesting that "commitment to dialogism may be seen as a type of radi-

cal pluralism, a more relativized openness, concerned to state meanings provisionally in recognition of the legitimate claims of otherness and difference. Norms, here, are decidedly established but these are not seen as denying—the denial enforced by legitimated violence—the proposal of alternatives" (*Voice* 196–97). Rather than speaking of "the truth," then, one might speak of "the truth process" as a constantly evolving search for the truth that can never be reached in human finitude.

Nonetheless, within this process, human beings often must act, making an ethical decision—to kill or not to kill, to confess or not to confess. Acts undeniably must achieve closure, while words can remain unfinalized. But within the Kantian tradition of fixed norms, Bakhtin claims, ethical acts are mechanical. He believes that ethical judgments are not generalizable or a matter of rules, but rather are particular, involving careful analysis of a particular situation within a unique relationship with specific people. Each act must thus be judged within its own "eventness": "obligation . . . arises in and responds to each particular situation in a way that cannot be adequately generalized without depriving it of its very essence" (Morson and Emerson 26).

Dialogue thus does not preclude ethical behavior; rather, for Bakhtin, dialogue is both an empirical reality and an ethical imperative. He claims, first of all, that the self, speech, and society are inherently dialogic. Individuals and cultures have no clear boundaries: "To be means to be for another, and through the other for oneself. A person has no sovereign internal territory" (*Problems* 287). Languages' boundaries exist only provisionally in specific situations: "Every utterance participates in the 'unitary language' (in its centripetal forces and tendencies) and at the same time partakes of social and historical heteroglossia (the centrifugal, stratifying forces)" (*Dialogic* 272). Nonetheless, many social and discursive practices attempt to impose an authoritative, monologic voice and to suppress or subordinate other voices. Thus, Bakhtin rejects Stalin's totalitarianism and clearly prefers the heteroglossia of the novel as a literary form to the monologic language of poetry or the epic.

Although the self-contained monologic self is a fiction for all people, previously colonized people, with their multiple cultural experiences, offer particularly striking examples of dialogic selves. Kwame Anthony Appiah (dialogic in his very name) describes the polyphonic quality of his sister's wedding, which took place in a Methodist church in Kumasi, Asante, used the words of the Book of Common Prayer, incorporated a prayer by the local Catholic archbishop, and concluded with the pouring of libations to the family ancestors (119). Achebe similarly finds himself in a world of multiple identities. Most simply put, he occupies a no-man's-land between two cultures, African and European. Christened Albert Chinualumogu ("Named for Victoria, Queen of England," as he describes it in an essay with that title), Achebe grew up at "the crossroads of cultures" in the small eastern Nigerian village of Ogidi in the 1930s (*Hopes* 34). His father, converted as a young man and renamed Isaac, had married a fellow convert and served as an evangelist, teacher, and catechist for the Church Missionary Society. Yet Isaac's maternal uncle, who had raised him, was a respected traditional elder in Ogidi, having taken the second highest title that a man could assume. At home, Achebe read Shakespeare and Bunyan, but he also drank in his mother's folk stories, which "had the immemorial quality of the sky and the forests and the river" (*Hopes* 38). Eventually, he earned a degree in English literature, religious studies, and history from the University of Ibadan, which was affiliated with the University of London.

Far from being torn by the "dual consciousness" W. E. B. Dubois attributed to the African American or enacting the romantic myth of the modern African as agonizingly poised between two cultures, Achebe has frequently affirmed the benefits of his complex heritage. As a child he moved between both sides of his family, sneaking over to his neighbor's house to share in heathen festival meals as well as participating in the monthly evangelical outreach service held (without much success) in the village. In a much-quoted passage, Achebe describes the contrasts in his life: "On one arm of the cross we sang hymns and read the Bible night and day. On the other my father's brother and his family, blinded by heathenism, offered food to idols." However, the passage continues, revealing a complex irony in the apparently simple dichotomy: "That was how it was supposed to be anyhow. But I knew without knowing why that it was too simple a way to describe what was going on. Those idols and that food had a strange pull on me in spite of my being . . . a thorough little Christian" (*Hopes* 35). As an adult, Achebe deliberately began to visit tribal elders, shrines, and festivals in an attempt to explore his ancestral past (Moore 124). His earlier distance from traditional culture, he explains, "made it possible for me not to take things for granted" (Duerdon and Pieterse 12) and allowed a "necessary backward step which a judicious viewer may take in order to see a canvas steadily and fully" (*Hopes* 35). Similar distance from European culture came by virtue of his political and social position as a colonial subject.

Achebe's identity is more complicated, though, than a simple dichotomy of European and African, Christian and traditional. He is African, but also Nigerian and Igbo, and his Western world is similarly polyphonic, with its differing realms of academia, religion, and politics. Although Achebe believes that "it is part of the writer's role to encourage the creation of an African identity," he also recognizes the difficulty in such a monologic term.[3] "I think we are still wrestling with the definition of African," he told one interviewer. "There's no one tradition that we are talking about. We do have several traditions. We have the indigenous tradition, the oral tradition, the vernaculars, the ancient traditions of literature before, but we also have today. You can't disappear back into the past, so we need to create a synthesis out of these two" (Jussawalla and Dasenbrock 79–80). Achebe's multifaceted life results in his being unusually well placed to represent and deploy the different voices of his culture in such a synthesis.

Already in some of Achebe's earliest published writing as an undergraduate he was rendering this polyphonic reality of modern Africa, with particular reference to Christianity. "In a Village Church," published in the Ibadan *University Herald* in 1951, ironically contrasts "the semi-literate fumblings of the elderly bible reader with [Achebe's] own easy acquaintance with Wordsworth" (Innes 10). This short story exemplifies Bakhtin's notion of "hybrid construction," with at least four different strata of discourse: the confused English of the African Bible reader, the King James English against which the comic version is created, the original language of Wordsworth, and the employment of that language for certain purposes by the narrator.

Achebe's best known work, *Things Fall Apart*, contains an even more elaborate heteroglossia.[4] Linguistically, Achebe employs Igbo, so-called "African English" or vernacular English, and more formal English. Although the Igbo terms are almost always translated or explained in the text, their very presence "rarely lets [Achebe's] reader forget the otherness of Igbo culture and the language which embodies it" (Innes 34). Furthermore, in this novel, Achebe inaugurated the African English style; as Bernth Lindfors has noted, most previous African works spoke monologically in stiff, formal English prose, full of quotations of Sir Walter Scott and Shakespeare (Innes and Lindfors 6). Achebe also includes literary allusions, most notably in his novels' titles, but such allusions now appear in a world full of differing voices. *Things Fall Apart* retains the multiplicity of the Nigerian world during colonization, and Achebe does not reduce the heteroglossia of that world to a single, univocal language. Rhetorically, this novel contains several different kinds of discourses identified by Bakhtin:

the language used by the characters, the posited author, and incorporated genres (*Dialogic* 323).

Different characters possess distinctive voices: "In dialogue, for example, a Westernized African character will never speak exactly like a European character nor will he speak like an illiterate village elder. Achebe . . . is able to individualize his characters by differentiating their speech" (Lindfors, "Palm-Oil" 48). Throughout the novel, we hear a complex chorus of English and Igbo, Africans and Europeans, district commissioners and missionaries, Igbo speakers from Mbanta and from another region.

A particularly unique and effective kind of dialogism emerges in the Igbo characters' use of proverbs, a frequently noted aspect of Achebe's art. These proverbs are directly quoted by characters, indirectly quoted, and presented in the words of the posited author. Often a character will initiate a proverb with the phrase, "our elders say," and the posited author often repeats, "As the elders said" (*Things* 11, 12), building up a great chorus of ancestral voices providing interpretation and judgment. But the ancestors do not always speak with a single voice. The same ancestral wisdom that declares "that if a man said yea his *chi* also affirmed" also states, "A man could not rise beyond the destiny of his *chi*" (121). Similarly, one proverb holds that children will resemble their parents: "When mother-cow is chewing grass its young ones watch its mouth" (68). Yet Okonkwo's ability to go beyond the failures of his father prompts another proverb: "Looking at a king's mouth . . . one would think he never sucked at his mother's breast" (28). Even such an apparently monological form as the traditional proverb thus becomes polyphonic both in its content and in its rhetorical presentation.

The voice of the posited author moves with ease between such traditional forms and references to the classics of Western literature—Yeats, Wordsworth, and the Bible. On another discursive level, Abdul JanMohamed has demonstrated how the style and structure of *Things Fall Apart* bring together oral and written cultures—the language of traditional Igbo epic and proverbs and the European realistic novel—in a new formal synthesis: "The narrative, like the style, is a product of a double consciousness, of a syncretic combination of chirographic and oral techniques" (30). Although he grants that the novel "is delicately poised at the transition from the epic (oral) to the novel (chirographic)" (34), JanMohamed concentrates on the novel's use of oral discourse, such as the paratactic sentences, the use of periphrasis that resembles Igbo conversational patterns, the representative and flat characterization, and "monotonous" narrative voice—all of which

are characteristic of the monological epic. He does not note the more complex heteroglossia of the work. Thus, instead of dialogics, JanMohamed
sees the work as enacting a "negative dialectics" that deterritorializes both
"the English language and the novelistic form" (21). Ultimately, though,
he argues that Achebe's form and content clash: "While the content laments
a loss [of a vanished heroic culture] and points an accusing finger at colonialist destruction, the form glories in the pleasures of a new formal synthesis and transcends the manichean antagonisms of the colonizer and the
colonized" (38).

Such a monological reading of the novel's content as celebrating Igbo
culture and criticizing Western values and religion is common, but depends on silencing other voices in Achebe's narrative. As other readers have
noticed, biblical language, images, and stories also play an important role
in the unfolding of the novel. Okonkwo's moral dilemma concerning his
participation in the ritual sacrifice of his foster-son, Ikemefuna, parallels
both the Old Testament story of Abraham's near-sacrifice of Isaac and the
New Testament account of God the Father's sacrifice of Jesus Christ. Textual allusions reinforce these parallels; for example, Ikemefuna—like Isaac
and like Christ on his way to his crucifixion—carries the vessels to be used
in his own sacrifice. And when Nwoye, Okonkwo's first son, converts to
Christianity, he adopts the name of Isaac.[5]

These echoes of biblical language and themes suggest that the authorial
voice is much more complex than JanMohamed acknowledges. Much of the
narrative contains what Bakhtin calls "double-voiced discourse," "speech
serving simultaneously two intentions and internally dialogized" (*Dialogic*
324). Let us look at the opening of the novel for one example of this kind
of construction:

> Okonkwo was well known throughout the nine villages and even beyond.
> His fame rested on solid personal achievements. As a young man of eighteen
> he had brought honor to his village by throwing Amalinze the Cat. Amal-
> inze was the great wrestler who for seven years was unbeaten, from Umuofia
> to Mbaino. He was called the Cat because his back would never touch the
> earth. It was this man that Okonkwo threw in a fight *which the old men agreed
> was one of the fiercest since the founder of their town engaged a spirit of the wild
> for seven days and seven nights.*   (7; emphasis mine)

Beginning in the "common language" of factual narration, the passage
shifts in the italicized portion into the speech of another (indirectly rendered). But this is not just another's speech in the same "language," it is

another's utterance in a language that is itself "other" to the author as well, given the traditional beliefs that govern it. Furthermore, we can also hear, in the historical heteroglossia of the words and images, a faint echo of Jacob's wrestling match with an angel. Thus, in one utterance we can identify the voice of the author, the voice of the village elders, and the voice of Biblical tradition.

Another key passage in the novel similarly demonstrates Achebe's skillful use of polyphony and double-voiced discourse. It occurs when the missionaries first arrive in Mbanta:

> "If we leave our gods and follow your god," asked another man, "who will protect us from the anger of our neglected gods and ancestors?"
>
> "Your gods are not alive and cannot do you any harm," replied the white man. "They are pieces of wood and stone."
>
> When this was interpreted to the men of Mbanta they broke into derisive laughter. These men must be mad, they said to themselves. How else could they say that Ani and Amadiora were harmless? And Idemili and Ogwugwu too? And some of them began to go away.
>
> Then the missionaries burst into song. *It was one of those gay and rollicking tunes of evangelism which had the power of plucking at silent and dusty chords in the heart of an Igbo man.* The interpreter explained each verse to the audience, some of whom now stood enthralled. It was a story of brothers who lived in darkness and in fear, ignorant of the love of God. It told of one sheep out on the hills, away from the gates of God and from the tender shepherd's care. (136; emphasis mine)

The passage begins with the marked discourse of a villager and the missionary, the latter presented directly, although, for the villagers, it is mediated through the voice of the interpreter. We have at least three voices already. The third paragraph quoted begins in the authorial voice, which then shifts into an indirect rendition of the villagers' scornful comments. The final paragraph presents the most interesting discourse. By the end of the passage we clearly have the missionary's voice presented in the double-voiced discourse of the narrator, but do we also hear the villagers? Or at least some of them? And whose voice speaks in the italicized section?

These stylistic (or prosaic, as Bakhtin would call them) concerns lead to important interpretive questions: "all languages of heteroglossia . . . are specific points of view on the world, forms for conceptualizing the world in words, specific world views, each characterized by its own objects, meanings and values" (*Dialogic* 291–92). My two examples demonstrate how ideologically significant Achebe's use of these various discourses is when it comes to issues of postcolonialism and Christianity. Achebe's refusal to privilege one discourse over another provides a way to understand the thematic question of the novel's treatment of colonizer and colonized, of Christian and pagan. Rather than an authoritative celebration of the traditional past or a dialectical convergence of two traditions, Achebe's heteroglossia suggests a dialogical relationship in which each tradition continues to question both itself and each of the others. This complex dialogism throws the burden of interpretation upon the reader: the author presents us with the different voices but does not himself choose among them. He thus causes us to think about our own conceptions of justice and right action, and to question whether they are adequate to the moral dilemmas presented in the novel.

Within Igbo societal norms, for example, it is not completely clear whether Okonkwo should participate in the ritual killing of Ikemefuna.[6] The Oracle of the Hills and the Caves has pronounced the death sentence, but the oldest man in Umuofia, a well respected and fearless warrior, advises Okonkwo, "But I want you to have nothing to do with it. He calls you his father" (56). Although he himself represents the most rigid, authoritarian, and masculine aspects of Igbo society, even Okonkwo has unspoken doubts and imperfect motivations for participating in the ritual. He sits with his head in his hands for a long time after receiving the official decision of the oracle, and he impulsively cuts down Ikemefuna, "dazed with fear" and "afraid of being thought weak" (59). The day after he has killed his son, his old friend Obierika criticizes his action and prophesies a great punishment, "If I were you I would have stayed at home. What you have done will not please the Earth. It is the kind of action for which the goddess wipes out whole families" (64). The Oracle's commands could have been carried out without Okonkwo's direct participation in the death, Obierika argues.

The tension implied in the question of whether Okonkwo acted justly or not in the death of Ikemefuna highlights within the central character a continuing duality in Igbo life of masculine and feminine (*agbala*) values. Okonkwo's struggle to resolve that duality ultimately is unsuccessful, as he denies the feminine values that dominated his shiftless father, Unoka, values that he sees reappearing in Nwoye. "His whole life was dominated by fear," Achebe writes, "It was the fear of himself, lest he should be found to resemble his father. Even as a little boy he had resented his father's failure and weakness, and even now he still remembered how he had suffered when a playmate had told him that his father was *agbala*. That was how Okonkwo first came to know that *agbala* was not only another name for a woman, it could also mean a man who had taken no title" (16, 17). Yet Igbo society has a proper place for *agbala:* Ani, the earth goddess, "played a greater part in the life of the people than any other deity. She was the ultimate judge of morality and conduct" (37). While Okonkwo tells "masculine stories of violence and bloodshed," his wives, like Achebe's mother, tell tales of animals and nature (52). Okonkwo's monologic determination to construct a purely masculine world and his inability to live within a polyphonic society ultimately lead to his downfall.[7]

The depiction of Christianity is similarly complex. On one hand, we find the sympathetic Mr. Brown, modeled on the missionary who had married Achebe's parents (Innes 4), who "trod softly" on the faith of the clan (*Things* 163). He spends long hours in dialogue with the tribal leader Akunna talking about their different religious beliefs: "The picture given is that of two men who respect each other and are able to communicate in a way that clears up misunderstanding. In their relationship Mr. Brown learns that he has been wrong: that the Igbo do share the Christian concept of a supreme creator God . . . . Likewise, the elder Akunna is helped to see that his Igbo concept of God is dominated by fear . . . . Together, they work towards a fuller understanding of not only God, but life" (Bascom 73). Such nuanced dialogue stands in marked contrast to the authoritarian pronouncements of Brown's successor, who "saw things as black and white. And black was evil. He saw the world as a battlefield in which the children of light were locked in mortal conflict with the sons of darkness. He spoke in his sermons about sheep and goats and about wheat and tares" (169). Christianity, like the Igbo traditions, is depicted as having both a monologic and dialogic voice.[8]

For the most part, however, the forces of colonialism avoid dialogue and refuse to recognize alternative voices. Following the destruction of the church, the British District Commissioner invites six Umuofia men to "palaver," as he terms it (177). "I have asked you to come," he begins, "because of what happened during my absence. I have been told a few things but I cannot believe them until I have heard your own side. Let us talk about it like friends and find a way of ensuring that it does not happen again" (177). Such an exchange never takes place, as the Commissioner brings in his men ostensibly to hear the story and learn of the Igbo customs but in reality to seize and handcuff the unarmed Africans. Such monologic "justice" is in marked contrast with the more flexible Igbo legal system. In one instance, the *egwugwu* sit in judgment over a marital quarrel, hearing two very different accounts from the husband and the wife's brother. Their verdict is reached by "a very fluid system of negotiation," as David Carroll explains. "No attempt is made to extract a true version from the conflicting accounts; no principles of traditional law are invoked to apportion blame. . . . The peace and continuance of the tribe are the only criteria and these allow considerable freedom in dealing with internal dissention" (36). "Among the Igbo," Achebe tells us at the outset of the novel, "the art of conversation is regarded very highly" (10).

The District Commissioner's monologic oppression provides the heavily ironic conclusion to the novel, in a double-voiced discourse in which the narrator and the preceding rich tragedy loom behind the cold, scientific tone. The Commissioner is planning to write a book called *The Pacification of the Primitive Tribes of the Lower Niger:* "Every day brought him some new material. The story of this man who had killed a messenger and hanged himself would make interesting reading. One could almost write a whole chapter on him. Perhaps not a whole chapter but a reasonable paragraph, at any rate. There was so much else to include, and one must be firm in cutting out details" (191). Both thematically and stylistically, then, *Things Fall Apart* upholds dialogue.

The polyphonic voices of Igbo tradition and Christianity interrogate each other particularly with respect to the question of justice. It is not the monologic language of doctrine that captivates Nwoye, but rather the lyrical strains of the hymns that seem to echo his own questions in a double voice: "It was not the mad logic of the Trinity that captivated him. He did not understand it. It was the poetry of the new religion, something felt in the marrow. The hymn about brothers who sat in darkness and in fear seemed to answer a vague and persistent question that haunted his young soul—the question of the twins crying in the bush and the question of Ikemefuna who was killed" (137). The new church exercises a similar appeal for the *osu*, the outcasts who lived in isolation but who were enthusiastically embraced by the church. This complicates the presentation of Christianity in the novel, making it neither black nor white. Zohreh T. Sullivan, who teaches *Things Fall Apart* from a dialogical perspective, says, "Students confess to confusion as they side with and against the church that, because of its early support of weak outcasts and the wretched of the clan, prepares the way for colonial conquest" (106).

While Christianity questions the Igbo lack of concern for the sanctity of individual human life, the Igbo tradition similarly questions the professed Christians' lack of concern for the sanctity of community life in their summary imposition of foreign governmental structures, their disregard and disrespect for traditional practices, and their brutal slaughter of the entire Abame clan in retaliation for the death of a single missionary. Both traditions include failures of justice. However, the very notion of justice is also put into an unfinalizable dialogue: How could a just God order Abraham to kill his own son? Within Igbo society, Obierika wonders, "Why should a man suffer so grievously for an offense he had committed inadvertently?" after Okonkwo is banished for seven years for accidentally killing a young man (118). Two sets of values—the tribal and the personal—continue to question each other. The Oracle says that Ikemefuna must be killed. From the boy's perspective, this is unjust; from the community's perspective, it is ultimate justice necessary to provide reconciliation for the community. How can we harmonize the two?

Such uncertainty is particularly compatible with the Igbo mind, which, as Gikandi notes, "thrives on a temporal reversal of concepts and categories" (20). Achebe points to "the central place in Igbo thought of the notion of duality. Wherever Something stands, Something Else will stand beside it. Nothing is absolute. *I am the truth, the way and the life* would be called blasphemous or simply absurd, for is it not well known that a man may worship Ogwugwu to perfection and yet be killed by Udo?" (*Morning* 161). Gikandi concludes that Achebe is thus a poststructuralist: "Duality appeals to Achebe precisely because it produces a multiplicity of meanings and indeterminate zones of representation which generate narrative invention. In another sense, I believe, this duality allows the author, like his Igbo ancestors, to contest the central claims of Western metaphysics and its dependence on 'Reason'" (20). However, one does not have to deny the idea of reason in order to embrace either the notion of dialogue or that of unfinalizability. We can still see, hear, and talk logically about the competing and sometimes contradictory claims of personal and communal commitments, even though we may be unable to definitively resolve those dilemmas.

The context in which such conversations take place, their "eventness," is extremely important. Achebe's own comments on *Things Fall Apart* demonstrate a kind of duality, or reversal, dependent on their particular point of reference. On the one hand, in the context of the European novel about Africa, Achebe feels called to give a more accurate picture of African life, both for the colonizer but also for the colonized. As he explains in an interview with Lewis Nkosi, the composition of *Things Fall Apart* originated in his desire to retell Joyce Cary's *Mister Johnson:* "it was clear to me that it was a most superficial picture of—not only of the country—but even of the Nigerian character and so I thought if this was famous, then perhaps someone ought to try and look at this from the inside" (Duerdon and Pieterse 4).[9] Given the "savage" account of Africans so prevalent in Western thought, Achebe wanted to demonstrate the true profundity and complexity of Igbo culture. Yet one of his primary audiences, he believes, is his own people. The African writer is responsible to serve his or her community as a teacher. "I would be quite satisfied if my novels," he says, "did no more than teach my readers that their past—with all its imperfections—was not one long night of savagery from which the first Europeans acting on God's behalf delivered them (*Hopes* 45).

However, even within his defense of traditional culture for his Nigerian readers, Achebe maintains a critical distance, noting "all its imperfections." Within a different kind of conversation, Achebe can be critical of the past that he also simultaneously wants to defend: "We cannot pretend that our past was one long, technicolor idyll. We have to admit that like other people's pasts ours had its good as well as its bad sides" (Killam, *Writings* 9). *Things Fall Apart* is not a blindly romantic celebration of a perfect indigenous culture. In response to the question of who he really blames for the destruction of Igbo culture, Achebe replies: "[T]he coming of the missionaries is very complex, and I cannot simply assign blame to this man or that man. The society itself was already heading toward destruction . . . [but] Europe has a lot of blame . . . . [T]here were internal problems that made it possible for the Europeans to come in. Somebody showed them the way" (Egejuru 125). Achebe's willingness to criticize his own culture may appear politically incorrect to some, for it is not fashionable in Western scholarly circles to note the shortcomings of Igbo, or any other traditional culture. However, we must consider again the "eventness" of different kinds of readings and criticisms, "the peculiar needs of different societies" (*Hopes* 43). For example, in the tumultuous struggle for African independence and American civil rights during the 1960s, celebrations of the African past were unusual, provocative, and inspiring. Today, in light of the political and social chaos that dominates the African continent, African writers are aware of the need to dialogue with and critique their own cultures and societies—both traditional and contemporary.[10]

As readers, we too dialogue with Africa. One final kind of dialogue to which Bakhtin refers is that between cultures, and a Christian view of justice and peace depends on such dialogue to unite nation with nation. Postcolonial novels, especially such a significant cultural icon as *Things Fall*

Apart, provide an important way to acknowledge and to know the Other. Too often Foucault's exploration of how knowledge has constituted control throughout Western history has resulted in the complete equation of knowledge with power. But Bakhtin suggests another view of knowledge in his theory of dialogics, which pertains not only to language, literary works, and the individual psyche, but also to the process of interacting with cultures foreign to our own. Bakhtin rejects the extremes of objective fact gathering and subjective relativism, locating knowing instead as a dialogical process involving the ideas of outsideness, nonfusion, and active dialogue. How do we typically attempt to interact with Otherness, to read postcolonial texts? Too often, we opt for attempted empathy. "There exists a very strong, but one-sided and thus untrustworthy, idea that in order better to understand a foreign culture, one must enter into it, forgetting one's own, and view the world [entirely] through the eyes of this foreign culture" (*Speech* 6–7). This statement describes, for example, the assay of the American middle-class critic who tries to learn how to "think like an Igbo" when reading *Things Fall Apart*. Alternatively, readers "modernize and distort" the Other without recognizing significant differences ("The Igbo people are just exactly like us"). Both approaches demonstrate "the false tendency toward reducing everything to a single consciousness, toward dissolving in it the other's consciousness" (*Speech* 141). Both approaches are monologic, reducing two voices and two perspectives to one.

As we read postcolonial literature, and Achebe, our goal should be what Bakhtin terms "creative understanding": "*Creative understanding* does not renounce itself, its own place in time, its own culture; and it forgets nothing. In order to understand, it is immensely important for the person who understands to be *located outside* the object of his or her creative understanding—in time, in space, in culture. For one cannot even really see one's own exterior and comprehend it as a whole, and no mirrors or photographs can help; our real exterior can be seen and understood only by other people, because they are located outside us in space and because they are *others*" (*Speech* 7). By maintaining our "outsideness," we can discover meanings in the self that we did not previously see, as well as generate previously untapped meaning in the Other.

Active dialogue between self and Other, Western critic and postcolonial text, reveals the potential hidden in each and gives rise to unexpected questions and discoveries. Morson and Emerson explain, "Only dialogue reveals potentials. It does so by addressing them, by provoking a specific answer that actualizes the potential, albeit in a particular and incomplete way. At the same time, the questioner necessarily undergoes the same process, which helps him comprehend unsuspected potentials in his own culture. The process, then, is multiply enriching: it educates each side about itself and about the other, and it not only discovers but activates potentials. Indeed, the process of dialogue may itself create new potentials, realizable only through future activity and dialogue" (55). According to Bakhtin, "A meaning only reveals its depths once it has encountered and come into contact with another, foreign meaning: they engage in a kind of dialogue, which surmounts the closedness and one-sidedness of these particular meanings, these cultures" (*Speech* 7).

Such is the complex action that takes place with the clash of traditions in *Things Fall Apart*. This kind of dialogic process between cultures or between cultural texts does not result in a simple synthesis of ideas nor even in a dialectical resolution, but rather in a mutual enrichment. New meanings emerge for both the text and its interpreter: "[In] a dialogic encounter of two cultures . . . [e]ach retains its own unity and *open* totality, but they are mutually enriched" (*Speech* 7). Conrad's *Heart of Darkness* has been made more profound by Achebe's questioning, just as *Things Fall Apart* has been enriched and made possible by its (often stereotypical and racist) European precursors.[11] This understanding of meaning has significant implications for canonical expansion and the value of postcolonial studies, for according to this view "the great texts of any culture require the perspective of other cultures to develop their potential" (Morson and Emerson 289). Western readers thus need to read Achebe with a spirit of openness and curiosity about Igbo culture, as well as with a recognition of their own Western perspective, which, in dialogue with the text, may itself be altered.

Let us not be overly optimistic, however. As Achebe himself has pointed out, in "Impediments to Dialogue Between North and South," one cannot simply talk about "cultural exchange in a spirit of partnership between North and South," because "no definition of partnership can evade the notion of equality," a notion that is sorely lacking in North-South relationships (*Hopes* 22, 23). History has created a situation of asymmetrical dialogue, in which one voice has continually subdued or dismissed the other. Bakhtin notes the disparity in power between what he terms "official" discourse and that coming from the margins, but he concludes that the subaltern voice gains its own power through "the corrective of laughter and criticism," which "force[s] men to experience . . . a different and contradictory reality that is otherwise not captured in them" (*Dialogic* 59). Parody and travesty arose among the lower classes—Roman soldiers ridiculing their commander's triumphal entry march, Sancho's rendition of the knightly world of Don Quixote. Achebe's novel embodies such carnivalesque assertions in its occasional comic renditions of official discourse. For example, the African who translated for the first missionaries visiting Mbanta provides a healthy infusion of laughter that helps to blur the hierarchical distance between Christian and pagan: "Many people laughed at his dialect and the way he used words strangely. Instead of saying 'myself' he always said 'my buttocks.' But he was a man of commanding presence and the clansmen listened to him" (*Things* 134).

Dialogue between North and South, European and African, is admittedly difficult. Given the reality of colonial and postcolonial history, Anglo-American readers need to be far more willing to listen to the voices of postcolonial people than we have been. Does that mean that we are granting oppressed people a greater moral authority?[12] Not necessarily. As Nicholas Wolterstorff has argued, without denying universalism, we can still acknowledge a particularism of cognitive access; some people occupy certain positions that give them access or initial access to things unavailable to the rest of us ("Can Scholarship"). Bakhtin, as Caryl Emerson explicates, makes a similar point: "Bakhtin begins his discussion of self-other relations in his early manuscripts with a simple observation: we are distinguished from one another by the quality and contours of the 'surplus' that each one of us enjoys in relation to every other. I can see you, but I cannot see what is behind my own head; from your position you can see me, but only in your own way, not as anyone else sees me" ("Russian" 116). Thus, a writer like Achebe may have a better perspective from which to judge the clashes of colonialism, Christianity, and Igbo traditionalism than we do. At the very least, his perspective is of inestimable value in our attempts to deal justly with our fellow human beings.

9

"The Sound of the Horn of Justice" in Ngũgĩ wa Thiong'o's Narrative

OLIVER LOVESEY

In Ngũgĩ wa Thiong'o's latest fictional work, *Matigari* (1987), two desti-tute peasants, obeying the order from the Orwellian radio program "The Voice of Truth" to arrest all political madmen, turn in to the police the pictures of two subversives: Jesus Christ and Karl Marx. In a strange twist, in 1987 the Kenyan government sought to arrest Ngũgĩ's fictional creation Matigari as a troublemaker, in response to rumors that he was roaming the countryside demanding truth and justice. Realizing their mistake, the po-lice banned the book, which, with its English translation in 1989, has joined its author in exile. These references to Kenyan peasants, Jesus Christ, and Karl Marx demonstrate the deep social consciousness of Kenya's fore-most novelist, the mission-educated "James Ngugi," who rejected "the slave tradition of acquiring the master's name" (Ngũgĩ, *Detained* xxi), and now uses his Gikuyu name, Ngũgĩ wa Thiong'o. In his recent work, as clearly as in John Bunyan's confrontation between Christian and Apollyon in *The Pilgrim's Progress,* the narratives of Christianity and Marxism battle with the "macro-narrative of imperialism" and neocolonialism (MacCabe x).

In all of Ngũgĩ's writing there is a concern with the twin issues of society and spiritual liberation, but his last two narratives, composed in Gikuyu for an intended audience of literate and illiterate peasant "reader/listeners" (Ngũgĩ, *Matigari* ix), signal a radical departure. The novels before *Devil on the Cross* (1980), which employ a form Ngũgĩ defines as "the Afro-

European Novel," contain many biblical parallels and references, but Ngũ-gĩ's last two allegorical works, examples of "the African novel," have biblical patterns and themes embedded in their narrative structure.[1] These works emerge out of the crucible of Ngũgĩ's political detention and represent a radical departure in terms of narrative form, implied audience, and political engagement. Ngũgĩ's discourse in these writings constitutes a revolutionary experiment in language, ending his own "self-colonisation" (Ngũgĩ, "On Writing" 152). In them Ngũgĩ makes explicit his desire to empower his audience and to make the act of reading one in which the audience participates and one that awakens the people to direct, revolutionary political action. In *Devil on the Cross*, he attacks the hypocritical religiosity of the country's present rulers, and in *Matigari* he employs, in part, the narrative pattern of a demythologized Gospel.

There is obviously much ambivalence in the Marxist Ngũgĩ's appropriation of such narrative. In his use of the Bible, generated partly by his Mau Mau aesthetics, Ngũgĩ seems to be trying to produce a type of radical antidote to mass Fanonian mental colonization and moral degeneration.[2] However, Ngũgĩ's recent work demands "the sound of the horn of justice" (*Matigari* 21), which contains the transformative, regenerative spirit of the biblical call to justice and entails a critique of the traditional novel form. This essay examines the significance of Ngũgĩ's departure in form— a movement from the bildungsroman to the postmodern carnival of his last two works—and especially his use of Bunyanesque allegory and biblical parable, and his works' thematic demand for justice, in light of biblical notions of justice. Ngũgĩ's narratives sound a call for choice and truth, justice and liberation.

Ngũgĩ wa Thiong'o was born in Limuru, Kenya, in 1938, and after a Protestant mission school education he began postsecondary studies at Makerere University in Uganda—where he first became aware of the notion of a truly African literature for an African audience, edited the creative writing journal *Penpoint*, and published his first short stories. In 1964, he undertook postgraduate studies at Leeds University in England. His contact with the seat of former colonial power was not especially productive: "I attempted to write about my encounter with England and failed. Yorkshire Moors, Brontës' Countryside . . . all these were beautiful yes, but they only made me vividly live the Limuru landscape with its sudden drop into the Rift Valley. Memories of beauty and terror" (Ngũgĩ, "Preface" xi). *Weep Not, Child* was published in 1964 and was followed by three novels before Ngũgĩ made his departure from English in 1980 and began to tackle the unique problems of writing a work in a hybrid of various Western and indigenous narrative forms, but using Gikuyu and attempting to stir his readers to direct political action. However, as early as 1967 at the African-Scandinavian Writers' Conference he had said: "When we, the black intellectuals, the black bourgeoisie, got the power, we never tried to bring about those policies which would be in harmony with the needs of the peasants and workers. I think it is time that the African writers also started to talk in the terms of these workers and peasants" (Zell and Silver 158).

Devil on the Cross was written on rough toilet paper during his one-year detention without trial after the closing of his play, *I Will Marry When I Want*, written with Ngũgĩ wa Mirii. The rural playhouse where it was performed, the Kamiriithu Community Education and Cultural Center, was razed on March 12, 1982, by armed police (Ngũgĩ, *Barrel* 1). Ngũgĩ's own account of his arrest demonstrates his familiarity with the Bible and conveys hints of his anguish at the abrupt end of the Kamiriithu experiment. In rural Limuru, at midnight on the last day of December 1977, "A police saloon car remained at the main gate flashing red and blue on its roof, very much like the Biblical sword of fire policing the ejection of Adam and Eve from the legendary Garden of Eden by a God who did not want human beings to eat from trees of knowledge, for the stability of Eden and his dictatorship over it depended on people remaining ignorant about their condition" (*Detained* 15). Ngũgĩ lost his position as the head of the Department of Literature at the University of Nairobi, and not long after his release—receiving an ominous warning that "A red carpet awaits you at Jomo Kenyatta airport on your return" (Ngũgĩ, *Moving* 103)—he went into exile in London, where, in a small apartment in Noel Road, Islington, he wrote *Matigari*. Ngũgĩ has found exile very painful, almost a second imprisonment. Most recently, he has been exploring the potential of video as a medium for reaching the masses in his homeland (Diawara 117). Indeed, as Ngũgĩ explains in an interview, *Matigari* was much influenced by film technique: "the whole novel is a series of camera shots" (Eyoh 166). Such a medium is "the ideal means for breaking through the barriers of illiteracy" (Ngũgĩ, *Decolonising* 71). In July 1990, Ngũgĩ was named as one of the declared supporters of the radical Kenyan political organization Mwakenya, believed to be the force behind the protests in Nakuru, Naivasha, Muranga, Nyeri, and Nairobi during that summer ("Kenya" 7). However, Ngũgĩ's radical political stance may be perceived in his writings and statements from as early as the late 1960s.

As I have argued elsewhere, Ngũgĩ's recent narratives mark a shift in focus from the individual's social integration and spiritual healing to the community's economic and cultural alienation.[3] Moreover, the subtext of *Devil on the Cross*'s and *Matigari*'s allegories of angelic workers and capitalist devils is a discourse on political economy, identifying the narratives' intended program of struggle with the fight against cultural imperialism, and looking to Nyerere's conception of a precolonial African socialism as a model for a new Kenya. Like the officials who fail to recognize Matigari for what he is—a savior, the representative of the Kenyan people's struggle—non-African readers, Ngũgĩ's narrative intimates, may well be unable to identify his recent fictions for what they are, a new African literature designed primarily for a Kenyan audience of exploited peasants and workers. Ngũgĩ's *Devil on the Cross* departs from models of the European realist novel, taking up instead the challenge of fantasy and allegory and using *The Pilgrim's Progress* in a radically subversive way as a narrative model. This formal departure is itself a critique of the conservative, individualistic ideology embedded in the structure of the classic realist text.

The "native man of culture," the artist-intellectual, writing to give expression to the awakening social consciousness of the masses, "ought to use the past with the intention of opening the future, as an invitation to action and a basis for hope," argues Frantz Fanon (232). All Ngũgĩ's novels trace the story of the Kenyan people's history (Sicherman, "Ngũgĩ" 347–70), but his last two narratives concentrate on a revolutionary allegorical rereading and rewriting of Kenya's struggle before and after independence, pointing to missed opportunities and injustices in this history, particularly after independence, and indicating a direction for future political action. In these works, Ngũgĩ contributes to the postcolonial "process of 'revisioning' history through the reappropriation of allegory" (Slemon, "Post-Colonial" 163). In this project, Ngũgĩ counteracts the persistent view, held by Hegel and more recently Hugh Trevor-Roper (Achebe, *Hopes* 2), that Africa has no history. In the Kenyan context, Ngũgĩ's work, and especially its future orientation, however ambivalent and romantic, act against the "stagnationist views of dependency theory," which place neocolonial peoples, locked in a symbiotic and parasitic relationship with international capitalism, into a "historical deep freeze" (Ogot and Zeleza 424).

Devil on the Cross and *Matigari* may be read as parables of Fanon's account of the rise of the national bourgeoisie in the period after independence. *Devil on the Cross* offers an interpretation of the economic condition of Kenya in its neocolonial stage, singling out for censure the national

bourgeoisie, so lacerated by Fanon. *Matigari* continues the interrogation
of neocolonialism, but seeks the origins of neocolonial oppression in the
disenfranchisement of Mau Mau freedom fighters. These fighters, emerging from the forest after the Emergency, "were left to seek their personal
Uhuru in the open market" (Hargreaves 195). Celebrated in the frenzied
rhetoric of nationalism on the eve of independence, the tribally-based movement would eventually be "denied the right to inherit the political kingdom" (Ogot and Zeleza 406). As Fanon points out, "Now that they [the
militants] have fulfilled their historical mission of leading the bourgeoisie
to power, they are firmly invited to retire so that the bourgeoisie may carry
out *its* mission in peace and quiet" (171). In Fanon's terms, "Nationaliza-
tion . . . means the transfer into native hands of those unfair advantages
which are a legacy of the colonial period" (152).

Ngũgĩ's perception of the function of the artist-intellectual as prophet
and as tool of the masses has roots in both the Bible and Fanon's writing,
and partly dictates his choice of alternate narrative models. Nevertheless,
in Ngũgĩ's last two narratives, the position of the artist-intellectual is markedly different from that of Njoroge in *Weep Not, Child,* who desires a
grandiose transformation into a Matigari-like savior of the people. In Fanon's view, as in Ngũgĩ's nonfictional writing, the artist-intellectual has a
significant historical role, not leading the masses, but being a part of them
and giving voice to their "fierce demands for social justice" (204). For
Fanon and Ngũgĩ, the engaged artist must contribute to the political education of the masses, instructing them about and impelling them to assume
their guiding role in the struggle. This task is especially difficult given the
degraded psychological state of peoples subjected to the vicissitudes of colonial racial attitudes, which, as Achebe suggests, derived from "the desire—one might indeed say the need—in Western psychology to set Africa
up as a foil to Europe, as a place of negations at once remote and vaguely
familiar, in comparison with which Europe's own state of spiritual grace
will be manifest" (*Hopes* 3). While acknowledging the importance of literature for social transformation through changing people's perceptions
about personal and national realities, Achebe, writing of literature's place
in a postcolonial development strategy in 1986, fails to acknowledge the
problems of uncritically adopting the genre of the oppressor. The conditions of subalternity must be challenged, Fanon argues (and Ngũgĩ would
agree), before the masses are prepared to accept that "everything depends
on them" (Fanon 197). Fanon recommends that the artist, engaged in this
task, substitute "muscular action" for "concepts" (220). Ngũgĩ was im-

paired in achieving this goal of acting as a teacher by his suspicion of the intellectual elite and his lack of an appropriate narrative form. His last narratives show how he discovered a new method of combining history and prophetic but demythologized biblical narrative, linking them in his readers' minds and drawing on the transformative power of the Gospels' promise of a new dispensation.

There are a number of reasons for Ngũgĩ's use of biblical narrative in his last works' rehistoricizing the narrative of modern Kenya. While space does not allow a complete exploration of this notion here, one of Ngũgĩ's reasons for using biblical narrative may derive from the perceived power issuing from a violation of taboos associated with the Bible in the peasant mind. Ngũgĩ's "heretical" use of biblical narrative, therefore, may be seen to correspond to Mau Mau oathing rituals, which derived power from the violation of "universal taboos" (Hargreaves 130) regarding the eating of the "other" and the disregarding of the "pure/impure distinction" (Kristeva 91–95). A more immediate impetus for Ngũgĩ's debts to the Bible derives from a similar appropriation within the Mau Mau liberation movement, which, as Ngũgĩ explains in *Writers in Politics,* "created a popular oral literature embodying anti-exploitation values. They took Christian songs; they took even the Bible and gave these meanings and values in harmony with the aspirations of their struggle. . . . The Mau Mau revolutionaries took up the same song and tune and turned it into a song of actual political, visible material freedom and struggle for land. The battle was no longer in heaven but here on earth, in Kenya" (27). Ngũgĩ's Mau Mau aesthetic, his transformation of what he perceived to be the tool of the oppressor into a weapon to fight oppression, has revolutionary precedents. He felt his implied African audience, composed of peasants and workers, weighed down by subalternity, could be empowered by witnessing such a transformation. Furthermore, as he explains in *Decolonising the Mind,* Ngũgĩ mingled biblical parable with oral narrative forms in order to reach his audience: "People would be familiar with these features and I hoped that these would help root the novel within a known tradition" (78).

Ngũgĩ's narrative mode draws on the Bible and on a carnivalesque fusion of Bunyanesque allegory, oral folk tale, exemplum, cinematic techniques, and symposium. It also owes much to García Márquez and the South American practitioners of magic realism. Linda Hutcheon argues that magic realism is a genre which signals "works which encode . . . 'resistance' " ("Circling" 169). Furthermore, this genre incorporates indigenous mythologies; in *Devil on the Cross,* characters meet with ogres derived from Kenyan popular folk tales and the "human shaped rocks" of Idakho in western Kenya (Ngũgĩ, *Decolonising* 81). In their use of such intertextual diversity, Ngũgĩ's narrative experiments belong to the postcolonial literary project that, in Ashcroft, Griffiths, and Tiffin's formulation, involves a "subversion and appropriation of the dominant European discourses" (195). Such cultural practices create a "hybridized" art, enabling a dialogical relationship between European and local culture.

Bunyan's influence is of particular importance in this context. With Bunyan's allegory, Ngũgĩ evolved a form sufficiently hybridized to hold fantasy, political instruction, and moral earnestness, and the potential for transformation. A further attraction for Ngũgĩ must have been the fact that *The Pilgrim's Progress* was well known by African readers (Ngũgĩ, *Decolonising* 69, 70). In *The Pilgrim's Progress* and perhaps yet more clearly in *Divine Emblems*, Bunyan symbolically sets forth moral truths; Bunyan's choice of form and his bold narrative style both reflect his work's incorporation of popular narrative forms and his desire to communicate with the barely literate seventeenth-century readership, a relatively small community of "sharers in a particular text" (Hunter 160), like Ngũgĩ's own rural peasant/worker Kenyan audience. As Great-heart says, "I make bold to talk thus metaphorically, for the ripening of the wits of young readers" (319).

Like the politically radical Bunyan who wrote *The Pilgrim's Progress* in Bedford jail after completing his spiritual autobiography *Grace Abounding to the Chief of Sinners*, Ngũgĩ's impetus towards allegory derived from his experience in political detention and his sheer exasperation with his country's monstrous state of affairs.[4] Ngũgĩ's prison experiences, detailed in *Detained: A Writer's Prison Diary*, made him rethink the role of individuals within the Kenyan struggle. In *Detained*, the committed individual's incarceration without sentence becomes an allegory for the confinement of the nation. Ngũgĩ's chief act of resistance in detention, an attempt to resist psychological imprisonment by remaining in mental contact with the outside world, was writing *Devil on the Cross* in Gikuyu. In *Detained*, with the sense of validation that his detention gives him, Ngũgĩ situates his own imprisonment within colonial and postcolonial Kenyan history. Through writing his autobiography, Bunyan was able to recognize the universal application of the allegory of an individual life (Batson 13); Ngũgĩ, similarly, having produced an allegorized history of the nation in his personal account of unjust political imprisonment, next wrote an allegorical journey of an individual who embodies a nation's future aspirations. If autobiography looks backwards, the plots of *The Pilgrim's Progress*, *Devil on the Cross*, and

Matigari lead into the future. After Ngũgĩ's encounter with collective authorship in the Kamiriithu theatre group, the terrible education of prison—and prisons have been schools for many of Africa's national leaders and writers—freed him as a working intellectual to abandon the hapless, fence-sitting, liberal artist-intellectual Gatuiria, and to obey the injunction from the people and the "voice, like a great clap of thunder" (*Devil* 8). Ngũgĩ's *Devil on the Cross* writes history infused with prophecy, sanctioned by the masses and God: "The voice of the People is the voice of God" (8). *Devil on the Cross*'s narrator, the "Gicaandi Player, Prophet of Justice" (8) tells of all that happened that "now lies concealed by darkness," giving an account of what "I . . . saw with these eyes and heard with these ears when I was borne to the rooftop of the house" (8). Bunyan's work similarly begins with an apology about how he "Fell suddenly into an allegory / About their journey" (43).

One of Ngũgĩ's primary borrowings from Bunyan, aside from his work's strident apocalyptic tone and moral seriousness, is his use of allegorical characters. Ngũgĩ's rhetoric of character exploits caricature, partly because the national bourgeoisie is not a "replica" of the colonial or imperialist bourgeoisie but merely a "caricature" of it: "It is already senile [without having experienced] youth" (Fanon 175). *Devil on the Cross*'s capitalists happily acknowledge their debt to colonial forms, regarding themselves as conduits for multinational corporations' exploitation of the masses. The participants in the competition for the prize in international theft and robbery are animalistic caricatures, representing national and international capitalism. For example, one of the competitors has a "mouth . . . shaped like the beak of the red-billed ox-pecker, the tick bird. His cheeks are as smooth as a new-born baby's. His legs are huge and shapeless, like giant banana stems or the legs of someone who is suffering from elephantiasis" (186). Another proposes that in his vision of the future, "Every rich man could have two mouths, two bellies, two cocks, two hearts" (181). Similarly, in *The Pilgrim's Progress*, in addition to many personified vices, Christian encounters Giant Despair, and, in the Valley of Humiliation, Apollyon, a monster "hideous to behold . . . clothed with scales like a fish, [who] had wings like a dragon, [and] feet like a bear, and out of his belly came fire and smoke, and his mouth was as the mouth of a lion" (102).

Ngũgĩ's monstrous figures are contrasted with the characters traveling from Nairobi to the fictional town of Ilmorog to attend the feast, such as the representative peasant, Wangari; the worker in blue overalls, Muturi; and the petty bourgeoisie intellectual, Gatuiria. The fantastical competi-

tion, a praise-singing feast of grotesque proportions, is routed by a band
of peasants and students. The biblical parallels are obvious. This section of
the work ends with Wariinga's nightmare, in which the devil, representing
colonialism and imperialism, is crucified by the people and then, on the
third day, resuscitated by a new breed of Kenyan neocolonialists. The second part of the novel depicts Wariinga's transformation from a "fallen
woman" to a "heroine of toil," the embodiment of the cultural aspirations
of the Kenyan people. Wariinga's heroism underscores not Ngũgĩ's attempt
to formulate a type of "feminotopia" (M. Pratt 166), but his faith in a
worker/peasant society of complete gender equality which enables a transformation of all social relations. *The Pilgrim's Progress* also advocates a
radical realignment of familial obligations and gender roles. Christian, for
example, abandons his family responsibilities when he departs from the
City of Destruction, and in Vanity Fair, the tempting but dangerous mer-
chandise on sale includes "delights of all sorts, as whores, bawds, wives,
husbands, children" (137). Like Bunyan, Ngũgĩ stresses the responsibility
of the individual in seeking revolutionary salvation, but both writers use
not individualized characters, but representative, allegorical types to embody this notion.

 Matigari also employs a Bunyanesque allegory with biblical echoes. Matigari is a leviathan, a representative of the collective past of his people,
and their champion and savior. He was a freedom fighter during the anticolonial Mau Mau struggle and, laying down his arms, has returned to
reclaim his lands. He asks again and again, "Who can tell me where a
person who has girded himself with a belt of peace can find truth and
justice!" (92). In his return, he encounters the injustice, oppression, and
fear of neocolonial Kenya. He rescues the prostitute Guthera from a brutal
police attack and is transformed from a wizened elder into a vital young
warrior. Imprisoned, he breaks bread and is recognized as a leader by
twelve prisoners, all but one of whom (Giceru, the informer) were arrested
on false charges. The prison doors open miraculously, although all miracles
are shown to have materially verifiable causes (miracles here signal that
narratives have become mythic and the property of the community), and
he completes a tour of the country, where he finds a people stifled by fear.
He wanders and meditates in the wilderness—a timeless, metaphysical
landscape—and then seeks representatives of different classes, questioning
them about justice. In despair, he takes up arms.

 Matigari's past is Kenya's anticolonial struggle, and his present the state
of neocolonialism, but his future is left up to his readers. His mature life

span encompasses the collective history of Kenya, and the novel intimates that he will see the dawn of a socialist Kenya. This use of a fluid time scheme—both radically expanded and compressed—implies that past, present, and future are all categories of consciousness. An awareness of the role of consciousness in organizing these temporal categories (and therefore in the structuring of personal identity) is central to the insight Matigari offers his listeners and the text's readers. He makes them aware of their involvement in a historic consciousness that can transform the nation.

Both narratives also incorporate Bunyan's journey motif, and much of the narration in each is delivered in the framework of story cycles told by groups of characters. They meet on the journey to the feast at Ilmorog in *Devil on the Cross* or on the trek to John Boy's house in *Matigari*. Like *The Pilgrim's Progress*, both works depict life as a journey containing very real moral battles. As in the Puritan spiritual autobiography, a genre that draws on the "parallel between the plight of modern Puritans and ancient Israelites" (Batson 39), the journey motif enables the writer to represent existence as a progress through material and spiritual trials. On his way to the River of Death before the Celestial City, Christian passes through the gates of temptation and despair. Through suffering and persecution he experiences spiritual growth, and in bypassing "the Britain Row, the French Row, the Italian Row, the Spanish Row, the German Row" (137) in Vanity Fair, he comments upon the historical present. Matigari, like Christian, laments, "So many traps, oh so many temptations, in the way of the traveller on this earth" (6). Matigari's journey is a simple one. He merely desires to return to his house, symbol of the country, and gather his relatives there: "Spread the message: Settler Williams [the colonialist] is dead. John Boy [the traitor] is dead. We must go home, light the fire and rebuild our home together" (23–24). These narratives also incorporate Bunyan's use of monsters on the journey who terrify the small band of pilgrims. In *Matigari*, these devilish forces are much more directly derived from the oppressive power of the state, as represented by vicious police, in a period when "[o]ur leaders have hearts as cold as that of Pharaoh" (53).

At the work's close, Matigari enters a river that resembles Bunyan's. As Mr. Stand-fast says in Part 2 of *The Pilgrim's Progress*: "This River has been a terror to many, yea the thoughts of it also have often frighted me. But now methinks I stand easy, my foot is fixed upon that upon which the feet of the priests that bare the Ark of the Covenant stood while Israel went over this Jordan. The waters indeed are to the palate bitter, and to the stomach cold; yet the thoughts of what I am going to, and of the conduct that waits for me on the other side, doth lie as a glowing coal at my heart" (384). For Matigari, however, the River will eventually lead to the Gates of the restored City of new Kenya, and to a reassertion of the rights and dignity of the community. At the end of Part 2 of *The Pilgrim's Progress*, Christiana is welcomed at the Gate by trumpeters, but Matigari finally hears "the distant sound of the siren" before the voices of the patriots close the novel, anticipating a future victory. Unlike Christiana and Christian, Matigari's arrival at the Celestial City is deferred. The kingdom of heaven on earth, Matigari intimates, will be established only by collective action. Like Bunyan, Ngũgĩ wants readers to envision the parallels between the City of Destruction and present social realities. Engaging with Ngũgĩ's narratives, readers must not merely play "with the outside of my dream," but "turn up my metaphors" (219) and, inspired by a kind of vicarious identification with the hero of the allegory (who in *Matigari* represents the people's social aspirations), take action to establish the Celestial City on earth.

Ngũgĩ also draws directly on the Bible for his narrative form. *Devil on the Cross* radically transforms this material. The sacrifice of Christ is metamorphosed into the judgment and punishment of the devil of modern capitalist exploitation, and the Eucharist is distorted into a cannibal feast in which oppressors vie with one another over the prize for modern theft and robbery. The central biblical narrative with which *Matigari* engages is Luke's account of the two despairing disciples, walking to Emmaus and meeting a man on the road who walks with them, but whom "their eyes were kept from recognizing" (Luke 24:16). It is nearing evening, and they urge him to stay with them. When he breaks bread, "their eyes were opened, and they recognized him; and he vanished from their sight" (Luke 24:31). In *Matigari*, which charts the course of one long day, its apocalyptic weather reflecting the rising tension in the narrative, the recognition of Matigari by the twelve in prison follows his breaking of bread. The drunkard is then moved to recite the words of the Eucharist. As in George Eliot's *Adam Bede*, in the scene in which Bartle Massey offers Adam a "bit and a sup" on the morning of Hetty's trial, the use of biblical references in *Matigari* at first appears to convey merely a demythologized, humanistic feeling, but in Ngũgĩ's work the scene is followed by miracles and by the explanation of miracles. In Ngũgĩ's parable the biblical narrative retains the potential of transformative power. As Diana Culbertson writes in *The Poetics of Revelation*: "Picture a world in which all values are reversed, where prostitutes and taxpayers eat at the tables in the Kingdom, where the righteous will be last. The parables called for a new kind of vision" (23). Ngũgĩ's call to justice in *Matigari* makes this demand, and it specifies that this radical, political transformation is contingent upon recognition and cleansed perception, which must take place in the context of community.

In the topsy-turvy economy of blood that characterizes modern Kenya for Ngũgĩ, hostility and revenge overwhelm reconciliation. In *Matigari*, however, the story of Christ's return in Luke's Gospel is used as the basis of the narrative. While Ngũgĩ de-emphasizes the metaphysical nature of Christ's promise of the Second Coming, his work does employ the spirit of the Gospels and uses their language. Matigari warns, for example, that "Jesus will find you asleep . . . when he returns" (153). Here, the idea of justice for all contains the Hebraic notion of righteousness. Ngũgĩ situates this religious truth in a political context:

> The God who is prophesied is in you, in me and in the other humans. He has always been there inside us since the beginning of time. Imperialism has tried to kill that God within us. But one day that God will return from the dead. Yes, one day that God within us will come alive and liberate us who believe in Him. I am not dreaming.
>
> He will return on the day when His followers will be able to stand up without worrying about tribe, race or colour, and say in one voice: Our labour produced all the wealth in this land. So from today onwards we refuse to sleep out in the cold, to walk about in rags, to go to bed on empty bellies. Let the earth return to those to whom it belongs. Let the soil return to the tiller, the factory to the worker . . . But that God lives more in you children of this land; and therefore if you let the country go to the imperialist enemy and its local watchdogs, it is the same thing as killing that God who is inside you. It is the same thing as stopping Him from resurrecting. That God will come back only when you want Him to. (156)

This passage emphasizes the role of imperialism in stunting the individual's spiritual nature, but also challenges readers to perceive the relationship between both personal and collective bondage and spiritual well-being. It challenges readers to perceive the value of their effort in handling the gift of choice. The climate for a second coming depends on the enabling will of the masses. While Ngũgĩ departs from a traditional interpretation of the Gospel here, his narrative embodies a mystical view of the divine as contained within a vision of a completely unified community.

While this view expounds a demythologized Christianity, it draws on the Bible's transformative power and recognizes the truth of narrative theology, "the discovery of individual and communal identity through the intersection of our personal stories with the 'master-story' of Christian revelation" (T. Wright 83). The appropriation of the Gospels in narrative form may itself be part of the process of revelation. It is "their openness to different interpretations in different historical conditions which helps myths to survive, adapting, in evolutionary terms, to the demands of the times" (86). One might add to Wright's analysis that, in Ngũgĩ's case, cultural difference is a significant inscribing feature of interpretation. In Ngũgĩ's work this use of Gospel storytelling blends with the traditional story cycles told at African praise-singing feasts and with the notion of oral narrative as a mode that contains a people's collective history and seals their cultural and spiritual identity.

For the call of the "horn of justice" to be sounded, the oppressed must first realize that they must make a choice. Ngũgĩ's narrative is an attempt to "decolonize" the minds of his implied readers, who are not the leisured, introspective readers of his past work but active, participating readers who "command" the narrator to "tell his tale" (Ngũgĩ, *Devil* 247). The latest novels assume an implied audience of hearers, and their implied reception is a collective and communal undertaking rather than the experience of private introspection so important in the early English novel. *Devil on the Cross* is a written oral tale; in Kenya it was read aloud, and in this way "appropriated" into the "oral tradition" (Ngũgĩ, *Decolonising* 83). The narrator urges preparedness for future struggle. This urging is accomplished yet more explicitly and stridently in *Matigari*, where the narrator has a collective voice that includes the implied reader, as, for example, in the children's admission: "We are the children of Matigari ma Njiruungi. . . . We are the children of the patriots who survived the war" (139). The final action and conclusion are left up to the reader: "Reader/listener: may you allocate the duration of any of the actions according to your choice!" (ix). Reading itself is not a passive act but one that implies a resultant action. The reader must be empowered and seize the right of choice because "people starve only because they choose to" (142). The type of action demanded here is not the peaceful restructuring of society but its violent transformation. The demand for decision and for reader participation recognizes that reading itself is a revolutionary act. It involves, like Mau Mau initiation and ceremonies of ritual circumcision, the repetition of almost liturgical words. Clearly, the reader, at the narrative's end, is positioned with Muriuki by the mugumo tree, digging up the pistol, cartridge belt, and sword, and prepared for conflict with the forces of neocolonialism.

In *Matigari* an AK-47 replaces words of peace; the pious and revolutionary father of Guthera hides bullets in his Bible. *Matigari,* like *Devil on the Cross,* acknowledges the corruption and degradation of language. The name for the devil, for example, as the rogues and villains are called, has been appropriated and sweetened by capitalist exploiters. In *Matigari,* similarly, the "honeyed tongues" are full of deceit (79). Choosing to compose *Devil on the Cross* in Gikuyu, Ngũgĩ wrote "in the very language which had been the basis of incarceration" in the security prison (*Decolonising* 71). The language of his story represents his commitment, a resistance to the imperialism embedded in English for the African writer—who has sometimes had the experience of being punished for speaking a mother tongue in colonial schools. Control over language is one of the most pervasive and insidious aspects of colonial domination. Part of Ngũgĩ's problem was that Gikuyu had first been transliterated by non-native speakers such as missionaries, and the orthography was inadequate. As a result, words would "slip and slide under my own eyes. They would not stay in place. They would not stay still" (*Decolonising* 75).

Like Bunyan's, Ngũgĩ's narrative project entails a revision of the interpretation of the relationship between language, the Word, and the world (Damrosch 142, 151). For Bunyan, representing biblical myth using "feigning words" (45) in an allegorical fiction was a dangerous undertaking, justified only by the presence of similar "types, shadows and metaphors" in the Gospel (46) and the demands of his audience. For Ngũgĩ, the corrupted state of the language in which he was writing compounded his difficulties in evolving a narrative form for his work. In this problem he discovered one of colonialism's and neocolonialism's most devious effects: the reification of the means of communication. Achebe writes of the power of language, in a discussion of Fulani creation myths: "when language is seriously interfered with, when it is disjoined from truth, be it from mere incompetence or worse, from malice, horrors can descend again on mankind" (*Morning* 59). In *Devil on the Cross,* which is in many ways a parable of naming, the language of the exploiters has turned things "upside down." The neocolonial proponents of this language have done violence to history, saying that "all freedom fighters returned from the mountains the day the independence flag was hoisted" (*Matigari* 83). They have a science of Parratology, a method of canceling the truth of language. The law of this system resides in the Minister of Truth and Justice. These hypocritical "professional truth-tellers" guarantee that "lies are decreed to be the truth, and the truth is decreed to be a lie" (117, 137). In such a world,

"The robber calls the robbed 'robber.' The murderer calls the murdered 'murderer,' and the wicked calls the righteous 'evil'" (150). The hyperbole of this hypocrisy reaches a crescendo in the blasphemous words of the Minister about the Second Coming: "There is no way that Jesus could return without first going to pay a courtesy call on His Excellency Ole Excellence" (84). In the neocolonial state, language has been corrupted, and for the postcolonial artist, the problem of finding an appropriate linguistic vehicle embodies the contradictions of neocolonialism.

To counteract these effects, the power of allegorical naming must be commanded. The colonial representative, Settler Williams, must be identified as "the white-man-who-reaps-where-he-never-sowed." Matigari asks, "Does he think that he is God's representative here on earth?" (46). Next to this figure stands his black neocolonial servant, "Mr Boy," a name implying the absurdity and disgrace of the uncircumcised. Matigari himself has a name that stands for a collectivity, and this name sometimes stands in apposition to the pronoun "we," thereby including the Kenyan masses and the implied reader. Elsewhere he is variously figured as a legend, a dream, and as both male and female, young and old. He is called "Mr Seeker of Truth and Justice," "the prophet," and "A giant who could almost touch the sky above" (75–76). Many who meet Matigari in market places, eating places, farmlands and law courts "added salt to his story," embellishing his myth and claiming it as a legitimate part of their own oral tradition. Matigari finally comes to the realization that words must be given significance by the power of choice and reinforced with action. Matigari, who is searching for truth and justice, finally seems to recognize the truth of Mao Zedong's words about truth coming from the barrel of a gun. "Justice for the oppressed comes from a sharpened spear," he declares, because "the enemy can never be driven out by words alone" (131, 138). Words must become "armed": "One had to have the right words; but these words had to be strengthened by the force of arms. In the pursuit of truth and justice one had to be armed with armed words" (131). In order for justice to have meaning, words must regain their truth. The motto of the oppressed will be "Saying is doing" (141). Language is important in interpreting reality and in empowering the speaker, but this understanding is insufficient, Ngũgĩ argues, unless it leads to revolutionary action. Discourse must enable action, and language must initiate events. Words must take up arms.

This demand that the empowering force of naming be restored and be extended to encompass action is therefore directly related to the novel's engagement with the biblical call for truth and righteousness. This biblical call to justice lacks the orthodox Marxist insistence on the economic and dialectical basis of social transformation. In its Hebraic form, justice constituted a moral contract between nation and God, and was not merely a "supramundane idea" ("Justice" 652–53). The Jews conceived of justice as deliverance. Theologian Marjorie Hewitt Suchocki sees justice as having three levels of meaning: (1) a sense of individual well-being and dignity; (2) a recognition of the individual within the human community; and (3) an openness to self-development within this community context ("In Search"). The final stage in Suchocki's system itself leads to a multiplicity of forms comprising freedom and openness. Ngũgĩ's recent fiction seems to incorporate this understanding inasmuch as it comprises a call for the liberation of all members of the community, including children and women. The homeless children who inhabit the "vehicle cemetery," a wasteland marked by the tempting brand names of multinational capitalism, are those who by the end of *Matigari* may build "A new heaven on a new earth" (16). It is they who have the power to imagine a future without fear.

There is, in these recent fictions and especially in *Matigari*, a powerful recognition of the interpenetration of secular and sacred interpretations of reality, and an overlapping of Marxist and biblical calls for justice. The awareness of this interpenetration of the secular and the sacred, and of the relationship between Gospel narratives, oral tales, and real events, begins with a change in readers' perception. With this attempt to produce a change in perception comes a call to name fear as "the enemy of the people," and to answer the character who says, "my life has been without meaning" (*Matigari* 171, 140).

Fredric Jameson notes the special problems presented by formal narrative closure for the contemporary African artist, writing "after the achievement of independence, when once again no political solutions seem present or visible" ("Third-World" 75). While remaining rooted in the material conditions of Kenyan reality, Ngũgĩ's closure must include the possibility of future change. *Matigari*'s closure draws upon the belief that the end of evil, of history's sorrows, may be realized through the power of God (Suchocki, *End of Evil* 80). Matigari, in the role of prophet, warrior, and messiah, explains to the peasants that the potential to realize the kingdom of heaven upon earth dwells within them. "Mr Seeker of Truth and Justice," Matigari comes to recognize that neither truth nor justice exist in present-day Kenya, but he renews his devotion to a belief in the realization of a type of justice that is itself "mightier than force" (80). He proclaims that the people will only overcome their social and spiritual alienation when they discover their necessary relationship to that which is beyond them but to which they essentially belong. Such an overcoming of alienation is conceived of as an acceptance of the reality of "social and economic justice" (Suchocki, *End of Evil* 50). The dispossessed, in their demoralized state of subalternity, must be empowered to seize upon the possibility of transformation and to acknowledge their role in this metamorphosis. To accomplish this political education, Ngũgĩ relies on the instructive qualities of allegory and parable, and on the Bible's promise of social justice.

Ngũgĩ's last two narratives reject the imperialist ideology embedded in the rhetoric of the classic realist novel, drawing inspiration instead from a carnivalesque variety of texts: folk tales, Bunyanesque allegory, and biblical narrative. The very forms of *Matigari* and *Devil on the Cross* indicate their strident revolutionary stance, just as their rhetoric of character downplays the subjective experience of individuals, focusing instead on the portrayal of community action. This emphasis on the community is particularly significant in the reading of these novels, as this activity must lead to revolutionary struggle, not merely quiet epiphany or intellectual awareness. To trigger this reaction, given the psychological demoralization of his readership and the corrupted state of the artist's linguistic vehicle, Ngũgĩ follows the direction of Fanon and employs a "harsh style, full of images, for the image is the drawbridge which allows unconscious energies to be scattered on the surrounding meadows. It is a vigorous style, alive with rhythms, struck through and through with bursting life; it is full of color, too, bronzed, sunbaked, and violent" (Fanon 220).

Ultimately, too, Ngũgĩ draws on the transformative power of the Gospels, which point to the possibility for personal and communal regeneration and offer the promise of social justice. The prayer for such a dispensation, however, demythologizes Christianity, substituting "the people" for "God": "Let the will of the people be done! Our kingdom come as once decreed by the Iregi revolutionaries" (*Matigari* 63). In Ngũgĩ's last narratives, hearing "the sound of the horn of justice" is recognizing the truth of the relationship between the individual and community; past, present and future; the finite and the infinite. These calls for truth, justice, and liberation demand a revolutionary response.

10.

Comrade Jesus
Postcolonial Literature and the Story of Christ

NORMAN R. CARY

The definitive treatment of the Jesus figure in literature is Theodore Ziol-kowski's *Fictional Transfigurations of Jesus* (1972), which surveys earlier criticism and concludes that the term "Christ figure" is vague and of limited use. He observes that fictional characters resembling Jesus are presented by word or deed, and bear a salutary or at least moral message, though their psychology and the content of their messages vary so widely that they may not resemble the biblical figure or the kerygmatic Christ of Christian tradition. So Ziolkowski brackets out the question of spiritual meaning and confines his definition of the Jesus figure to the character whose portrayal structurally resembles the form of New Testament accounts of Jesus, "whose life consisted of a series of traditionally associated motifs or mythologems: baptisms, temptation, gathering of disciples, performing of various 'miracles,' proclaiming a new way of life, a last supper, lonely agony, betrayal, trial, and crucifixion" (10). Ziolkowski's study charts the effects of Western secularism, psychology, myth studies, politics, and theology on representations of Jesus in Euro-American fiction, most of which was written before World War II. In this essay, I consider such Jesus figures in four postcolonial novels from Latin America, the Caribbean, Africa, and the Middle East.[1] In the light of postcolonial studies, such figures emerge as subversive responses to the oppressions of colonialism.

The concept of postcoloniality is rooted in Michel Foucault's study of power as it relates to discourse, the necessarily linguistic expression of human thought (Shumway 16). Foucault is interested in how power relations function not only in regard to discourse in its limited sense, but communications in the wider sense, which encompass exhortations, surveillance, reward and punishment, definitions of sexuality and the health of the soul, as well as institutions like the family, schools, asylums, and prisons—all are symbols, signs, actions, "elements of meaning" that affect other people (Foucault 218). But, perhaps in reaction against the Marxist view of the dynamism of history, he so assiduously avoids judgment on the systems he analyzes that he has been accused of quietism and fatalism in the face of what he assumes to be an irresistible and omnipresent network of power in modern society. Edward Said takes Foucault to task for describing only the "actual realization" of cultural and political power evident in "official discourse" rather than opposing the destructiveness of social domination, a task that Said says has been left to political and literary critics, as well as feminist, minority, and Third-World writers ("Foucault" 150–51, 153). This is an observation of the highest importance for the study of postcolonial literature.

Other commentators pick up from Foucault the notions of resistance and the Other. His essay "The Subject and Power," which deals with how human beings are subjected or made subjects, gives them their cue. Here Foucault focuses on discursive strategies that resist "knowledge, competence and qualification: struggle against the privileges of knowledge . . . against secrecy, deformation, and mystifying representations imposed on people," against forms of "economic and state violence which ignore who we are individually, and also refusal of a scientific or administrative inquisition which determines who one is" (212). A second important term is the *Other*. Foucault remarks that "a power relationship can only be articulated on the basis of two elements which are each indispensable if it is really to be a power relationship: that the 'other' (the one over whom power is exercised) be thoroughly recognized and maintained to the very end as a person who acts; and that, faced with a relationship of power, a whole field of responses, reactions, results, and possible inventions may open up" (220).

The concept of "othering" comes into play when the Other's cultural discourse is perceived as empty, valueless, or inferior, a rationalization that facilitates the projection onto the Other of the discourse of one's own culture and values (Slemon, "Cultural" 103). Representatives of Western Christianity exemplified this process by believing that their religion emanated from the Word of God (Christ, the Bible), and that they were the communicators of the only means to salvation. Indigenous religions were regarded as idolatrous, devilish, or at best preparatory to the superior revelation of Christianity. It is hardly surprising that the Europeans and their early converts suppressed or marginalized the "heathenish" alternatives to their revelation and authority. Christianity thus often helped in the creation of Others.[2]

Many postcolonial authors responded to the religion brought by the missionaries and conquerors by countering and mimicking the Eurocentric Christian story. The novelists considered in this essay adapt the most radical of such strategies; they subvert and replace the central figure in the Christian discourse they have received with "hybridized" figures who are interpreted in terms of the very religions and cultures the Europeans sought to supplant. The postcolonial Jesus becomes an indigenous Jesus.

This being the case, we need to consider the European/indigenous tensions and religious history in the settings of the novels I will be discussing. Two are situated in what might be described as "Christian" countries, Paraguay and Jamaica, though in each of these cultures there is a non-Christian tradition associated with the culture and political aspirations of an indigenous population. Paraguay retains a layer of pre-Columbian Indian tradition under its Roman Catholic piety brought by the Spanish. The settling of Europeans in the West Indies, however, was for other than religious reasons, and because various peoples were imported as slaves and laborers, the islands became a meeting-place for Christianity, Hinduism, and African traditional religions (Cary, 98, 103). Similarly, in Kenya, remnants of indigenous religion vie with a Christianity that is viewed paradoxically as both antithetical and helpful to native aspirations. Egypt, the setting of the fourth novel, is a predominantly Muslim country. The ancient Christian faith in the Middle East was largely superseded by Islam, and since the nineteenth century Christianity has often been associated with European colonialism or neocolonialism. There is also, however, the countervailing belief that Judaism and Christianity are preparatory to Islam, that Jesus is a precursor of Mohammed. Such variances in geography, history, and culture make these novels distinct from those discussed by Ziolkowski; no longer can we say that the Jesus figure is a European literary construction.

Augusto Roa Bastos's *Son of Man* (1961) is the most famous Paraguayan novel and the epic of that country's sad political history from 1912 to 1936. Roa Bastos is not interested, however, in historical veracity or religious dogma but in creating "a prophetic vision of mankind as a continuing struggle of self-liberation and self-progression toward the ultimate resolution of a vital and sensitive human fraternity" (Foster, *Myth* 87). In more specific terms, he transforms the Christian mythos introduced by the Spanish conquerors into a story that celebrates the this-worldly salvation of Paraguay's indigenous people. Roa Bastos accomplishes this by producing a Latin American version of what Ziolkowski terms "Comrade Jesus," a novel whose Jesus figures deliver the people from political and economic oppression.

The initial section of *Son of Man* describes how Caspar Mora, an instrument-maker, contracts leprosy and becomes a hermit in the hills. Mora is a saintly figure: he is not greedy, keeping only enough money for tools and materials and spending the rest on the poor. Associated with him is a Mary Magdalene figure, Maria Rosa, who like her namesake was once a prostitute. She devotes herself to searching for Mora, and after his death goes mad, proclaiming that he will return as the savior. After finding Caspar Mora's body, the people from his village, Itapé, discover a life-size figure of Jesus that the old man made for company in his isolation. In the face of the opposition of the local priest—the institutionalized religion brought by the Spanish is antagonistic to the natives' freedom—the people mount the wooden Jesus on a hill above the village. From that time on, every Good Friday, "as an expression of their rebellious spirit," they bring it to the church porch and "shout out their own angry liturgy" (9). Roa Bastos thus uses the yearly village ritual to make Mora live on symbolically among the people. Although Ziolkowski deletes the resurrection from his structural pattern, remarking that it is the kerygmatic Christ rather than the historical Jesus who was resurrected (10), authors who invest the Jesus figure with the moral weight of their fictions, like Roa Bastos, often attempt to make his influence outlast his physical existence.

The corpus thus embodies and encourages the spirit of the villagers, a spirit that periodically produces revolutionary heroes who suffer to deliver the rural proletariat. There are, as old Macario remarks, "innumerable, anonymous martyrdoms" (Roa Bastos 21), but the author focuses on two sufferers, Casiano and Christobal Jara. After a peasant rebellion is put down by the military, Casiano goes with his wife, significantly named Natividad (Christmas), to become a laborer in a state plantation that is a microcosm of the oppressive state. Like Jesus, the peasants here rest only on Friday, and are "buried alive in the catacombs of the plantation . . . only for these obscure, barefoot Christs there was no glorious resurrection; they died unredeemed and forgotten" (73). In a chapter labeled "Exodus," Casiano and Christobal manage to escape with their son, as Joseph and Mary fled into Egypt, and a generation later the child—whose name "Kirito" is the Guarani rendition of "Christ" (Bareiro and Baldran 41)—is involved in a second failed revolt. He is released from prison to fight in the Chaco war and dies leading a caravan of trucks (including a water truck) to the isolated and dying troops; thus he dies serving his thirsting compatriots. The narrator of the novel, Vera, functions as a Judas figure: despite his initial sympathy for the rebellion, he betrays Christobal to the authorities, kills him during the Chaco war, and finally commits suicide.[3]

Following the main action is an "Aftermath" depicting the killing of Meliton Isasi, the village political boss, by the brothers of a woman he abused. His body is hung on the cross occupied for twenty-five years by Caspar Mora's wooden Christ. At this point we have moved from the carved corpus as a symbol of individual faith that counters isolation to a hanged body as a symbol of communal judgment against sexual outrage, for now the peasants are beginning to exact justice on their own. Again the priest is horrified, and the image is rededicated. It is not clear, however, whether those who attend the ceremony are honoring the image or the assassinated Meliton, for even the Christ of Itape with whom the novel begins can be associated with the abusive power structure. Roa Bastos's Jesus figure is not the canonical Savior of European religion, but rather a native who is "a powerful symbol of the redemption of man by man himself, a symbol that has been perverted by official religious dogma and its subservience to oppressive political regimes" (Foster, *Augusto* 40). The novel portrays the suffering of the poor rather than the achievement of liberation and can be read as a fictional foreshadowing of the analysis of oppression by more recent Latin American liberation theologians.

The liberationists' political and religious concerns also appear in the work of Jamaican writer Roger Mais, whose childhood, as is the case with most of the authors cited in this chapter, was infused with Christianity. Kenneth Ramchand refers to "themes from the Bible which were part of [Mais's] upbringing in a society nurtured on the Christian Book and in the home at the hands of parents who were members of the Non-conformist Fundamentalist Brethren Movement" (ix). But as an adult, Mais became a political radical, "a thinker committed to the remaking of Jamaican society, a commitment which included for a start an improving of the lot of the proletarian masses in the city and on its perimeters" (viii). Edward Brathwaite and Norman Manley agree that Mais's work is political in nature, though Oscar Dathorne sees it a bit differently, interpreting his writing to include both the pain and the vision of the human condition.

Both readings are supported by the depiction of the title character of Mais's most famous novel, *Brother Man* (1974), a Jesus figure who is also convincingly Jamaican. His name establishes a certain egalitarianism about him, that he is not defined as superior to other people. It also associates him with the hybridized Afro-Christian Rastafarian movement, as does his greeting of "Peace and Love" and his beard; this association also provides a motivation for Bra' Man's persecution. The racialism and apocalypticism of the Rastafarians are almost entirely absent, however. So is their typical disregard for the status of women (Morish 83). Instead, Mais emphasizes Bra' Man's care and respect for Minette, a waif he has rescued from the street and protected. Mais has also built in many parallels to the New Testament Jesus, both in terms of Brother Man's life and words, and in terms of the people's treatment of him. Brother Man is a craftsman (not a carpenter but a cobbler); he cares more for others than for himself and sees a fallen bird as a sign of God's care, surely an echo of Matthew 10:29. As Jesus did not fit his contemporaries' expectations for the Messiah, Brother Man does not fit his contemporaries' stereotype of the holy man. Like Jesus at his baptism and temptation, Brother Man hears a voice from God instructing him, "Go, and anoint yourself, and fast for three days," but the wording suggests a humanistic rather than supernaturalistic authority. On the other hand, Brother Man speaks in parables, preaches to the crowd like Jesus preached from the mountain, and performs miracles; the healing of a little girl, during which he calls in a "loud voice" and feels power draining from him (31), is particularly dramatic. Mais may have in mind such biblical incidents as the healing of the woman with a hemorrhage and the raising of Jairus's daughter. For a time these wonders make Brother Man very popular with the common people; this emphasis on the common people, like his egalitarianism, suggests that this novel presents another "Comrade Jesus." Brother Man is so popular, in fact, that he can hardly escape the crowds, and he hides himself from them, as Jesus did from the multitudes.

In view of these Gospel analogies, one expects opposition to the Christ to develop. Bra' Man's enemy is also a Jamaican, a greedy *obeah* man called Brother Ambo. Instead of offering peace and love and giving his money to the poor, Ambo demands money for his advice. When Brother Man becomes popular, Ambo becomes jealous (perhaps Mais is here drawing on the tradition of Satan's jealousy of God). Mais alters the gender of the Judas, adding a sexual dimension both to Brother Man's concern for others and to his downfall. The betrayer is young Cordelia, who comes to Brother

Ambo after Brother Man fails to heal her baby; she is so filled with hatred for Brother Man that she puts counterfeit coins in his room to frame him. For this her sister calls her a Judas, and later Cordelia hangs herself. After his arrest for counterfeiting, and after it is reported that a bearded man has committed rape and murder, the people start to distrust Brother Man. He feels their growing suspicion and goes up the hills to pray (like Jesus in the Garden of Gethsemane), but he will not leave the city. Finally the mob turns on him and beats him almost to death. He is rescued by his friends, and as he convalesces, "two women [sit] by the side of his bed, and [keep] watch through the night" (189), as do the women at the tomb of Jesus. Mais recalls the biblical resurrection when he has Brother Man recovering after three days, at which point "[a] great light [glows] across the sky" as a heavenly sign (190).

For all his similarities to the New Testament portrait of Jesus, we have seen that Brother Man is distinctly Jamaican and human. Not only are his mannerisms, speech, and religious outlook influenced by Rastafarianism, but his sexual mores are West Indian. Earlier he was framed by a woman he had lived with and was sent to jail, and for much of the novel he rejects anything but a fatherly relationship with Minette. Her background, however, leads her to expect that a close relationship be expressed sexually, and eventually he responds to her overtures and becomes her lover. In keeping with the novel's humanism, Brother Man defines himself not as a miracle worker but a "channel for life." His is a gospel of human dignity, not of spiritual salvation from sin. Even his growing unpopularity does not undermine his faith in the common people, for he understands that their mistreatment of him is driven by rumor, fear, and political manipulation. He knows that the people need faith in "something" to save them from poverty, disease, and frustration (174). Combining political activism with a concern for the human condition, Brother Man is a thoroughly secular Jesus.

In a more striking manner than the fiction of either Roa Bastos or Mais, the work of the noted Kenyan writer Ngũgĩ wa Thiong'o becomes progressively more critical of Christianity as a means by which Europeans colonized and oppressed Africans. In his early novels, though, Ngũgĩ attempts to combine the power of Christian symbols with the Gikuyu cultural and political tradition, which he has championed as an adult (Jabbi 210). In A Grain of Wheat, the third of Ngũgĩ's novels to be published, an important symbol of resistance to this oppression is the Mau Mau leader Kihika, an African version of "Comrade Jesus." The biblical parallels here are not so much in action as in language: quotations from the Old and New Testaments put into the consciousness of the Jesus figure, into the mouths of those who function as his disciples, or supplied directly by the author. Ngũgĩ, who went to a mission school, has said he is no longer a believer, charging that the missionaries preached love while serving the cause of a colonialism based on racial and cultural inequality. In an essay titled "Church, Culture, and Politics," he claims that the missionary attitude meant "rejection of these values and rituals that held us together; it meant adopting what, in effect, was a debased European middle-class mode of living and behaviour. The European missionary had attacked the primitive rights of our people, had condemned our beautiful African dances, the images of our Gods, recoiling from their suggestion of satanic sensuality. The African convert did the same, often with even greater zeal, for he had to prove how Christian he was through his rejection of his past and roots" (qtd. Killam, *Writings* 8). Abandoning Christianity as the agent of colonial and more recent neocolonial control by the West, Ngũgĩ came to see Africa's salvation in socialism rather than religion ("Literature and Society"). But this has not prevented the claim that his vision is "essentially Christian" in its advocacy of moral and spiritual freedom (Sharma, "Ngũgĩ's" 208), despite the fact that in *A Grain of Wheat* Kihika hacks to death a pastor who opposes the insurgents and whose last words are those of a Christian martyr.

The first references to the Christian Savior in the novel are made by the narrator when he recounts the arrival of the white missionary, who comes to the Gikuyu people with a "tongue coated with sugar." "About Jesus, they could not at first understand," Ngũgĩ writes, "for how could it be that God would let himself be nailed to a tree? The whiteman spoke of that Love that passeth all understanding. Greater Love hath no man than this, he read from the little black book, that a man lay down his life for his friends" (11). Yet other Europeans came not with Bibles but with swords, expropriating the Gikuyu land. Soon biblical language is associated with Gikuyu heroes who resist and suffer execution, their deaths inspiring continuing struggle against the white man.

As the prophets anticipate Jesus, these sacrificial figures anticipate the coming of Kihika, who inspires the insurgency. While a student in the mission school, Kihika begins seeing parallels between himself and the biblical deliverers he learns about, dreaming of leading his people to freedom as Moses led the Israelites out of Egypt (85). Then at a political meeting he announces, in Christ-like words, "A day comes when brother shall give up brother, a mother her son, when you and I have heard the call of a nation in turmoil," and he closes with the admonition, "Watch ye and pray" (15). Later Kihika tells his friends: "Take up my cross is what Christ told his people. . . . If any man will come after me, let him deny himself, and take up his cross, and follow me. For whosoever will save his life shall lose it: and whosoever will lose his life for my sake will find it. Do you know why Gandhi succeeded? Because he made his people give up their fathers and mothers and serve their one Mother—India. With us, Kenya is our mother" (88–89). The political situation, he continues, calls for new Christs, because the death of the Christ of Christianity didn't change anything: "I die for you, you die for me, we become a sacrifice for one another. . . . I am Christ. Everybody who takes the Oath of Unity to change things in Kenya is a Christ. Christ then is not one person. All those who take up the cross of liberating Kenya are the true Christs for us Kenyan people" (95). When Kihika kills a British officer, he compares this assassination with the vengeance God sent against the Egyptians. But as a Kenyan Christ, he is betrayed to the colonial authorities and hanged from a tree, "crucified" (176).

In spite of his salvific role, Kihika is less fully developed than his betrayer Mugo, who ironically sees himself from the same biblical perspective. Like Kihika, he identifies with Moses. After working in the field one pleasant day, he lies down at noon and receives a vision: "Moses too was alone keeping the flock of Jethro his father-in-law. . . . And the angel of the Lord appeared unto him in a flame of fire out of the midst of a bush. And God called out to him in a thin voice, Moses, Moses. And Mugo cried out, here am I, Lord" (125). But later, under the influence of a consuming jealousy of Kihika, he secretly divulges Kihika's whereabouts to the authorities. In its ignorance, the community regards Mugo as a hero of the British detention camps and a reincarnated Kihika, and he himself initially thinks that he has survived the camps to play a special role: "Surely he must have been spared in order that he might save people like Githua from poverty and misery. He, an only son, was born to save. The exciting possibilities of his new position agitated him and lured him on. . . . he would lead his people across the desert to the new Jerusalem" (134). Yet he is also hounded by guilt and sometimes sees himself as Judas—though isn't Judas "a stone from the hands of a power more than man?" he rationalizes (176). In agony, he sees Christ's blood dripping from the walls of his hut, and finally he confesses his crime at a public commemoration of Kihika's sacrificial death: " 'You asked for Judas,' he started. 'You asked for the man who led Kihika to this tree, here. That man stands before you, now. Kihika came to me by night. He put his life into my hands, and I sold it to the whiteman. And this thing has eaten into my life all these years' " (223). Mugo is condemned to death for his betrayal, but this unusual fusion of Jesus and Judas nonetheless continues to transform his people's lives. Kihika's sister Mumbi, who has not told the community that Mugo confessed to her his betrayal of her brother, is prepared after Mugo's death to be reconciled to her estranged husband. He, in turn, who has been angry with his wife for being unfaithful to him, prepares to carve a peace offering to her, "a woman big—big with child" (247). Thus the novel concludes with regeneration, even as the title from St. Paul suggests.

Unlike the three previous novels we have considered, the next one places the Jesus figure in an Islamic society. *Children of Gebelaawi* (1959), also known as *Children of our Alley*, by the Egyptian Nobel Laureate Naguib Mahfouz, is an allegorical *Heilesgeschichte* of prophetic monotheisms to which is added modern scientism and the political totalitarianism it has supported. Because it deals with religion in an unorthodox way, the story so offended conservative Muslims in Egypt that when it was serialized in the leading newspaper *Al-Ahram*, mobs demanded that it be banned, and it was published as a novel only outside the country in Lebanon (Stewart vii); to this day it is not listed among Mahfouz's publications in Egyptian editions of his works (Le Gassick 4). Mahfouz's novel allegorically represents in miniature four thousand years of religious history, using biblical and Koranic material in a setting of desert and urban alleyways that resemble nineteenth-century Cairo. The novel recounts the stories of four men who free or attempt to free the people from the chiefs who terrorize them, and from the trustees who deny them their inheritance.[5]

Mahfouz begins at the onset of sacred history with a God figure, Gebelaawi, the mountain man who tamed the desert. The account follows the lines laid down by the Hebrew and Muslim Scriptures, and includes the fall of Adham (Adam) and his subsequent expulsion from the Big House (Eden). Adham spends the rest of his life laboring to survive, but just before he dies, Gebelaawi appears and promises the estate to his children. However, the trustees keep the income from the estate and oppress the people, until Gebel (Moses) frees them. He is interested, though, only in the inhabitants of his own quarter, and misery returns.

A second liberator is Rifaa (Jesus). Mahfouz places him in the prophetic tradition by having him remember the old stories sung in the opium dens about Gebelaawi and Gebel; the Muslim emphasis on the recurrent need for God's prophets is hinted at when Rifaa wonders why Gebelaawi has shut himself away for so long. But Rifaa's approach differs from that of Gebel; though he speaks against the chief of the Gebelites, he is not interested in winning back the estate by violent means, for he views this as leading to more oppression. He focuses instead on the inner life of the people by casting out their evil spirits. His concerns seem to be legitimized when he wanders off into the desert and hears Gebelaawi's voice calling him as "the beloved son" to liberate all the people, not just those of Gebel's quarter, from evil spirits—the universalism of Rifaa's call is important. There is also a new identification with the disreputable, symbolized by his marriage to a woman of easy virtue instead of the chief's daughter. For this he is repudiated by the Gebelites, so he moves out of their quarter and takes non-Gebelites as his patients; here is the Christian theme of the Jesus rejected by his own people. Rifaa begins to gather a group of followers, telling them that the Gebelites have forgotten the virtue of happiness without estate or power. This antagonizes the chiefs, who plot against him. Unwilling to resort to violence to protect himself, Rifaa is eventually betrayed and killed. After his friends bury him, it is said that Gebelaawi took his body to the garden of the Big House; in this way the novel enacts the growing opposition of the religious establishment to Jesus, which culminates in the passion and resurrection—the name Rifaa itself suggests "rising" or "elevation" (El-Gabalawy 93).

Injustice reigns again until the appearance of the next salvific figure, Kassem (Mohammed), who defeats the chiefs in battle and proclaims that all the alley-dwellers are Gebelaawi's heirs. This story dramatizes the Muslim criticism that Judaism is ethnically limited and Christianity too pacifistic. The final liberator is Arafa the magician (scientist), who has no faith in the old stories and wants to use his knowledge to end oppression. However, he inadvertently causes the death of Gebelaawi, and his magic comes to be used to ruthlessly enslave the people. He is buried alive by a trustee, but afterwards the people hope for liberation from Arafa's dwarf brother, who is rumored to have escaped with the magic secrets.

The novel's religious implications are complex. Mahfouz was trained in European philosophy and for a time lost his faith, so it is no coincidence that one of the major themes in his fiction is the conflict between Islam and modern skepticism.[6] The presentation of the willful Gebelaawi raises questions about the justice and love of God; the author seems to recognize this issue in his comment that Gebelaawi represents "not God but a certain idea of God that men have made" (qtd. Stewart vii). The novel also calls into question the veracity of the contradictory versions of the old stories in the various quarters of the alley. However, the presentation of human history as wretchedness relieved only periodically by deliverers does not suggest skepticism about God's interest in human wretchedness (El-Gabalawy 96), but instead, in typically Muslim fashion, recognizes the power of the divine breaking into history. Though Somekh claims that the portrait of Rifaa is so hastily drawn that he is "ridiculous rather than saintly" ("Sad" 107), the depiction of Rifaa is more Christian than the usual Muslim interpretation of Jesus: Gebelaawi addresses him as his son (a relationship unacceptable to Islam, which holds that God neither is begotten nor begets), and his death is real rather than an illusion. The story of Kassem joins religious devotion with social justice, a combination that may grow in part out of the author's commitment to socialism (Milson 178). The final section appears both to acknowledge that God has been killed by modern science, and to lament the loss of the old stories—a theme in Mahfouz's earlier novels (Nijland 123–24). Certainly the author is not happy that the people put their hope in science, for a scientist has caused their ancestor's death and science enforces their present oppression.

Critics differ in their reading of the novel's ending. Nijland feels that Mahfouz has abandoned hope in science (154), while other commentators view Mahfouz as ambivalent, seeing the destructiveness of atheism and knowledge used for totalitarianism but also recognizing its great potential for social good.[7] But by building his plot upon the accepted Islamic view of Moses and Jesus as prophetic precursors of Mohammed, and then ironically portraying the prophets as precursors of the modern secular scientist whose knowledge is wielded by tyrants, Mahfouz appears to return to a belief in the supernatural.[8]

Why do novelists who affirm the indigenous values of cultures that the West has "othered," who transform European political ideology so that it harmonizes with local tradition, and who envision sympathetic natives in conflict with oppressive Europeans, resort to a symbol associated with the imperialism of missionary and colonialistic Christianity? The answer is that these authors replace the European Christian story, which they associate with the religious and cultural subjugation Foucault observed, with an indigenized or hybridized Christianity, which they associate with liberation and justice.

Since the novelists create their Jesus figures from various personal and religious perspectives, can we be more precise about the kind of affiliation these figures have with biblical justice? I think we can name three characteristics that are typical. First, there is the Jesus figures' identification with the poor and disreputable. Second, in the modern world, identification with the poor often has political and cultural ramifications that are not nominally religious. The political impact is likely to be in the form of anti-imperialism, since all the novels come from territories colonized or controlled by Europe. Concern for the subjugated in these areas first led to protest against overt political rule, but since the colonies were granted political independence protest has been directed against neocolonialist economic and cultural control. Finally, protest against Eurocentrism entails affirmation of the indigenous tradition; significantly, the Jesus figures have all been incarnated, brought into the historical world, in new cultures.

All the Jesus figures identify with the poor and oppressed; they avoid and oppose the powerful and respectable, or are opposed by them. Roa Bastos's Caspar Mora is a humble instrument-maker who isolates himself from the village, and the wooden *Christus* he carves becomes the focus for the villagers' hatred of the European-oriented church that so often in Latin America has allied itself with the elite. The other Jesus figures in *Son of Man* are persecuted by the military. Mais's Brother Man has been a Rastafarian, a member of a sect that had absolutely no social status in Jamaica; its adherents came from the underclass and literally lived in the garbage dump outside Kingston. Brother Man's appeal is to the street poor of the city. Ngũgĩ's Kihika gives up the privileges which his mission-school education could have given him in the church or colonial civil service, and flees to the hills to fight for his people. And all of Mahfouz's liberators identify with the alley-dwellers against the trustees. Gebel and Kassem overthrow the power structure, while Rifaa and Arafa are killed by the rich and influential.

To resist those in power is not just a matter of personal conviction but a social-political act. It is hardly a coincidence, then, that Ziolkowski's concept of "Comrade Jesus" can be considered relevant to the novels of Roa Bastos, Ngũgĩ, and Mais. The Jesus figures in Roa Bastos's novel oppose "internal colonialism" by the powerful military, land-owning, and ecclesiastical elite in Paraguay. Mais's Brother Man is linked with Rastafarianism, whose adherents are continually harassed by the political authorities. Ngũgĩ's Kihika participates in the Mau Mau struggle against British colonialism; the gospel he preaches is Gikuyu solidarity against the white man, and his death empowers the survivors to continue the struggle. Mugo betrays not only Kihika but also his people's political aspirations. Mahfouz's vision is broader, since his story dramatizes millennia of injustice, not just modern oppression. He recounts stories of the monotheistic liberators repeatedly rebelling against their rulers and of the political powers of this century manipulating the modern secularist.

These novels dramatize unsettling, even revolutionary values, but we also need to recognize that these values are not Eurocentric. The Jesus figures and the outcasts they consort with tend to reject what is European and to affirm or be interpreted in terms of marginal or indigenous cultural principles. The Jesus figures in Roa Bastos's novel are village Indians. The Afro-Caribbean origins of Brother Man's sanctity have already been mentioned; Rastafarianism took the Christianity brought by the missionaries and indigenized it into a black messianic movement that questions the superiority of Euro-Christianity. Kihika employs the language of the European missionaries to affirm an ethnic tradition that is in revolt against European hegemony, and he fuses this language with the more ancient wisdom of his people: "'Watch ye and pray,' Kihika said, calling on his audience to remember the great Swahili proverb: *Kikulacho Kimo ngeuni mwako*" (15). The religious liberators in Mahfouz's novel are placed in a Muslim scheme of religious history to which the European-style secularism represented by Arafa does not offer a viable alternative.

These novels, written since World War II by authors who are neither European nor American, replace the Euro-American Jesus figures with Jesus figures who are localized. Breaking free from the strictures of Western Christianity, the newly incarnated Jesus figure has become an effective postcolonial character who protests against injustice.

11.

The Nightmare of History Revisited
André Brink's *An Instant in the Wind*

ALAN JACOBS

The biblical understanding of justice cannot be divorced from the biblical understanding of history: the achievement of a permanent just order, in the vision of the Hebrew prophets, will occur in human time as the culmination of human history. Whether this vision is unique among the world's cultures is questionable, but in any event it has proven adaptable to an astonishing variety of peoples and has met an astonishing variety of needs. One may or may not understand Marxism as a secular, desacralized version of the biblical quest for *shalom*—this too is questionable—but there is a distinct tradition of linking the two. In African literature, for instance, the novels of Ngũgĩ wa Thiong'o, especially *A Grain of Wheat* (1967), consti-tute a notable example. Again and again Ngũgĩ clothes the precepts of Marxism in the imagery of the prophets and the historical narrative of Israel, as other essays in this collection have demonstrated. And since he is using these biblical materials to interpret the history of the Gikuyu people, he provides for us a distinctive (but wholly natural) blend of Marxist polemics, biblical literature, and historical fiction. In short, Ngũgĩ is engaged in biblical typology—the thematic linkage of distinct historical events, the interpretation of contemporary events according to patterns es-tablished in biblical narrative. And this is a characteristic use of the Bible in African culture (including African culture outside of Africa, for ex-ample, the Rastafarians of Jamaica): it enables one simultaneously to depict the injustices of the colonial past and to show how those injustices are part of a larger pattern of justice and liberation.

Like many African novels, then, Ngūgī's *A Grain of Wheat* understands justice in strictly historical terms. It should not be surprising that the historical novel has been prominent in the development of written literature in Africa; most African cultures possess a strong historical consciousness, bequeathed them by oral traditions rich in character and event.[1] But if the arrival of the European in Africa did not bring history, typically it did bring a sense of cultural crisis amenable to Western (and again, in many cases biblical) narrative forms, whether historical or fictional. Thus the representation and interpretation of historical crises may be seen as a fundamental impulse of the African novel. Ngūgī aside, we may note Chinua Achebe's tragic *Things Fall Apart* (1959) as a standard example, but Sembene Ousmane's *God's Bits of Wood* (1960), which describes a successful railway strike on the Bamako-Dakar line in 1948, shows that a satisfactory resolution of the conflict is possible as well.

In any event, the confrontation of native Africans and Europeans clearly provides the main impetus for the historical novel in black Africa. In South Africa, however, other rules apply. To be sure, the Zulu people memorialize their greatest achievements as a nation (under Shaka Zulu in the early nineteenth century) and their ultimately unsuccessful wars with the white settlers, in a fashion that closely follows the familiar pattern of crisis history.[2] Afrikaners, though, have their own very different perspective: their culture has for at least a century and a half been characterized by a rigorous, biblically based interpretation of their place in history, an interpretation within which the English, more than the Zulu, are the chief antagonists. (The Zulu and other tribes, considered less than fully human, could not be raised to the level of antagonist.) This historical world view has rarely had significant detractors within the Afrikaner community.[3] But in recent years, South African novelists—in Afrikaans and English alike—have often attempted to use fiction to challenge or provide an alternative to that monolithic Afrikaner history. One of the more fascinating documents to emerge from this reinterpretive urge—because of, rather than despite, its many and serious flaws—is André Brink's *An Instant in the Wind* (1976). In the modern world, when so many intellectuals have (like Joyce's Stephen Dedalus) seen history as a nightmare from which to awake, the agony of South Africa both reinforces that sense of nightmare and demands that it be confronted. Brink's novel, as we shall see, illustrates this double bind.

A brief summary of traditional Afrikaner self-interpretation may be useful here. The first premise of what T. Dunbar Moodie has called "the Afrikaner civil religion" is one shared by many Christians in all times and places, but that traditionally has received a special emphasis in Calvinist thought: that God exercises sovereign control over history, indeed had formulated a plan for human history before the foundation of the world, and works (even through the evil done by humanity) to bring forth in the fullness of time the eternal Kingdom.[4] It is the second premise that makes this civil religion distinctive and controversial: that God has chosen the Afrikaner people to be a special people, perhaps *the* specially favored people, in the modern world.

According to this view, Afrikaners are to the Christian age what the nation of Israel was in ancient times. In fact, the history of the Afrikaners is usually seen to correspond closely to the history of Israel. Believing themselves oppressed by the English yoke, the Afrikaners in 1835 began the Great Trek across the desert to a new land of their own—a perfect analogue to the Israelites' divinely guided Exodus from Egypt, wandering through the wilderness, and eventual arrival in the Promised Land. The Afrikaners' later defeat in the Second Anglo-Boer War, which subjected them to the British crown, reenacted the Babylonian captivity of Israel. But while the Israelites, depending upon one's point of view, either never regained their national status or have only done so recently, the Afrikaners—who, they believe, differ from Israel in that they chose more-or-less consistent faithfulness rather than recurrent apostasy—were quickly able to rebuild: they achieved political power and eventually forced secession from the British Commonwealth.

In short, the Afrikaners apply the same typological method of scriptural interpretation to their history as Ngũgĩ does to that of his Gikuyu people, which suggests that the recurrent popularity of this hermeneutical strategy may be due in part to what might politely be called its flexibility. Michael Walzer has shown in *Exodus and Revolution* (1985) how the story of the Israelites' flight from Egypt and their ultimate victory over their oppressors has given strength and sustenance, and has suggested a pattern of action, to innumerable quests for liberation. But at times this vital connection is achieved only by reducing the biblical story to an elementary structure that can be shared with any number of other events, some of which bear little or no resemblance to the Exodus narrative. One thinks of the structuralist A. J. Greimas's claim to be able to reduce all stories to three pairs of *actants* (Subject and Object, Sender and Receiver, Helper and Opponent); it is a wonderfully clever thing to do, but to make all stories the same story is inevitably to withhold a substantial portion of their interest and value. Typological interpretation originates in a concern for history, but in the wrong hands can calcify into a rigid structuralism that denies historical difference.

The Afrikaner typology, for instance, works in this way: If the Gospel of Christ succeeds the Mosaic Law, and Christian believers (as the Body of Christ) succeed the Jewish adherents to that law, and if these are not just spiritual but historical events, then it follows logically that there must be a Christian nation to succeed the nation of Israel. The pattern of Afrikaner history shows that the Afrikaners are that nation. Furthermore, since other typologically comprehensible biblical events indicate that God always does the job better the second time around, they are on earth to do what the Israelites failed to do. The question then becomes, what sets them apart from other peoples, other cultures? What distinctive message are they able, are they *called*, to bring to the world (as Israel brought its message of the oneness of God and the universality of the moral law)? The obvious answer—obvious, in any case, to many Afrikaners—is the system of sociopolitical organization based on the separation of the races and known as apartheid. Thus apartheid is no relic of a racism passing from the earth. It is theologically necessary, in order to preserve the progressiveness of God's action in bringing history toward its culmination in the Kingdom, to see that apartheid in fact provides the proper pattern for the structuring of society. As the anthropologist Vincent Crapanzano has written, many Afrikaners "are messianic and actually see in apartheid a new social order that, according to God's will, will eventually spread to free the world of its serious social problems" (xx).

The development of modern fiction in South Africa has been strongly influenced, one is tempted to say dictated, by the stringency and cultural authority of the Afrikaner view of history. The insistently biblical character of Alan Paton's *Cry, the Beloved Country* (1948) is best understood as an alternative Christian interpretation, one that convicts the Afrikaner determination to separate the races of a profound violation of Christian love and equality. But more recent developments are, not surprisingly, marked by an explicit and complete rejection of biblical history. Furthermore, since Marxist influence among South African whites has not been strong, and, since the fading of Hegelianism from the intellectual scene, other substantial interpretations of history are hard to come by, in practice the rejection of Christian history often means a rejection of historical meaning altogether.

In J. M. Coetzee's allegorical *Waiting for the Barbarians* (1980), for instance, the Empire and the Barbarians are presented as vague and confused antagonists: the reader is never given a distinct context for the events that occur and the attitudes that people hold in the book. The Magistrate (the story's protagonist) replies to rumors of possible barbarian invasion in this way: "Of this unrest I myself saw nothing. In private I observed that once in every generation, without fail, there is an episode of hysteria about the barbarians. . . . Show me a barbarian army and I will believe" (8). And in the last sentence of the book the Magistrate compares himself to "a man who lost his way long ago but presses on along a road that may lead nowhere" (156). What appears at first to be a deliberate withholding of vital information is actually an assertion that there *is* no vital information. Any attempt to construct a meaningful history, in order to explain the violence of the novel's world, can be nothing more than an empty rationalization of essentially irrational acts. Historical interpretation, in this view, is merely the self-justification of oppressors. Coetzee's vision stands in direct opposition to the Afrikaner typology: it suggests that the passage of time reveals no divine order, that if events have a pattern, it is the pattern of a worn needle stuck in the worn groove of an old record. Using another metaphor, Frank Kermode has seen the clock's *tick-tock* as the minimum of plot and argues that we need something much more complex than "the humble genesis" of *tick* and the "feeble apocalypse" of *tock* "if we persist in finding 'what will suffice'" (45). But the Magistrate hears not even that: he hears *tick . . . tick . . . tick*. It may be argued that the Magistrate indeed possesses a theory of history, but its premise can only be that history will not "suffice."

André Brink's novel *An Instant in the Wind*, however, embarks upon another course: it seeks an understanding of history—of South African history—that is neither fatalistic nor Christian nor, for that matter, Marxist. Brink selects an apparently insignificant episode from the early history of white settlement in South Africa and, in expanding upon the few available facts, makes it serve and illustrate a philosophy of history that radically opposes Afrikaner thinking—especially regarding the role of the individual's experiences and convictions. It is a fictional method that bears significant resemblance to Clifford Geertz's "thick description" in its assumption that a few nuggets of historical information can be fraught with enormous implications.

The facts are indeed few, and Brink presents them in the very first paragraph of his story:

The names are known—Adam Mantoor and Elisabeth Larsson—and something of their history has been recorded. We know that in 1749, the last
year of the rule of Governor Swellengrebel, Elisabeth accompanied her husband, the Swedish traveller Erik Alexis Larsson, on a journey into the interior of the Cape of Good Hope where he died some time after; that she
was eventually discovered by the runaway slave, Adam; and that they reached
Cape Town together towards the end of February 1751. An interesting trifle,
a mere footnote adding nothing to one's knowledge of the land or the course
of history.[5]

This invocation of the data of conventional history—dates and places, a
governor's name—is characteristic of the book's brief opening section.
There we are even presented with a list of the contents of Larsson's wagons
(as preserved in Larsson's inexplicably recovered journal). But the purpose
of such information is strictly contrastive. Once the story itself begins, the
character of "history" undergoes a metamorphosis. History becomes the
province of individual experience; history is what happens to Adam and
Elisabeth. Their experience is not, or is not intentionally, an *alternative* to
history, such as Coetzee presented. (If Brink had been seeking an alternative, he would not have chosen a real event from South Africa's past.) The
essence of history is what happens within and between Adam and Elisabeth
there in the unmapped interior of the Cape: "It is to this end that the crust
of history must be scraped off. Not simply to retell it but to utterly expose
it and to set it in motion again" (15). Political history is the crust; Adam
and Elisabeth, the pulsing and vibrant core suffocating beneath it.

Brink's exposition of this theme is sometimes predictable and unimagin-
ative, as "individual experience" is defined according to the hoariest tenets
of the Romantic philosophies of self: it consists chiefly of communion with
nature and sexual intercourse. These are the experiences that best promote
the quest for authentic selfhood because they present the self with an Other
that is not (or need not be) alien, an Other with which it is possible to
reconcile. This is Brink's conviction, and he holds to it with a religious
passion. Throughout the book he repeats a phrase introduced at the begin-   ·
ning, in the paragraph about the "crust of history": "It is not a question of
imagination, but of faith." He is not inventing or imagining but retrieving
that which he must believe is really there, that which the crust of political
and social event hides.[6] The frightening implication of Brink's secular fide-
ism is that in the absence of such Romantic individualism, the traditional
Afrikaner view goes effectively unopposed.

   Contributing to the possibility of such individualism finding genuine expression are the social positions of the two main characters. Elisabeth, a woman, and Adam, a runaway slave, are to Brink alike in their powerlessness, in their subordinate positions within their racist and patriarchal society. But this likeness is not enough. It is necessary, in addition, that the meeting of Adam and Elisabeth occur in the wilderness. Cape Town, there at the edge of the continent, is crust; to go inland is to find (as Coetzee might say) the heart of the country. The two characters' early relationship is dominated by attempts to understand the significance of their separation from society, to grasp what rules, if any, still apply: she orders him to bring her water, he refuses; she calls him a "slave," he denies it. Eventually she tells him, "You don't seem to know your place" (22), but even then she seems half-aware that in this wilderness there is no "place" for either of them. The wilderness is by definition *not* a place in the human sense of that word. On the very next day she finds herself, without knowing why, telling him stories about her past (25).[7] That pattern continues until he asks, after she has described her horror at once having seen a pack of dogs kill a bull, "Why did you tell me all this?" (31)—to which she has no answer. Clearly, in the absence of the social structures that would ordinarily describe their communicative possibilities, the instinctive need to tell and be heard takes over. Thus both Adam and Elisabeth find themselves continually falling into memory, recalling the events that have shaped their lives, as though they are testing the personal history they have so far written against this wilderness's vast integrity. In the absence of a communally dictated history, a political history of races and classes, a new history based on personal exchange and made possible by the context of a desocialized natural order begins to take shape.

Thus the wilderness in this novel is not something that the characters pass through on their way to a Promised Land; this is no Great Trek, no Exodus narrative. Adam and Elisabeth, by different paths to be sure, enter the wilderness from Cape Town, and in the end they return to Cape Town. Rather than being a link in a narrational chain, the wilderness is one pole of a binary opposition, the other pole being society itself. Brink thus resurrects the familiar dichotomy between Nature and Culture. If in Culture the self is externally circumscribed and defined, in Nature there are no confinements: the self is free to discover its own range of force and expression. After remembering the constrictions placed upon her because of her gender, Elisabeth thinks: "But this once I refuse to obey them, I shall break free. This once I'll trek into my own wilderness" (65). (The word "trek" here has an obvious ironic force.) In Romantic mythology, with its commitment to spiritual freedom, the wilderness is thus Eden. Is it necessary to say who Adam and Elisabeth are? Brink here swerves quite explicitly from the historically grounded, linear narrative of the Exodus to the more fabulous set piece of the Garden myth, and in so doing swerves from a story whose thematic vocabulary involves justice and injustice to one whose polarities are wholeness and brokenness, or unity and separation.

Romanticism tells several stories revolving around the themes of Genesis. The most common is, of course, the fall from unitary being into self-consciousness. Another, less frequent in Europe after the spiritual and moral failures of the French Revolution but exemplified in America by the early essays of Emerson, is the recovery of unitary being through the dissolution of the subject-object opposition.[8] For a while, it looks as though *An Instant in the Wind* will be this kind of story, as Adam and Elisabeth confirm the freedom learned from the wilderness by establishing a passionately sexual relationship. Significantly, at the moment that Adam realizes and expresses his desire for Elisabeth, Brink repeats his *leitmotif:* "Not a question of imagination, but of faith" (108). Sexual communion, he thereby insists, is a necessary element of their spiritual growth, and, what is more important, of the alternative history they are enacting—it constitutes a refutation of apartheid, of the very idea of miscegenation, not only in idea but in act.

Moreover, the natural imagery of the next chapter (109ff) persistently reinforces their communion. Elisabeth even learns Adam's real name, Aob, which previously only his mother had known. The restoration of prelapsarian, transpersonal identity is apparently complete. But the story does not end here, and it soon becomes clear—if it were not clear already—that Brink is not telling the Emersonian story after all. Instead, we begin to sense the characteristic traits of a third kind of story: the merely apparent recovery of unitary being. For Adam and Elisabeth never intend to remain in the Edenic wilderness. Elisabeth is pregnant—not by Adam but by her now-lost husband. "But there is still the child. For his sake I must get back to the Cape" (45).

Adam too wishes to return to the Cape, a desire that may be surprising in view of his status as a runaway slave and criminal (possibly a murderer), but his needs are as primal as Elisabeth's: "I didn't choose the wilderness because I wanted to. I simply had to. And by now I've learned to stay alive, to survive like an animal. But I'm not an animal. I'm a human being. And I want to live with people again." He holds desperately to the hope that he need not return as a criminal, "crawling like a runaway dog," and the key to that hope is Elisabeth: "If you tell them I brought you back, if you will tell them I saved your life, if you demand my freedom, they'll give it. You can buy me my freedom. No one else can. I am in your hands" (91). Eventually, Adam's need becomes the one which compels their movement toward the Cape, for Elisabeth loses her child.[9] Enormous suffering, including near-starvation, unites them even more deeply, yet they continue to move toward the Cape—even though Elisabeth sometimes thinks that they might have a better chance at happiness in one of the Hottentot settlements they occasionally come across. Even the name Aob, which at first promised perfect union, becomes a point of conflict: when Elisabeth uses the name Adam, as she tends to do, he feels alienated and distressed; but sometimes he becomes angry at her use of the real name, finding it an impertinence (see 122, 136, 177). Clearly Adam is torn between the desire to dissolve the subject/object dichotomy and the fear that such dissolution might bring about not an augmentation but an erasure of selfhood.

The tragic separation that must occur when they reach the Cape they manage somehow not to consider, but the reader is constantly aware of its inevitability. It is prefigured when the travelers come across an Afrikaner farm and Elisabeth chooses to lie about her relationship with Adam, fearing the farm family's reaction (219). After they escape the farm, where Elisabeth is almost raped and the revelation of their relationship produces horror among the family members—all of which should indicate what is to come—she nevertheless holds desperately to the illusion that their arrival at the Cape will be a joyous one: "'For neither of us it will be the Cape we knew.' She tried to convince him with the intensity in her eyes. 'It will be a new place altogether. To start from the beginning'" (230). But Adam is not persuaded; he is beginning to confront the necessary chasm between the personal history they have made and the political realities of society. "You're a new person now," Elisabeth tells him, to which he replies, "But will the Cape be a new Cape?" (231).

Of course, the Cape to which they return is unchanged. Brink is forced to accommodate the factual record: Adam was executed less than a month after their return. For this fact Brink offers no explanation, and he (through Elisabeth), on the book's final page, imagines—or rather, as he would have it, faithfully believes—that Adam, after a brief period of confusion, "would realise, and accept [his death]. He would not even consider an alternative any longer: it had been given from the beginning" (250). Or is this Brink's condemnation of Elisabeth's acquiescence in Adam's unjust execution?

I do not believe that Brink sees this dénouement as an utter failure; to do so would be to see the inner history built by Adam and Elisabeth as empty and meaningless. In the end Brink seems to place his hope—his insistence on faith rather than imagination—in a sentence written by the real Elisabeth Larsson and, remarkably, preserved. At the end of a "dreary" account (too blandly factual for Brink) of her wilderness experience, she writes, "This no one can take away from us, not even ourselves" (12, 250). The inner history, once made, is not unmakeable, Brink interprets her as saying. It stands as firmly as political history on the most vast scale. It cannot be unmade, we are encouraged to think, even by those who made it; if Elisabeth rejects Adam in Cape Town, she cannot unwrite their love in the wilderness (nor, it should be added, could she erase his presence from the child Brink believes they had). Without a stable and ineradicable personal history, political history has the final word, has no opposition in the long and painful record of South African experience—and this Brink's faith will not allow.

It is hard to imagine that for many readers this faith will seem justified, or that even if it is true it provides much comfort. For the message of the book, against Brink's will, seems to be that history in the familiar sense will win out, that personal history cannot succeed against it. The Afrikaner worldview cannot be challenged by this peculiar Romantic quietism. For in the end personal history does prove to be an escape from history. It is a journey into the permanence and impartiality of nature, but persons and societies share neither of those traits. This irreconcilability of Nature and Culture makes Adam's fate tragic. And it is, let us note, only *his* fate that achieves this stature: Elisabeth is reabsorbed into society, while Adam's execution dramatically completes his long alienation. At the end of the book, he is even exiled from Brink's goal to "utterly expose [their personal history] and set it in motion again" (15), for he is present only in Elisabeth's imagination. His capture and execution are beyond the novel's reach because they are also beyond the reach of history as it has come to be defined by its chroniclers.

Early in the novel, Elisabeth had thought of herself as "making history" by becoming "the first person" to reach the part of the desert through which they are travelling. Adam sardonically replies, "You think you're taking history with you wherever you go"—a proper response, but in the practical sense Elisabeth's assumption is of course true. History is what is recorded. A record of their journey remains simply because one of them was white. Adam's angry invocation of other inhabitants and makers of history—

"every weak old Hottentot bundled into a porcupine hole, . . . every name-less wanderer crossing this river"—is necessarily incomprehensible to Elisabeth (84). At this point in the story, though, Elisabeth's exclusion of Adam from history is counterbalanced by the reader's access to Adam's consciousness—perhaps more than counterbalanced, considering Brink's commitment to re-situating history in the individual. What happens at the end is a twofold tragedy: first, the reduction of Adam to an object of socio-political history; and second, the collapse of Brink's faith in his mytho-graphic ability to "imagine the real." What was a question of faith becomes one of (fallen) imagination, for imagination is only necessary to compensate for what is absent. In the book's last paragraphs, Adam is absent to Elisa-beth and Brink alike.

The story itself, then, pronounces a verdict that Brink seems unwilling to accept upon Brink's own Emersonian insistence that Nature, passionately embraced, can overcome the depredations of history. Early in his career, Emerson said, "history is an impertinence and an injury, if it be anything more than a cheerful apologue or parable of my being and becoming" (270). This could be the motto for Elisabeth and Adam's trek into the wilderness. But when they return to the Cape, to the opposite pole of the dichotomy, they find themselves in the situation Emerson describes in "Ex-perience," in a passage written after the death of his young son Waldo (a death he felt he could never sufficiently grieve for): "Some thing which I fancied was a part of me, which could not be torn away without tearing me, . . . falls off from me, and leaves no scar." Emerson has discovered the insinuations of time into the apparent permanence of love: "Our rela-tions to each other are oblique and casual" (473). Further, "Two human beings are like globes, which can touch only at a point" (488). Though their desire to meet more completely ever increases, that union cannot be achieved; eventually, perhaps, they cease to touch at all. This is what hap-pens to Adam and Elisabeth.

Brink, then, cannot provide a historical answer to the Afrikaner view of history. His Romantic individualism presumes an impossible creature: a self independent of any social Other, reliant only on the natural and sexual mirrors of its own being. This philosophy of autonomous and internal "history" cannot be reconciled with the self always or already immersed in (and, after a fashion, created by) culture and society. As Robert Bellah and his coauthors have written, in the context of American culture's recurrent infatuation with this philosophy, "the culture of individualism has diffi-culty coming to terms with genuine cultural or social differences, [and] it

has even more difficulty coming to terms with large impersonal organizations and institutions" (207).

This problem occurs in large part because of what I can only call an
enormous category mistake—perhaps the most characteristic category mistake of the post-Romantic world. The Afrikaner understanding of history
constitutes a violation of justice masquerading as the realization of justice;
the purpose of its biblical typology is to cover the unjust truth with a
plausible fictional mask. One can only respond to such an understanding
by positing an alternative conception of the just, a conception that discovers
and unmasks the contradictions in the Afrikaner account. But Brink seems
incapable of such a response, and thereby tries, through the story of Adam
and Elisabeth, to convert a problem of justice into a problem of epistemology. Confronted with the need for just action, he responds with a recipe
for right seeing. One is reminded of all those bumper stickers reading
"Visualize World Peace." But does one work at *visualizing* world peace—
"not a question of imagination, but of faith"—if one can think of anything
to *do?* The chief irony among many in this novel is that Brink's chosen
story powerfully illustrates, even as he himself attempts to deny, the inevitability of tragedy in South African life.

But it is one thing to say that history is tragic, quite another to call it a
nightmare and argue that the proper response to it is to shake oneself
awake—especially if what one wishes to wake *into* is a radically de-
contextualized individualism. Walzer has recently argued that the desire
for such detachment (from history, from one's culture and one's people) is
the characteristic flaw of the modern social critic, whose "hard-won impartiality" often becomes "a cold indifference" (*Company* 142). I do not say
that Brink is guilty of indifference, only that the program of detachment
and retreat presented in his novel courts that danger. It is not unlike Buddha's injunction to shun love, for he who has many loves has many woes.
Buddha's observation is acute, his recommendation dubious. For, as Frederick Buechner has written, "side by side with the Buddha's truth is the
Gospel truth that 'he who does not love remains in death'" (55).[10]

To the detached critic, Walzer offers as an alternative the "connected
critic," perhaps best exemplified by Albert Camus. Camus was born an
Algerian Frenchman, a *pied noir,* and throughout his life, in the face of
sometimes vitriolic condemnation from his fellow French leftists, acknowledged his debt and responsibility to *pied noir* society even as he (often
bitterly) criticized it. The example of Camus, Walzer argues, "invites us
to doubt the standard view of the social critic as someone who breaks loose

from his particular loyalties and views his own society from the outside—from an ideal point, as it were, equidistant from all societies." Instead, "Camus conceived of the critic as one of the crew [on the ship of society], who can't leave before the passengers."[11] Brink, in contrast, invites us to abandon the unsalvageable ship of South African society, of history—but to accept such an invitation is to set forth upon waters now and forever uncharted, without form and void.

As a South African alternative to detachment, Walzer holds up the great Afrikaans poet Breyten Breytenbach. But the author of *The True Confessions of an Albino Terrorist* (1985) has promoted violence so enthusiastically—and moreover, in the 1970s, proved himself to be so strangely inept and confused as a terrorist (Walzer, *Company* 213–15)—that he has lost most of the moral authority that his early and vocal resistance to apartheid once won him. Others see Nadine Gordimer as an example of persistent and forthright condemnation of an unjust regime from within the culture itself, and this view (as far as it goes) can scarcely be contested. But Gordimer's value as an exemplar of resistance and protest, and as a chronicler of manners and mores in a tormented society, far exceeds her value as an interpreter of that society. For one could never learn from Gordimer's fiction (or her nonfiction, for that matter) that the political struggles of South Africa are so deeply implicated in biblical prophecy and narrative, and in the interpretation of the Christian gospel. Gordimer writes as though there were simply no religious element in the great *agon* of South African life, and this remains an incomprehensible and irredeemable lack in her otherwise brilliant fiction. For the great majority of South Africans, the question of justice is and will continue to be a spiritual as well as a political one; and therefore Gordimer—along with, in their different ways, Brink and Breytenbach—is vulnerable to the powerful critique leveled against Marx by Simone Weil.

Weil points out that the Marxian (and not just the Marxian) hopes for the transformation of society are predicated on two assumptions: first, "that everything is exclusively regulated by force," and second, "that a day will suddenly come when force will be on the side of the weak. Not that certain ones who were weak will become strong—a change that has always taken place; but that the entire mass of the weak, while continuing to be such, will have force on its side" (193). But for Weil these two assumptions taken together are contradictory and absurd, except when they take one form and only one form: "The idea that weakness as such, while remaining weak, can constitute a force, is not a new one. It is the Christian idea itself, and the Cross is the illustration of it. But it has to do with a force of quite a different kind from that wielded by the strong; it is a force that is not of this world, that is supernatural" (194).

If Weil's analysis is right, it has enormous consequences for how we assess the relative value of South Africa's internal critics, whether their work is literary or nonliterary. Among contemporary intellectuals, whether in Europe, America, or South Africa, few political positions could be more scorned than that of mere liberalism, especially if such liberalism is grounded in a Christian universal humanism. Yet Weil's analysis of materialist dreams of social transformation suggests that such a position may not be utterly misbegotten. Perhaps the time has come for reconsideration of a writer whose Christian humanism, while painfully aware of the tragedy of South African life, nevertheless held that that tragedy could be redeemed through the transformation of the oppressors' hearts. I refer to Alan Paton. [12] The sustained argument of Paton's career is that meaningful achievements in social justice depend upon a prior correction in the human will, and ultimately that that correction depends upon divine action. In short, it is the argument of the prophet Isaiah:

> For the palace will be forsaken,
>   the populous city deserted;
> the hill and the watchtower
>   will become dens forever,
> a joy of wild asses,
>   a pasture for flocks;
> until a spirit from on high is poured out on us,
>   and the wilderness becomes a fruitful field,
>   and the fruitful field is deemed a forest.
> Then justice will dwell in the wilderness,
>   and righteousness abide in the fruitful field.
> And the effect of righteousness will be peace,
>   and the result of righteousness, quietness and trust for ever.
>   (Isa. 32:14–17)

This is a hard saying; who can hear it? It swerves dangerously close to a recommendation for quietism. As Raskolnikov tells Sonya, if you wait around for God to step in, nothing will ever get done. But Paton's (and Isaiah's) position must be evaluated not only according to some putatively objective standard of probable success, but also in the context of available alternatives, some of which have been explored in this essay. In 1985 (two years before his death) Paton made a speech in which he referred to Nadezhda Mandelstam's two autobiographical volumes of her life, with her husband the poet Osip Mandelstam, in Stalinist Russia, the first of which is called *Hope Against Hope*, the second (describing her life after Osip's death in the Gulag) *Hope Abandoned*. "In South Africa we are still writing the first book," he said. "We trust that we shall never have to write the second" (qtd. Callan xxvii). With *An Instant in the Wind*, André Brink has written that second volume. To accept his detachment is to acquiesce in the verdict that history is without hope of redemption, and to deny the biblical vision of *shalom* as the culmination of human history.

12

The *Intifada* of the Intellectuals
An Ecumenical Perspective on the
Walzer-Said Exchange

MARK WALHOUT

Intellectuals, like other people, have their commitments. But what happens when an intellectual committed to a people or a cause carries that commitment into his or her work as an intellectual? Suppose, for example, I am a critic working in the West who is committed to the end of apartheid in South Africa or to a Palestinian homeland. Few of my fellow citizens will contest my *right* to carry this commitment into my work as a critic, though some may question my choice of career if I devote all of my criticism to it. By the same token, few will insist that I have a *duty* to carry this commitment into my work as a critic, though some may question my sincerity if I fail to devote any of my criticism to it. Of course, the more controversial my commitment is—if I support the African National Congress (ANC) or the Palestinian Liberation Organization (PLO), for example—the more my right to express it through my criticism will be contested by my opponents. And the closer my connection to the society in question—in this case, South Africa or Israel—the more my friends will insist that it is my duty to be a committed critic. In sum, committed criticism is regarded, in the West, as a right that may become a duty depending on the critic's connection to the people or cause in question.

Now suppose I am also a Christian. In that case, my commitments ought to be those that follow from the Christian *telos*, namely the Kingdom of God or *shalom*, that state of affairs in which God's creatures are in harmonious relationship with God, with their fellow creatures, and with God's creation. Few Christians (outside of the Dutch Reformed Church in South Africa) will dispute the judgment that *shalom* requires the end of apartheid and equal rights in South Africa. But how many Christians will agree that *shalom* also requires equal rights in Israel, or even a separate Palestinian state? The fact is that most Western Christians, even in the liberal ecumenical establishment, do not think of South Africa and Israel simply as parallel cases. For one thing, they are painfully aware that both blacks and Jews have been the victims of Western Christian oppression in the form of slavery and anti-Semitism. For another, they condemn apartheid as a specifically Christian heresy, whereas they see Zionism as a legitimate expression of Jewish hope and therefore a subject for ecumenical dialogue.[1] From the Palestinian point of view, however, the Zionist regime in Israel is precisely analogous to the apartheid regime in South Africa: both are expressions of Western colonialism, states created through violence against indigenous populations. In both cases, furthermore, the oppressed indigenous peoples include many Christians. All of this makes it very difficult for Western Christians to know what their commitments ought to be in the case of Israel.

Thus it is important for Western Christians to listen to the voices of Jews and Palestinians, especially on those rare occasions when they are engaged in dialogue with each other. For the Christian critic, the voices and exchanges of Jewish critics like Michael Walzer and Palestinian critics like Edward Said, both of whom bring their commitment to their respective peoples with them into their work as critics, are particularly noteworthy. Walzer is Professor of Social Science at Princeton's Institute for Advanced Study, the author of such important works of political philosophy as *Just and Unjust Wars* (1977) and *Spheres of Justice* (1983). He is also a coeditor of *Dissent* magazine—the voice of democratic socialism in America—and a contributing editor for the *New Republic*. Said is known to the general public as the leading American spokesman for the Palestinian cause, appearing regularly in this capacity both in print and on network television. He is also Professor of English at Columbia University and one of the country's most prominent literary critics, the author of major books on literary theory and the culture of imperialism. His most influential books, however, are those in which he brings his talent as a literary critic to bear on Middle Eastern studies and news reporting, including *Orientalism* (1978) and *Covering Islam* (1981).[2] The exchange I am referring to (whether it was a true dialogue or not is a question we shall consider later) began when

Said reviewed Walzer's book *Exodus and Revolution* (1985) in 1986, a year before the *intifada* erupted in the occupied territories. In retrospect, their exchange can be seen as a kind of intellectual prelude to the uprising and Israel's attempts to suppress it.

Before turning to the substance of the exchange between Said and Walzer, however, it might be helpful to illustrate briefly the contrasting political styles of these two public intellectuals as well as the opposing modes of criticism they practice.[3] Consider, first of all, their uneasy responses to the threat of war in the Persian Gulf as the January 15, 1991, United Nations deadline for Iraqi withdrawal from Kuwait approached. Writing in *The New York Times*, Said declared himself to be opposed both to the Iraqi invasion and to a United States attack. The problem, he stated, is that "the fundamental reason for the huge buildup of U.S. and Iraqi forces has been virtually ignored" by both sides. That reason is not a clash of principles, such as resistance to naked aggression over and against the rights of the Palestinians, for example. Rather, the reason for the buildup is "a collision between the anachronistic but still powerful ideologies of Western imperialism and Arab nationalism." "Clearly," Said asserts, "the major reason for the American buildup and the increasing likelihood of war is that the U.S. still believes in its right to project its power where it pleases, for its own ends, wrapped in its own 'higher' morality and principles." Yet Iraq, and indeed all of the Arab nations, come in for an equal measure of Said's scorn. "It is as if Mr. Hussein had collected all the tattered remnants— anger at colonialism, despair at being unable to deal with the challenge of Israel, noble rhetoric about Arab honor—and forced them into a row of banners people will salute because there is little else to like or respect" in a world where "no Arab president or king is accountable to his people," where Arab "intellectuals, writers, artists" are compelled to "choose silence . . . or join the battle," and where "it was the Arab states that deserted the Palestinian intifada." In short, virtuous motives—motives that are virtuous in reality, not merely in appearance—can be attributed to neither side ("Tragic").

Where Said is impassioned and dogmatic, Walzer, writing in the *New Republic*, is cool and ambivalent. Rather than taking sides in the debate over U.S. military intervention, he asks, "Why are so many people, myself among them, so confused about the confrontation in the Gulf? The confusion is particularly obvious," he continues, "on what might be called the near left of the political spectrum, where people were not confused at all in the Vietnam years." Instead, it is "almost as if they believe that the right response this time is radical uncertainty." That uncertainty lurks in the gap between motive and deed. "What makes for confusion on the near left," Walzer explains, "is precisely that this would be a clean war, so obviously just that one wants to see it fought. And yet the consequences of fighting it are so uncertain that one hesitates to begin." Its "cleanness" lies in the fact that "to come to the aid of a victim of aggression" is one of "the classic just causes of warfare"; yet one hesitates because "the Middle East is a terribly volatile place to start a war." Unlike Said, Walzer makes no attempt to stand above the fray by condemning both sides from a rhetorically impartial stance. Instead, he defends the justice of the American cause, hesitating to endorse a war only out of purely prudential considerations. As he says himself, "I don't think [my] worries express a specifically moral anxiety. Perhaps they only express a lack of moral courage" ("Perplexed"). By comparison, Said's stance might seem to be the epitome of moral courage. Yet he, too, is not indifferent to prudential considerations. "A sobering look at the concretely terrible consequences of a war that seems ever more likely," he concludes, "might set a different course . . . for Americans and Arabs alike" ("Tragic"). On this point, at least, Walzer might have agreed.

In view of their difference in political style, it is not surprising that Walzer and Said prefer opposing modes of criticism. In keeping with his commitment to his Jewish heritage, Walzer practices a form of hermeneutics, inasmuch as he conceives of criticism as the interpretation of the best sense of the traditions of the community by one who is a member of that community.[4] To see how this form of hermeneutics works, consider an example of Walzer's criticism from *Exodus and Revolution*. Numbers 16 narrates the story of Korah, who rebels against the authority of Moses and Aaron and is swallowed alive by the earth. This text traditionally poses a problem for those who seek liberal sentiments in the Torah, for Korah's argument is appealingly democratic: "You have gone too far! For all the congregation are holy, every one of them, and the Lord is among them; why then do you exalt yourselves above the assembly of the Lord?" (16:3). Walzer clearly has some sympathy for Korah, "the first left oppositionist in the history of radical politics." Yet he continues to approach the text hermeneutically, reading between the lines in the Mosaic spirit of the Torah where its letter fails:

> Moses doesn't reply in the text, but it is easy to imagine what he would have said. His whole experience, in Egypt and the wilderness, forced upon him a powerful sense of the people's unholiness. Despite the covenant, Israel had still to become holy. . . . And that would require a long and painful struggle. Korah had experienced the great moment of deliverance and the enthusiasm of the original covenanting not as a promise of what might be in

the far future but as an immediate reality. . . . Everyone was holy who had shared the Sinai experience, and so there was no need for a leader or a priesthood. But that, Moses would have argued, makes holiness too easy, like milk and honey. In fact, it is a hard business.

Nevertheless, despite his evident suspicion of Korah's oppositionism, Walzer is no mere apologist for the text. He adds immediately, "We might worry, though, that it was now in the interests of the Levites to make it even harder than it was," and concludes, "Perhaps the only way to avoid such a priesthood is to reduce the rigor of the required performances, to make holiness and virtue less troublesome. . . . I suppose that this is the democratic way" (*Exodus* 111–13).

Walzer's skepticism regarding the Mosaic theocracy lends credibility to his hermeneutic reverence for the biblical text; together, these apparently conflicting attitudes make for a complex, balanced interpretation of the Korah narrative. Still, Walzer's reading overlooks the nuances of the text. Turning Korah into a "left oppositionist" challenging the legitimacy of the Levitical priesthood, Walzer ignores the fact that Korah is himself a Levite. Far from challenging the legitimacy of the Levitical priesthood, Korah seems to be preoccupied with the threat that Moses and Aaron pose to its privileges. Dathan and Abiram, the Reubenites, come closer, perhaps, to the utopian political rebels of whom Walzer is suspicious; but their quarrel is with Moses (whom they accuse of setting himself up as a "prince" [16:13]), not with the priests. Indeed, Numbers 16 may well be a composite narrative incorporating two different rebellions. As Robert Alter explains, "Perhaps . . . considerations of narrative coherence seemed less important to the writer than the need to assert thematically that the two separate events—the attempt to seize political power and the usurpation of sacerdotal function—comprised one archetypal rebellion and so must be told as one tale" (*Art* 136). Fortunately, Walzer's erroneous reading does not invalidate the substance of his interpretation, which is consistent with the general intention of the narrative.[5] But it does point up the potential hermeneutical danger of prematurely harmonizing the text.

That danger is precisely the sort of trap that Edward Said's method of criticism is designed to avoid. Eschewing hermeneutics as a form of religious apologetics, Said opts instead for the secularism of ideology critique, debunking systematically distorted discourse from the standpoint of those excluded from and misrepresented by such discourse.[6] *The Question of Palestine* (1979) contains an example of such critique that is, for American

Christians, particularly painful. In the wake of the 1946 bombing of British headquarters in Jerusalem's King David Hotel by Menachem Begin's Irgun, Reinhold Niebuhr, the leading Christian pro-Zionist in America, challenged British policy in Palestine. Acknowledging the Labour government's anxiety regarding Arab opinion, Niebuhr admitted,

> There is, I know, not sufficient consideration in America either of Arab rights or of the embarrassment of Britain in dealing with the Arab world. I find it baffling, on the other hand, that the average person here [in Britain] speaks of Arab "opinion" without suggesting that such opinion is limited to a small circle of feudal overlords, that there is no middle-class in this world and that the miserable masses are in such abject poverty that an opinion is an impossible luxury for them. One difficulty with the Arab problem is that the kind of technical and dynamic civilisation which the Jews might have helped to introduce and which should have the support of American capital . . . would not be acceptable to the Arab chieftains though beneficial to the Arab masses. It would therefore have to be imposed provisionally, but would have a chance of ultimate acceptance by the masses. (qtd. *Question* 31–32)

Here is Said's commentary on this paragraph:

> Whether before this piece was written or after it, Niebuhr could not have been found guilty of discussing, much less supporting, "Arab rights." He simply never did. His opening sentence, therefore, is little more than a rhetorical ploy for making his main point, that Arab opinion doesn't count (for the bogus sociological reasons he gives, as if masses didn't also need some piece of land on which to conduct their ignorance, backwardness, and decadence). Even that is not his *real* intention, which is nothing more than saying that whether they have an opinion or not, Arabs ought not to be allowed to obstruct the "technical and dynamic civilisation" being brought into Palestine by the European Jews. It might have been easier to make such a point if, for example, he could directly assert (a) that Arabs are sui generis inferior and (b) that they were simply the creatures, without will or opinion, of a hopelessly decadent, small, feudal class of "overlords" who manipulated the "masses" as so many puppets. Instead, Niebuhr chooses the more culturally valid form of statement, and says that his argument in reality is being made not merely on behalf of the "technical and dynamic civilisation" brought in by Zionism, but that it has the Arab masses in mind.

"Had Niebuhr been speaking about the South African situation," Said concludes, "no such condescension or racial implications would have been tolerated, which is a situation the more to be appreciated when we realize . . .

that Niebuhr believes himself to be expressing an advanced, or progressive, liberal view" (*Question* 32–33).

What are we to make of this argument? It is true, as Said points out, that Niebuhr ignored both the modern history of Palestine, with its many instances of mass uprising against Zionism and the failure of Zionists to aid Arab peasants, and the idea of Palestinian nationhood. The record of Niebuhr's pronouncements, furthermore, bears Said out. Even as he was condemning the Dutch Reformed Church in South Africa for using "an obscurantist version of the Christian faith to elaborate policies as inhumane as those of the Nazis" ("Church" 53), Niebuhr was comparing Nasser to Hitler and accusing the Eisenhower administration of "appeasement": "Just as Hitler before him, he [Nasser] achieved all his ends by inordinate demands" ("Stake" 12). In short, Said's critique lays bare the double standard implicit in Niebuhr's pro-Zionist ideology. Still, it is important to note an inconsistency in Said's argument. On the one hand, Said hears nothing but cynicism and hypocrisy in Niebuhr's rhetoric; his talk of uplifting the Arab masses is just a verbal smoke screen for racism and imperialism. Yet Said goes on to grant, more generously, that Niebuhr believes his view to be a liberal, progressive one. The problem is that Said can't have it both ways: either Niebuhr believes what he's saying, in which case he is indeed a liberal concerned (however ineffectually) with Arab rights; or he doesn't believe it, in which case he is not really a liberal at all. It is hard not to conclude that Said's criticism is itself governed by rhetorical considerations more urgent than mere consistency.

Exodus and Revolution—part storytelling, part *midrash*, part history of ideas, part political manifesto—is Walzer's homage to the traditional culture of the People of the Book, a culture in which it was natural for intellectuals to conduct political argument in the form of biblical commentary. As an intellectual and a democratic socialist in America, Walzer knows the limitations of the jargons of the academy and of Left politics. As a Jew and a Zionist, he knows the power—even for a Zionist in the secular tradition of Weizmann and Ben-Gurion—of the words of the biblical text. As a social critic and a public figure, he knows the value of bringing these styles together in popular form. I do not mean to suggest that *Exodus and Revolution* is a calculated book (though, as we shall see, that is what Edward Said thinks). On the contrary, no one who still shares in the culture of the Book can read Walzer without acknowledging his genuine reverence for the text and his belief that interpreting it in some sense shapes politics, rather than serving merely as a useful disguise for it. Books like *Exodus and Revolution* represent, I think, popular criticism at its best.

Walzer's method is to retrace the Exodus story, with its stages of bondage and liberation, covenant, wilderness, and Promised Land; his claim is that this story is the culturally specific paradigm of radical politics, from the Puritans to Marxism to national liberation movements in the Third World. But *Exodus and Revolution* has a polemical purpose as well, inasmuch as Walzer defends a secular, this-worldly interpretation of the Exodus narrative, as opposed to a religious, millenarian one. In political terms, his aim is to uphold a moderate, realistic version of social democracy—what he calls "Exodus politics"—against the utopian dreams of messianism, "the great temptation of Western politics" (135). For a socialist who is also a Zionist, the specific forms of messianic politics to be resisted include both the radical socialism of Lenin and Stalin and the radical Zionism of Begin and Shamir. The irony is that these avowedly secular political movements are rooted in a religious reading of the Exodus narrative, one that Walzer rejects as utopian. Yet it is clear that the kind of secular, realistic politics Walzer defends is not meant to be incompatible with religious belief. On the contrary, he thinks of such politics as consonant with the deepest religious values of the Jewish community.

At the same time, Walzer's version of radical politics is not compatible with a literalist reading of the biblical text. He admits that "every reading is also a construction, a reinvention of the past for the sake of the present" (x), and that his interpretation, "like all interpretations, . . . highlights some features of the account and neglects or suppresses others" (134). In particular, the account of the conquest of Canaan, while it fits well into the messianic politics of the South African Boers or the radical Zionists, has no place in the mainstream of "Exodus politics" in the West, where it "does not survive the work of interpretation." Hence Walzer relegates the problem of Canaanite genocide to a brief section of his conclusion, granting that in "the text as it stands" the Canaanites "are explicitly excluded from the world of moral concern," but noting that the Jewish settlement of the land ended in "a rough accommodation," that Yahweh would not approve such an accommodation with idolaters, and that, seen as "an extension of the struggles in the wilderness," "the divine commandment and the failure of the Israelites to fulfill the commandment are, both of them, further examples of biblical realism." He concludes by rebuking right-wing Zionists for espousing a fundamentalism at odds with traditional Judaism, which, "like Exodus politics itself, is not found in the text so much as in the interpretations of the text" (141–44). It is necessary to rise above those "tendencies in Jewish thought that we might think of as territorialist" and to see that "the deeper argument of the Exodus story is that righteousness is the only guarantee" (107).

Interestingly, Walzer makes no use here of the means offered by the Higher Criticism for recognizing the genocide commandment as the invention of a time long after the original settlement, or for explaining the violence of the settlement period in terms of class conflict rather than invasion.[7] To his credit, he does not deviate from his literary approach to the biblical text (an approach advocated most notably by Robert Alter, who praises *Exodus and Revolution* in a blurb on the dust jacket). Unfortunately, excluding the conquest of Canaan from the "main" Exodus narrative is bound to seem suspicious to anyone whose interpretation of that narrative includes the conquest as one of its main stages. This would include not only colonizing literalists like the Afrikaners and the radical Zionists, but also those whose land has been colonized, such as the Zulus and the Palestinians. For the colonizer, the biblical conquest of the Promised Land is part and parcel of a national-religious ideology that was central to the founding of a modern state. For the native inhabitant, on the other hand, it is the suppressed subtext of Canaanite experience that is the key to the Exodus narrative and to the self-understanding of an oppressed people. The history of colonialism thus belies Walzer's claim that the conquest account has been marginal in Western politics.

This is precisely the point made by Edward Said in his typically scathing review of Walzer's book, "Michael Walzer's *Exodus and Revolution*: A Canaanite Reading." Though not the first time Said had challenged Walzer in print, the review represents his most sustained engagement with Walzer's work to date.[8] Just as Walzer presents himself in the book as both philosopher and Jew, so Said writes as both critic and Palestinian, denouncing Israel while bringing the Foucauldian analysis of discursive power to bear on Walzer's text. In doing so, he is continuing the project begun in *Orientalism:* the exposure of the tactics by which the West controls discourse about the Middle East, determining what can be said and who is permitted to speak. For Said, Walzer is first and foremost a member of a Zionist intellectual elite whose privileged position in the American media enables them to disseminate pro-Israeli propaganda under the guise of disinterested scholarship. By debunking such scholarship, Said hopes to open up a discursive space for the voices of Palestinians.[9]

Yet it is not just Walzer's book that Said sets out to debunk. As Mark Krupnick observes, Said could have met Walzer half-way by arguing "that modern-day Israel is unworthy of its biblical precursor. But he takes a different tack, trying to discredit the story of Exodus itself" ("Edward" 23). This approach is somewhat surprising in light of what Said tells us about his upbringing in his most autobiographical book, *After the Last Sky: Palestinian Lives* (1986). The Said family lived in Palestine, then a British mandate, until the Palestinian diaspora preceding the 1948 "war of independence." (Subsequently, Said learned, Martin Buber occupied the family home in Jerusalem until his death.) Said was raised a devout Anglican; despite the "dry Protestant atmosphere," he tells us, he feels a certain nostalgia for his pious childhood. He goes on to describe his grandmother:

> She was a literalist when it came to the Bible—it was God's word—but for her, as for us as children, it was the story that mattered, the exchanges between Moses and Pharaoh, Joseph and Potiphar's wife, Jesus and Pilate, exchanges that she led up to carefully and then rendered with a burning fidelity to the unadorned truth of how people—not plumed saints or imaginary heroes—could stand up for what they took to be right and just. Each of the narrations of the climactic scenes she did so well would invariably begin with the homely admonition "Now look here," and indeed we could look and be able to see plain men and women engaged in telling and speaking, exactly as we told and spoke.   (154–55)

One might have expected Said to come away from such formative literary experiences with a lasting reverence for biblical narrative. Indeed, the obvious emotion in his language suggests that such reverence has not wholly disappeared. Yet in his review of Walzer's book, he dismisses Exodus contemptuously as an "ideological text" (169).

At some point, Said must have realized that the stories told by his grandmother were the stories of her oppressors, written by the ancestors of the Jewish settlers and interpreted by the clerics of the British Empire's state church. Krupnick coins the term "discourse envy" to describe Said's frustration over the fact that his enemies turned out to have all the good stories. Whether this is fair or not, Krupnick rightly sees that Said's special scorn for Exodus is linked to a general theory of the relation between narrative and political power. In an essay called "Permission to Narrate," Said argues that "facts do not at all speak for themselves, but require a socially acceptable narrative to absorb, sustain, and circulate them." Thus "the idea of a Palestinian homeland would have to be enabled by the prior acceptance of a narrative entailing a homeland." The problem is that "Palestine is a privileged site of origin and return for both Judaism and Christianity" and is thus inscribed with "a Western master narrative, highlighting Jewish alienation and redemption," whereas "the archive speaks of the depressed condition of Palestinian narrative at present" (34–38). Krupnick suggests that this depressed condition is due in part to the fact that the Palestinians do not have "a sacred text of their own, like Exodus, to memorialize an original covenant between a people and its god" ("Edward" 23–24). But Said no longer has any use for sacred texts; otherwise he might have turned to the Koran, a non-Western master narrative that also privileges Palestine. The truth is that Said wants Palestine to be free to develop its own, secular narrative.

One can see, then, why Said feels the need to discredit both Walzer and the Exodus narrative itself. He challenges not only Walzer's reading of Exodus as the paradigm for revolutionary politics, but also his right to call his own politics radical or progressive, concluding that *Exodus and Revolution* and indeed all of Walzer's work is little more than a thinly veiled apology for whatever Israel does. Not only does it seem "unlikely to expect that the kind of secular and decent politics Walzer salvages from Exodus could coexist with the authority of the sole Divinity plus the derivative but far more actual authority of His designated human representatives," but Walzer himself "offers no detailed, explicit, or principled resistance to the irreducibly sectarian premises of Exodus" ("Michael" 166–67). In regard to Walzer's interpretation of the conquest of Canaan, for example, Said finds Walzer

> unperturbed that for the Jews "the Canaanites are explicitly excluded from the world of moral concern." This does not suggest a very elevated model for realistic politics, and it isn't clear how the dehumanization of anyone standing in Moses's way is any less appalling than the attitudes . . . of the founders of apartheid. To say that "thou shalt utterly destroy them" is a command that "doesn't survive the work of interpretation . . . ." is, I regret to say, to take no note of history after the destruction of the Temple in which Jews were in no position at all to collectively implement the commandment. Therefore, I think, it is Walzer who is wrong, not "the right-wing Zionists" in today's Israel whom he upbraids for being too fundamentalist. The text of Exodus does categorically enjoin victorious Jews to deal unforgivingly with their enemies, the prior native inhabitants of the Promised Land. As to whether that should be "a gradual infiltration" or "a systematic campaign of extermination," the fundamental attitude is similar in both alternatives: get rid of the natives, as a practical matter. In either case, Israel's offending

non-Jewish population is "excluded from the world of moral concern" and
thus denied equal right with Jews.   ("Michael" 167)

After such passionate words on behalf of the victimized Canaanites, Walzer's apology for the conquest narrative begins to sound a bit hollow. But,
as is so often the case when militant intellectuals take the moral high
ground, accuracy suffers. Walzer is correct to point out that Said "repeatedly credits me with the opinions I oppose—as if he can't believe . . . that
I really oppose them" (Walzer and Said, "Exchange" 248). As we have
seen, Walzer readily admits that the text means what it says when the Canaanites are "explicitly excluded from the world of moral concern," and he
is greatly perturbed when Jewish fundamentalists take the text as a justification for present-day Israeli territorialism. Indeed, that is why he wrote
Exodus and Revolution in the first place, insisting that it is not the text but
its interpretation that constitutes the real Jewish tradition. As for the post-
exilic beginnings of such interpretation, Said obviously means to imply
that the Jews only began to discount the genocide commandment when self-
interest necessitated such a strategy. But he ignores the ethical content of
the Jewish tradition that so impressed him as a child, denying it the moral
resourcefulness to overcome its own excesses through self-criticism. This
same assumption that racism is the primary motive governing Jewish behavior prevents Said from acknowledging any moral difference between
peaceful settlement and genocide.

After defending himself against such distortions, Walzer goes on the
offensive, attacking Said for failing to dissociate himself from PLO terrorism. Understandably, Said responds in kind, counterattacking Walzer for
failing to dissociate himself from Israeli human rights abuses. Exodus
quickly drops out of the picture altogether as the critics accuse each other
of "just going along with one's own people for the sake of loyalty and
'connectedness' " (Walzer and Said, "Exchange" 250–51). Said's reply is
notable for its extremely vituperative tone, unusual in criticism even in
these days of cultural warfare between conservative humanists and radical
postmodernists. The exchange ends with Said insisting that Walzer express
"compassion and atonement," dismissing him as "a small frightened man
who is completely unequal to the question of Canaan-Palestine, and barely
adequate for the easier bits of Exodus" (259). (Apparently compassion is
required only of Zionists.) It is hard not to see in this animosity the discursive equivalent of the *intifada*, with Said lobbing verbal rocks at Walzer,
who resents being pelted and is inclined to rely on the police, whose strong-

arm tactics he has never approved of, until the attack is over. One's final impression of the whole exchange is that American intellectuals are no more capable than Middle Eastern politicians of participating in true dialogue, the necessary prelude to any peaceful resolution of the conflict.

This failure of genuine dialogue is all the more disappointing in light of the fact that Walzer and Said agree, apparently, on a practical first step in resolving the conflict: the partition of Palestine. True, Said attacks the idea of partition in his reply to Walzer, asking, "What, other than divine injunction and military strength, gives him the right to recommend the partition of Palestine against the wishes of its majority [i.e. its original Palestinian] inhabitants? Are binationalism and pluralism so contemptible as goals . . . ?" (Walzer and Said, "Exchange" 254). This is not the first time that Said has expressed a preference for a secular democratic state embracing both Jews and Palestinians. At the same time, he has indicated that he would support partition should it come as the result of direct negotiation between Israel and the PLO, which is the official PLO position.[10] But Walzer, he thinks, does not believe in negotiation with the PLO, let alone binationalism in Israel. Walzer is certainly highly critical of the PLO, but so far as I know he does not oppose negotiation.[11] As for binationalism, it is true that Walzer wants Israel to remain, in some sense, a Jewish state: "Little Israel" alongside "littler Palestine." But that state ought to be, by the very fact of its Jewishness, a liberal, pluralistic state, with the rights of its Arab minority guaranteed. Indeed, Walzer goes so far as to say that "Jews who are fully aware of their own (Diaspora) history might well come to identify with the Arabs rather than with the Jews of Greater Israel" ("What Kind" 128).

In short, Walzer and Said are not as far apart on the shape of a workable political settlement as the rancor of their exchange over Exodus would suggest—far closer, certainly, than the demonized figures with which they unfairly link each other, such as Habash and Kahane. Why then are they unwilling to trust each other's sincerity and acknowledge their common ground, rather than volleying the charge of "just going along with one's own people for the sake of loyalty and connectedness?" Clearly, the answer is complicated and involves more than the hard facts of Middle Eastern politics. It also involves, as Said puts it, "unresolved problems about the role of intellectuals, about canonical texts concerning religion and tradition, about contemporary realities and ancient ideologies"—in short, the politics of criticism (Walzer and Said, "Exchange" 253–54). As one sifts through the hostile charges and countercharges of the debate, one finds two very different sets of assumptions regarding the role of the committed critic. It is tempting to see in the Walzer-Said exchange a classic instance of the difference Walzer discusses in his latest book, *The Company of Critics* (1988), namely, the difference between the critic connected with a particular people and committed to its religious and cultural traditions, and the alienated, cosmopolitan critic, committed only to reason and to humankind in general, who has severed all special connections to his people. Walzer identifies himself with the first type of critic, and Said, as an exile and a secular rationalist, seems to exemplify the second type.

Obviously, however, Said is every bit as "connected" as Walzer, if not more so. As a Palestinian nationalist, he would certainly agree with Walzer that "there are times when connection, for all its dangers, is morally necessary" (Walzer and Said, "Exchange" 251). Indeed, at the end of "Permission to Narrate," Said reproaches his friend Noam Chomsky, perhaps the most outspoken Jewish-American critic of Israel, for his "history-transcending universal rationalism." Only the "sense of communal or collective commitment" that "national narratives authorize and represent," Said insists, can motivate action on behalf of the Palestinians; Chomsky's facts alone will not suffice (47). Here Said sounds very much like Walzer, agreeing that the critic ought to be connected with a specific people and their fate. But this agreement doesn't go very far. "The real question . . . ," according to Walzer, "is how one works out the connection. No, says Said, the real question is, to whom is one connected? The only morally safe course is to be one of the 'Canaanites'—as if oppression always made for virtue." "Even the oppressed need their critics," Walzer concludes (Walzer and Said, "Exchange" 251–52). To this Said replies, "What Walzer cannot see is that there is a considerable moral difference between the connectedness of a critic with an oppressing society, and a critic whose connection is to an *oppressed* one" (253).

With this point we have reached the moral crux of the argument. For Walzer, all critics must be judged by the same standard—the ability to maintain that difficult balance between connection and opposition to one's people, whether oppressing or oppressed. To fail to oppose one's people is to cease to be a critic; to sever one's connection with one's people is to render one's opposition ineffectual. For Said, on the other hand, this balance is, in the case of a critic connected with the oppressors, illusory; such opposition will merely be co-opted so long as the connection is independently maintained. The critic who is connected to an oppressed people has, therefore, an a priori moral advantage. Who is right? The question, it seems to me, is an empirical one. History teaches that the oppressed are perfectly capable of becoming oppressors in their turn; one need look no further than the state of Israel itself for a classic example. Surely Walzer is right to fear that the Palestinians might, given the opportunity, behave likewise. As for the effects of connected criticism on oppressing societies, recent changes in the Soviet empire suggest that *glasnost*, whatever its original purpose, was something more than a means of co-opting internal opposition, as the peoples of Eastern Europe will gladly testify. Perhaps there are cases in which a society is so evil that any connection with it is culpable— Nazi Germany, for example, or the apartheid regime in South Africa, though even here one hesitates to condemn good critics whose opposition does not entail breaking the connection altogether. For these reasons, among others, I think Walzer is right: justice depends on how the critic works out his or her connection, something that can only be determined empirically in each particular case.

This holds true, I have just suggested, even for a critic whose connection is with a society as oppressive as that of South Africa. Take the case of Alan Paton, who tried consistently to work out his connection to his country in terms of the Christianity he shared with the creators and defenders of the apartheid regime. Looking back on Paton's life and work, J. M. Coetzee argues that he must, as a writer and social critic, be judged a failure. That failure was not a failure of ideals, for Paton's liberalism was, Coetzee admits, an honorable one. His failure was rather a failure of insight, an inability to understand the psychologies that made his liberal ideals impracticable. This failure of insight shows itself, Coetzee suggests, in the gap between the anguished eloquence of *Cry, the Beloved Country* (1948) and Paton's "politics of innocence," in which "a Christian commitment to non-violence co-existed, not entirely easily, with an implacable detestation of apartheid and a hawkish anti-communism" ("Too Late" 39–40). This peculiar combination of political attitudes led Paton to distrust the revolutionary nationalism of the ANC, to stake his hopes on an accommodation with Chief Buthelezi, and to oppose economic sanctions. "I don't understand," he once wrote to Archbishop Tutu, "how your Christian conscience allows you to advocate disinvestment" (qtd. Coetzee, "Too Late" 40). Even if Coetzee is right about Paton, however, the question remains as to whether the post-Christian conscience can serve as midwife in the birth of a just and peaceful South Africa. The remorseless killing in the townships, together with the threat of impending civil war, suggests that the commitment to nonviolence shared by Paton and Archbishop Tutu is not as naive as Coetzee implies.

It is still too early to say whether Walzer's criticism of Israel will prove to be any more effective than Paton's criticism of South Africa. One must be careful to distinguish between effectiveness and insight, something that Coetzee does not do very explicitly. He means to imply, I think, that Paton's social criticism was ineffective because it lacked insight. But more insightful critics might be just as ineffective because of circumstances beyond their control. Had Mandela died in prison, for example, his social criticism might have been judged as ineffective as Paton's. Yet one suspects that Coetzee would still have regarded Mandela as the more insightful critic; after all, it was largely as a result of Mandela's criticism that Paton and the Liberal Party embraced universal suffrage and began to engage in nonparliamentary political action.[12] The point I am trying to make is simply that a social critic ought to be judged by evaluating specific insights and effects in specific times and places. Said fails to do this because his theory of criticism predisposes him to find Walzer, as a critic connected with an oppressive society, guilty as charged.

Moreover, Walzer, like Paton, tries to work out his connection with his people by means of a hermeneutical dialogue with their sacred text, a critical method the dogmatically secular Said refuses to take seriously. Any interpretation that recognizes the authority of such texts, he assumes, is merely ideological. This is unfortunate, if only because it means that the Islamic tradition goes unrepresented in the Exodus debate. Said laments the fact that "*jihad* and Islamic law have the reactive force to stimulate young men and women for such suicidal struggle as the politics of secular liberation has never dreamed of" (*After* 153). But, as Walzer points out, Said "has made no effort to engage the religious fervor of contemporary Muslim Arabs, while *Exodus and Revolution* is at least an effort at engagement with the religious fervor of contemporary Jews" (Walzer and Said, "Exchange" 250). More to the point, Said's strident secularism prevents him from imagining how the Bible itself might speak for the Palestinians. Martin Buber's struggle for a binational state in Israel, for example, cannot be understood apart from his study of the development of the prophetic faith of the ancient Hebrews, which culminates in Deutero-Isaiah's vision of a new *tsadeqah* (order of nations) based on *mishpat* or justice (*Prophetic* 202f). Indeed, Said himself makes unacknowledged rhetorical use of the sacred texts he repudiates when he demands "compassion and atonement" from Walzer. What Said refuses to admit is that these powerful moral concepts are rooted in the monotheistic traditions he refuses to distinguish from their fundamentalist parodies.

I want to conclude by imagining the kind of ecumenical dialogue Walzer

and Said might have initiated had Said shared Walzer's hermeneutical attitude toward sacred narrative. Consider the Exodus story of young Moses'
slaying of an Egyptian:

> One day, when Moses had grown up, he went out to his people and looked
> on their burdens; and he saw an Egyptian beating a Hebrew, one of his
> people. He looked this way and that, and seeing no one he killed the Egyp-
> tian and hid him in the sand. When he went out the next day, behold, two
> Hebrews were struggling together; and he said to the man that did the
> wrong, "Why do you strike your fellow?" He answered, "Who made you a
> prince and a judge over us? Do you mean to kill me as you killed the Egyp-
> tian?" Then Moses was afraid, and thought, "Surely the thing is known."
> When Pharaoh heard of it, he sought to kill Moses.   (2 : 11–15)

Quoting verses 11–12 only, Walzer suggests that "there exists in the text
an argument about the moral and psychological effects of oppression," especially the internalization of "servitude and slavishness." But this argument must be discovered through sympathetic interpretation. On the basis
of the text alone, "we might think that Moses simply wanted to make sure
that he was not seen; killing a taskmaster would be a serious crime in the
house of bondage." Walzer, however, sides with the rabbis who refused to
accept this somewhat unflattering account of Moses's motives. They argued
that "when Moses looked this way and that way, he was looking for an
Israelite ready to intercede and defend the beaten slave; he was looking for
a *real* man, a proud and rebellious spirit" (*Exodus* 44–45).

This is an appealing political reading of the text, and Said might well
have pointed out that it puts young Moses on an equal footing with the
young Palestinians of the present-day *intifada*. By omitting the rest of the
pericope, however, Walzer misses the ethical core of the narrative and its
application to contemporary Middle Eastern politics. It is crucial that the
second struggle, which Walzer ignores, involves not a Hebrew and an
Egyptian but two Hebrews, and that Moses's response is very different
from his response to the earlier beating. Walzer might answer that the
second struggle merely further dramatizes his theme; it is a well-known
psychological fact that the oppressed person tends to sublimate hatred for
the oppressor into hostility toward his fellows, and Moses rightly protests
the futility of such internal dissension. This, too, is politically appealing,
yet it misses the moral force of the guilty man's questions. The point is that
Moses, by killing the Egyptian, has lost moral authority within his own
community. Having resorted to a cowardly murder in the case of the Egyptian, he is hardly in a position to serve as a mediator between his fellow

Hebrews or to restrain their wrongdoing. It does not matter that the Egyptian is one of the oppressors while the Hebrew wrongdoer is one of the oppressed; justice demands that they be treated in kind. It is not until Moses learns this that he is able to lead his people to freedom, confronting Pharaoh with the courage of genuine righteousness.

At this point Said (or Walzer for that matter) might have introduced Sura 28 of the Koran, Al-Qasas (The Story), which contains a slightly different version of the same episode:

> One day he entered the town unnoticed by the people and found two men fighting, the one of his own race, the other an enemy. The Israelite appealed for Moses' help against his enemy, so that Moses struck him with his fist and killed him. "This is the work of Satan," said Moses. "He is the sworn enemy of man and seeks to lead him astray. Forgive me, Lord, for I have sinned against my soul."
>
> And Allah forgave him; for he is the Forgiving One, the Merciful. He said: "By the favour You have shown me, Lord, I vow that I will never lend a helping hand to a wrong-doer."
>
> Next morning, as he was walking in the town in fear and caution, the man he had helped the day before cried out to him again for help. "Clearly," said Moses, "you are a quarrelsome man."
>
> And when Moses was about to lay his hands on their enemy, the Egyptian said, "Moses, would you kill me as you killed that wretch yesterday? You are surely seeking to be a tyrant in this land, not an upright man." (76)

Before Moses can reply, someone comes running "from the other side of town" to warn him that "the elders" are plotting against his life. As in the biblical version, the young Moses is shown to lack the moral authority of a just political leader. This time, however, it is an innocent Egyptian victim who brings this point home. It is also crucial that the wrongdoer, a Hebrew, is the same man in both cases, and that both times his victims are Egyptians. The Koranic account thus turns on the idea that the oppressed can act unjustly toward their oppressors.

For Moses, the dilemma is whether to be "an upright man" or to indulge the racial and political passions that lead to tyranny. The fact that he breaks his solemn vow to Allah in order to abet his fellow countryman's wrongdoing a second time indicates just how high such passions run in the house of bondage. Restraining that part of one's soul which automatically sympathizes with "quarrelsome" associates is part of what political leadership requires in such a situation, and Moses is not yet prepared to exercise such restraint. And if he cannot do so in Egypt, how will he be able to do so in the Promised Land, where quarrelsome associates will have the power to oppress in their turn? The point is not that Moses must suppress his natural sympathy for his people in order to attain a standpoint of perfect impartiality; neither Exodus nor Al-Qasas recognizes such a possibility. The point, rather, is that the attainment of moral reciprocity vis-à-vis the Other is the highest expression of that sympathy, and therefore a precondition for political leadership. Without such reciprocity, the cycle of oppression is bound to repeat itself. With it, dialogue becomes possible—and perhaps, someday, an approximation of *shalom*.

POSTSCRIPT, SEPTEMBER 1993

Since the time of the Gulf War, when the first published version of this essay was completed, events in the Middle East have happily rendered its original context obsolete.[13] With the signing of the peace accord between Israel and the PLO, *shalom* seems more proximate than anyone thought possible in the winter of 1991.

As for Said and Walzer, the rapprochement in Palestine has caused the two social critics to undergo a curious reversal of public roles, with Said denouncing Arafat's leadership and Walzer urging the PLO chief to establish his authority over Gaza and Jericho, by force if necessary. Said was the first to respond to the news of the accord, bluntly telling a reporter, "You can't have peace between a servant and a master" (qtd. Terry A8). Later, while insisting that he "still believe[s] in a two-state solution peacefully arrived at," Said condemned both the accord itself and the process by which it was achieved. For those who remain in the occupied territories, he objects, the plan "leaves Palestinians very much the subordinates, with Israel still in charge." As "for the more than 50 percent of the Palestinian people not resident in the occupied territories, the plan may be the final dispossession." In addition, Said laments the undemocratic character of the negotiation process itself. "Our struggle is about freedom and democracy," he asserts, and "for a long time . . . it was fairly democratic." But now "Arafat has canceled the intifada unilaterally," transforming the PLO "from a national liberation movement into a kind of small-town government, with the same handful of people in command" (Said, "Arafat's Deal").

Defending the peace accord in the pages of the *New Republic,* Walzer quotes this last remark of Said's as evidence that "militants and ideologues" will reject the plan on the grounds that "it is not instant statehood." Walzer's response is to draw an analogy with Israel itself: "So the Jewish

Agency in the 1930s and 40s took on many of the responsibilities of a small-town government, ran the occupation for the British (so far as Palestine's Jews were concerned)—and established itself as Britain's successor." But before the Palestinians can do likewise, he adds, their leaders "will have to learn what only the best of Israel's leaders [Rabin and Peres?] know: that it is better to rule justly in one small town than to march in triumph through the cities of one's neighbors (which is, I suspect, the secret fantasy of these militants)." Unfortunately, the moral force of Walzer's proverb is diminished, in a way that is not entirely uncharacteristic of Walzer's pronouncements on the Palestinian question, by the gratuitous parenthetical remark. He goes on to propose what he calls "a useful political maxim: no nationalist movement that has deliberately inspired fear in its neighbors—practiced terrorism, threatened their very survival—should be awarded sovereignty until it has found some way of reassuring those same people" ("On the Road" 23, 26). One can imagine Said's outraged response: What, other than brute force, gives the state of Israel the right to "award" sovereignty to the people it has dispossessed?

Moreover, Walzer's maxim cuts both ways; it is not clear that the maxim would legitimate the sovereignty of Israel itself. The question thus arises, Is it fair for the Israelis to hold the Palestinian nationalists to a standard of conduct that the Israelis themselves may have violated in their own pursuit of nationhood? Walzer, of course, does not claim moral authority for his maxim, only political practicality. On that score, he is probably right: international diplomacy is not governed by moral considerations. But for those who care about the morality of politics, the question of fairness remains. Perhaps all we can say is that the Palestinians will be making a courageous sacrifice in giving up their claim to strict justice in order to pursue a peace that holds the promise of greater justice in the future.

Notes

Introduction: New Conversations on Postcolonial Literature (Gallagher)

1. Jameson's essay originally appeared in *Social Text* with the title "Third World Literature in an Era of Multinational Capitalism." It was later reprinted in a collection entitled *The Current in Criticism*, with the new title, "World Literature in an Age of Multinational Capitalism." I am quoting from this reprint, pp. 141–42.

2. Katrak, 159. For a critical rebuttal to Jameson, see Ahmad; for Jameson's rejoinder, see Jameson, "A Brief Response."

3. See Darby 1–3 and Boahen.

4. For instances of this criticism, see Parker, and Rich.

5. Key texts in African versions of these debates include Achebe, *Morning Yet on Creation Day;* Appiah; and Ngũgĩ, *Decolonising.*

6. See Miller, and Darby 38.

7. The phrase is Wolterstorff's (*Until* 4). See also Walzer's *The Revolution of the Saints,* which contrasts the proactive Calvinist position to the separatist Christianity that characterized a medieval understanding of God (1–113).

1. Biblical Ideas of Justice in Postcolonial Fiction (Block)

1. In the *New Catholic Encyclopedia,* theologian Bernard Häring offers these further, related definitions of justice: "The complete integration of love and justice is the chief characteristic of Christian moral doctrine besides its Christocentric orientations. It is through love of God and neighbor that the kingdom of God is achieved within us" (68). "In the Biblical-theological view, justice among men deserves the name of justice in the full sense only if it is accomplished with a view toward God in that love and thanksgiving and obedience are owed to God absolutely" (69).

2. In an interview, Vargas Llosa alludes to a biblical dimension in the story, commenting that the novel was written "against revolutionary utopias—that is a symbol for the misdirection of a generation. . . . Indeed the idea of a socialistic

revolution has deep roots in Latin America. It has to do with the messianic tradition that has been anchored here for centuries, since the time of the Spanish Catholics. It has to do with belief" (Interview 17, 18; my trans.) Though he tries to distance himself from the "messianic tradition" of the "Spanish Catholics," that tradition speaks through both the form and content of his work.

3. "Hope" is an idea (if not an explicit word) continually in one's mind as one reads these works. It is significant that a number of postcolonial writers incorporate Marxist theorist Ernst Bloch's enigmatic notion of "hope" in their works.

4. Speech at Marquette University, Milwaukee, Wisconsin, April 1992.

5. A substantially different version of this essay appears in *Literature and the Bible*. Ed. David Bevan. Rodopi Perspectives on Modern Literature 9. Atlanta: Rodopi, 1993.

2. Ernesto Cardenal's *Salmos* (DeHay)

1. *Tocar* 46. This and all subsequent translations from Spanish to English are my own.

2. For a more detailed discussion of Cardenal's use of the Psalms as a historical reinforcement, see Ojeda.

3. References to Cardenal's *Salmos* will be made in the text by the number of the poem, in this case *Salmo* 16. All translations here are my own. An English translation of the *Salmos*—*The Psalms of Struggle and Liberation*—was published in 1971 (McAnay). Translations of individual *Salmos* have also appeared in various publications.

3. Biblical Justice and the Military Hero in García Márquez
(Morales-Gudmundsson)

1. *El coronel no tiene quien le escriba* (1961) was first published in English as *No One Writes to the Colonel* in 1968. The first English edition of *El otoño del patriarca* (1975) appeared as *The Autumn of the Patriarch* in 1976. Subsequent references are made parenthetically to these English editions.

2. Minta has carefully researched Colombian political history. Quoting James Payne, he states, "On a scale of political deaths per generation, Colombia has one of the highest levels of political conflict in the world" (5–6). In the first century of its independence, Colombia went through thirteen periods of violent political strife, some lasting four to five years. R. W. Ramsey, according to Minta, called this prolonged struggle the "western hemisphere's largest internal war in the twentieth century [which has] led to 1/4 of a million deaths" (6).

3. Janes aptly summarizes the novelist's political optimism: "García Márquez calls himself a revolutionary socialist, and it might be said that his confidence in the eventual triumph of a socialism that permits the bourgeois liberty of the imagination is as chimerical as levitating with cups of chocolate: neither seems to be occurring in the immediate present . . . . But the belief in a future order that is to transcend the present, curing all our social, political, and economic ills, freed him

from the internal compulsion and the external obligation to render those ills in a realistic mode, while the belief in the necessity of such a transformation keeps him anchored in our world where those ills are all too apparent" (9).

4. Gen. 1:2; Job 9:5−14; Ps. 74:12−17; 89:10−15; and Isa. 51:9−11. Forsyth traces the combat myth in the Bible from its pagan source through St. Augustine's "Genesis." The conflict between God and the adversary is a common thread that runs through the entire Bible into later Christian theology. In that context, the appearance of the dragon in the sea is a common combat image (44−66). Prophetic literature portrays nations as beasts that arise out of the tumultuous "sea," a reference to peoples or multitudes (Dan. 7:2−7, 16−17; Rev. 13:1). The sea as "mythological enemy" (Forsyth 256) and as peoples serves the novelist well as a means to contextualize the final triumph of justice. It also allows him to do what the Book of Revelation does: it lets him project political repression onto the cosmic stage (Forsyth 257) in order to work out the apocalyptic victory of good over evil.

4. Isabel Allende's Mechanism for Justice (Kovach)

1. Allende's novel was published in Spain in 1982 as *La casa de los espíritus* and was translated by Magda Bogin in 1986 as *The House of the Spirits*. In this essay I will cite the English edition.

2. Specifically, in his discussion of the modern distinction between self and soul, Dunne includes an explanation of the transformation required for such integration: "appropriating the God of Jesus, sharing in his relationship to God." This process includes building a "trust relationship" with God and communicating to others what one receives from God. A human being who succeeds in achieving these two steps "is not making himself so much as discovering himself, and thus receiving himself and his life as a gift in the very moment of giving everything away to others. He is, in fact, becoming himself, for this process is that in which the basic dimensions of human life, thought, feeling, and action are integrated" (222−23).

3. Scriptural stories repeatedly describe people who struggle with their God, with nature, with others: Ps. 51:1 supplies an instance of why the self should seek reconciliation with God; Ps. 33:5−6 shows an example of how God's love is revealed in all creation; Luke 23:34 gives an example of Jesus' desire for reconciliation with his enemies.

4. For a discussion of *shalom*, see the introduction to this volume.

5. Isa. 1:27 (NRSV). Translations other than the NRSV exchange the word "righteousness" with the word "integrity." The Jerusalem Bible, for example, makes this choice in this quotation from Isaiah. Often truth, honesty, righteousness, and integrity are juxtaposed and positioned in syntactic parallelism to emphasize the inner conversion required for justice to be attained; see, for example, various translations of Isa. 59:14−15, Job 27:2−6, and Ps. 7:6−8.

6. Richard McCallister describes at length how etymological meanings, textual

relationships, and historical/social/personal allusions in the novel provide a prophetic *nomenklatura* to "declare not only the nature, but also the destiny of each character and . . . of Chile itself" (30).

5. Julio Cortázar's Literature of Embodiment (Zamora)

1. See Weschler, Simpson and Bennett, and Dworkin; Beverley and Zimmerman discuss the political function of literature in Central America and its expressive relations to abusive regimes.

2. Unpublished interview with the author, 2 March 1983, Mexico City.

3. Cortázar's essays on contemporary sculpture, dance, photography, and painting are collected in *Territorios*.

4. Critical note has been taken of Cortázar's early reference to Merleau-Ponty's theory of language; see Castro-Klarén, Boldy (101–02; 117–18), and Alazraki (48, 51). There is as yet no critical discussion of Cortázar's and Merleau-Ponty's philosophical and aesthetic affinities.

5. See González Bermejo (136) for Cortázar's use of the term *permeability*.

6. I have discussed the apocalypticism in this story, and in Cortázar's work generally, in Zamora (76–96). Harlow considers the story's apocalypticism but concludes somewhat opaquely that it is "less apocalypse than it is history" (*Resistance* 79).

7. Some of the Solentiname paintings are reproduced in *The Gospel in Art by the Peasants in Solentiname* (Scharper and Scharper); see also Ferlinghetti and Cardenal, *El evangelio*.

8. Steinberg's emphasis in his indispensable study, *The Sexuality of Christ in Renaissance Art and in Modern Oblivion*, differs from mine, but he too is concerned with the depiction of Christ's humanity. He argues that beginning in the mid-thirteenth and continuing until the end of the sixteenth centuries, visual representations of Christ's sexuality are founded in the theology of the bodied Word. In its explicit depiction of incarnational theology, Steinberg argues that "we may take Renaissance art to be the first and last phase of Christian art that can claim full Christian orthodoxy" (72). My own argument suggests that Latin American depictions of Christ's suffering, if not explicitly sexual, escape "the modern oblivion" to which Steinberg's title refers.

9. The Brazilian film *Oue bom te ver viva* (*How Nice to See You Alive*, 1989), directed by Lucia Murat, treats the isolation of the survivors of torture and the ethical problems of torture narratives.

10. Among the works that comprise *la literatura de denuncia* are Reinaldo Arenas's *Cantando en el pozo* (*Singing in the Well*, 1982), José Donoso's *Casa de campo* (*House in the Country*, 1978), Angelina Muñiz-Huberman's short fiction in *Huerto Cerrado* (*Enclosed Garden*, 1985), Isabel Allende's *La casa de los espíritus* (*The House of the Spirits*, 1982) and *De amor y de sombra* (*Of Love and Shadows*, 1984), Elvira Orphee's *La última conquista de El Angel* (*El Angel's Last Conquest*, 1983), Osvaldo Soriano's *No habrá más penas ni olvido* (translated as *A Dirty Little War*,

1980), and Humberto Constantini's *La larga noche de Francisco Sanctis* (*The Long Night of Francisco Sanctis*, 1981).

11. Another version of this essay appears in *Literature and the Bible*. Ed. David Began. Rodopi Perspectives on Modern Literature 9. Atlanta: Rodopi, 1993.

6. Eastman, Black Elk, and the Construction of Religious Identity
(Monsma)

1. For more information on Eastman's life, see Wilson.

2. For studies of the role of the "Indian" in American mythology and ideology, see Berkhofer, Fiedler, Jennings, Pearce, Segal and Stineback, and Slotkin.

3. For a concise summary of scholarship on *Black Elk Speaks* and an exploration of its Lakota literary forms, see Wong.

7. The Search for a Language of Justice (Hawley)

1. In Africa, an interesting theology of liberation is being written by the Cameroonian Jean-Marc Éla, and in Asia by Aloysius Pieris, among others.

2. "God does not look for mute co-workers; God wants the words of Job. Because we, though a critical people, critical even of God, lack our own words, Job is our spokesman" (Schöckel 597).

3. An earlier version of this essay appeared as "José María Arguedas, Ngũgĩ wa Thiong'o, and the Search for a Language of Justice" (*Pacific Coast Philology* 27.1–2 [1992]: 69–76).

8. The Dialogical Imagination of Chinua Achebe (Gallagher)

1. One major source of uncertainty lies in the question of the authorship of certain disputed texts, such as *Marxism and the Philosophy of Language*, attributed to V. N. Voloshinov, and *The Formal Method in Literary Scholarship*, attributed to P. M. Medvedev. Subsequent interpretive dilemmas include the extent of Bakhtin's embrace or rejection of Marxist thought, whether he is a structuralist or poststructuralist, and the degree of his commitment to Russian Orthodox Christianity. For significantly differing accounts of Bakhtin, see Todorov, Clark and Holquist, and Morson and Emerson. Pechey has considered the use of Bakhtin's theories with relationship to postcolonial texts, in a Marxian reading very different from my own.

2. This passage is cited and translated by Caryl Emerson in an essay that explores Bakhtin's relationship to the Russian Orthodox Church (122).

3. Interview with Appiah, cited in Appiah 74. Appiah's book analyzes and critiques the concept of "an African identity," pointing out the reverse racism of many definitions depending on a racial essence and the extraordinary cultural diversity found on the continent of Africa.

4. Because of limited space, I will confine my discussion to *Things Fall Apart* and merely note in passing the dialogical nature of most of Achebe's subsequent work, particularly *Arrow of God* (with its concluding debate about the actions of a great man) and *Anthills of the Savannah* (with its multiple narrators).

5. For more detailed readings of biblical elements, see Bascom, Cobham, Weinstock, and Weinstock and Ramadan. Readers have come to different conclusions about the effect of the biblical language. Bascom sees these references (as I do) as a means of affirming certain aspects of Christianity as solutions to some of the flaws in Igbo society. Cobham takes a more skeptical view, claiming that Achebe uses such references in an attempt to address traditional aspects of Igbo life in a way that will engage western readers and resolve his own "search for a point of convergence between the two codes that inform his ethics" (95). We should not, Cobham argues, take his selective and strategic account of Igbo traditional society as definitive or objective.

6. Although most critics believe that Okonkwo committed an offense by participating in the killing of Ikemefuna (Carroll 42–43; Killam, *Writings* 20), Opata has argued that Okonkwo cannot be alleged to have committed any offense against the earth.

7. Innes argues that the clan itself is unable to balance these principles: "Ikemefuna's sacrifice is both a symbol of what the clan lacks and a realistic dramatisation of the clan's inability to maintain a harmonious balance between male and female principles, rather than an uneasy dialectic without synthesis" (29).

8. The posited author comments on this exchange: "In this way Mr. Brown learnt a good deal about the religion of the clan" (163). Lloyd W. Brown argues that this is double-voiced discourse, ironic in nature, "for Mr. Brown's grasp of the Igbo religion does not include real understanding or a sympathetic recognition of the African's morality" (30). Double-voiced discourse can be difficult to identify with certainty, but given the juxtaposition of Brown with Smith, I do not find this passage to be ironic.

9. A detailed study of the novel as a revision of *Mister Johnson* appears in Innes 21–41.

10. A particular concern is the treatment of African women in traditional culture. For example, see Achebe's *The Anthills of the Savannah* (1988), Buchi Emecheta's *The Joys of Motherhood* (1979), Tsitsi Dangeremba's *Nervous Conditions* (1988), and T. Obinkaram Echewa's *I Saw the Sky Catch Fire* (1992).

11. For differing analyses, see Robertson and Watts.

12. Mark Walhout argues that this is the position taken by Edward Said; see the discussion of this issue in the final chapter of this volume.

9. Justice in Ngũgĩ wa Thiong'o's Narrative (Lovesey)

1. Ngũgĩ, *Decolonising* 71. One of the best-sustained examinations of biblical references in Ngũgĩ's novels before *Petals of Blood* is by Govind Narain Sharma, who concludes that Ngũgĩ "is a religious writer" ("Ngũgĩ's" 208). Dianne Schwerdt and Abdulrazak Gurnah do not consider the use of biblical materials in *Matigari* exceptional in the Ngũgĩ canon. Schwerdt, for example, holds, "The narrative of this novel, as with that of others written by Ngũgĩ, is redolent with religious metaphors and allusions to various aspects of Christian mythology" (14).

However, David Maughan Brown perceptively regards *Matigari* as distinctive in this respect, and even speculates somewhat wildly about whether the exceptional handling of biblical materials in the work results from a crisis of faith in the author. He goes on to make a convincing case for his contention that Ngũgĩ's sympathetic handling of religious elements in *Matigari* may stem from Ngũgĩ's willingness to see the Church or "millenarian religious movements" (178) in Kenya as potential allies in opposing the state.

2. The importance of Fanon in Ngũgĩ's work is apparent in his persistent emphasis on mental decolonization and the importance of the role of national languages in this process. In a recently published interview, Ngũgĩ repeats this position, saying, "African thought is imprisoned in foreign languages" (Jussawalla and Dasenbrock 30). Sharma also provides a valuable discussion of Ngũgĩ's debt to Fanon's socialism ("Socialism" 24–27). Ngũgĩ's latest essay collection, *Moving the Centre* (1993), begins with an article in which Ngũgĩ explains that in the 1960s, "Frantz Fanon became the prophet of the struggle to move the centre and his book, *The Wretched of the Earth*, became a kind of Bible among the African students from West and East Africa then at Leeds" (2). However, Ngũgĩ is not uncritical of Fanon. While *The Wretched of the Earth* "was a very important eye-opener for me," Ngũgĩ said in an interview in 1979, Fanon's reading of Marx and Engels "began to reveal . . . serious weaknesses and limitations . . . , especially [Fanon's] own petit bourgeois idealism that led him into a mechanical overemphasis on psychology and violence, and his inability to see the significance of the rising and growing African proletariat" (Sicherman, *Ngũgĩ* 23).

3. See Lovesey, "Accommodation" and "Ngũgĩ."

4. See Herreshoff for a treatment of Bunyan.

10. Postcolonial Literature and the Story of Christ (Cary)

1. An earlier version of this essay discusses Shusaku Endo's *Wonderful Fool* (Japanese) and Patrick White's *Riders in the Chariot* (Australian) and appeared in *Christianity and Literature* 41 (1991): 39–59.

2. For more on this process, see Bhabha.

3. For more on these biblical parallels, see Foster, *Myth* and *Augusto*.

4. In the epigraph to *A Grain of Wheat*, Ngũgĩ quotes 1 Cor. 15:36.

5. A detailed reading of the allegory is in El-Gabalawy.

6. On Mahfouz's loss of faith, see Somekh, *Changing* 39. A particular strong philosophical influence on him was European rationalism (Cachia 178–79, 181). For Muslim views of Christianity, see Jomier 112–14, and Parrinder 105–21.

7. See Somekh, *Changing* 55, 140; Wessels 116–17; and El-Gabalawy 97.

8. A similar argument is made in Somekh, *Changing*.

11. André Brink's *An Instant in the Wind* (Jacobs)

1. See, for example, the transcription of the repertoire of one Malinké *griot* (or singer of tales) by the novelist Camara Laye.

2. For an excellent account of the Zulu nation's rise and its ultimate defeat, see Morris. The oral tradition of today's largely urbanized Zulus draws heavily on modern European accounts of the story, which in turn derive from quasi-journalistic reports written by Englishmen soon after the events recorded. But also see the very different emphases of Mazisi Kunene's novel, *Emperor Shaka the Great* (1979).

3. But see the important work of a few English-speaking African historians, notably Thompson and Elphick.

4. Moodie's is the best and most complete account of the Afrikaner world view, but also see de Klerk. The attitudes and beliefs I describe are, of course, not held by all Afrikaners; nevertheless, such attitudes have largely dictated the course of South African history in this century.

5. *An Instant in the Wind* was originally published, in 1976, in both English and Afrikaans. Brink—who considers himself an Afrikaans writer who occasionally uses English—has written of how in working on the book he found himself alternating between the two languages. In fact, the Afrikaans and English versions of the book, both of which he produced alone, are not at all identical. The essay in which he describes this experience also gives a fascinating general account of what it means (for him and for others) to live in a bilingual country in which the two dominant languages implicate one in very different structures of thought; see "English and the Afrikaans Writer" (*Writing* 95–115).

6. In an essay called "Imagining the Real," Brink offers a corollary notion, one that clarifies the goal of *An Instant in the Wind* and implicitly identifies it with mythography: "What is basically required, and what is offered by literature functioning as myth in a bewildering and secular age, is to *imagine the real*. Not to avoid what *is*, by offering a substitute or a palliative, but to experience what exists so intensely that through the imagination it realizes its full potential." Brink calls this approach a "difficult and indirect access to truth" (*Writing* 221).

7. Later Elisabeth continues to reflect on this problem of "place," addressing Adam in her thoughts and considering him as a natural force alien to culture and society: "*What* is your place? Have you any place—or do you come and go like the wind?" (66). Because Elisabeth is white and hence privileged, the lessons about selfhood and history with which the book is occupied are always more difficult for her to learn than for Adam. In their first exchange about "place," he, unlike her, is aware of the emptiness of the concept. We may assume that his awareness derives from his closeness to authentic nature—a closeness typically assumed to belong to native Africans, and not only by the Rousseau-influenced minds of Europeans; see the same argument, for instance, in Laye (19).

8. Thus the familiar argument of M. H. Abrams, argued in full in *Natural Supernaturalism* (1971) but presented with an admirable terseness in an essay published years earlier: "But the hope has been shifted from the history of mankind to the mind of the single individual, from militant external action to an imaginative

act; and the marriage between the Lamb and the New Jerusalem has been converted into a marriage between subject and object, mind and nature, which creates a new world out of the old world of senses" (59). Perhaps the recapitulation, in South African society, of the European and American move from biblical culture to Romanticism indicates an inevitable stage in the development of Protestantism—in which case my occasional comparisons between South African and American history are justified.

9. The historical record upon which Brink draws says that the Larssons left Cape Town in 1749, and that Elisabeth and Adam reached Cape Town in February 1751; it further notes that she remarried in May, and that she gave birth to a son in August. Brink's fantasia upon these bare facts, by making Elisabeth miscarry while in the wilderness, makes Adam the father of that son. "Not a question of imagination, but of faith."

10. The verse he quotes is 1 John 3 : 14.

11. *Company* 149–50. Walzer's insistence that absolute detachment is not possible is reminiscent of Alasdair MacIntyre's insistence that there can be no moral understanding independent of some tradition of moral inquiry. See his *Whose Justice? Which Rationality?*, especially chapter 1.

12. Some of the more common criticisms of Paton's work may be found well expressed in Ngũgĩ (*Decolonising* 69–70, 91–92) and in Coetzee's "Simple Language."

12. An Ecumenical Perspective on the Walzer-Said Exchange
(Walhout)

1. The World Alliance of Reformed Churches declared apartheid a heresy and suspended the Dutch Reformed Church of South Africa in 1982. See the documents and essays by South African theologians collected in de Gruchy and Villa-Vicencio. The suspension appears to have had some effect. In November 1990, for instance, the Dutch Reformed delegates to a conference of South African churches, black and white, agreed to a statement condemning apartheid as a "sin" (Wren).

2. Said's activities have earned him the title "Professor of Terror" among arch-Zionists; see Edward Alexander's essay in *Commentary* and the subsequent barrage of angry letters from leftist academics and Jewish supporters of Israel. Alexander was responding to a prior debate in *Critical Inquiry* prompted by an article in which Said had attacked Zionism as an "ideology of difference." The whole debate, which now spans a five-year period, has taken a vicious turn on both sides. See Said et al., "An Exchange on Edward Said and Difference."

3. Read together, Mark Krupnick's pair of essays constitute a fine introduction to the two social critics. For a different perspective on the Walzer-Said exchange itself, see Jonathan Boyarin, who emphasizes "the shared limitations of Walzer's and Said's ideologically secularist hermeneutics" (529). While I agree that such limitations mark both methods, I cannot accept Boyarin's conclusion that "Walzer's

insistence on the secularist reading of the ancient text is ultimately more comple-
mented than deconstructed by Said's attitude." (533).

4. Walzer's interest in hermeneutics is especially evident in his more recent
books, including *Exodus and Revolution* and *Interpretation as Social Criticism*.

5. One suspects that Walzer's interpretation is a slightly garbled version of
Martin Buber's chapter on the Korah episode in his book *Moses*, "The Contradiction," which is based not on the final Exodus text, but on a critical reconstruction
of the historical core of the narrative. (Walzer cites Buber's *Moses* elsewhere in
Exodus and Revolution.)

6. Although Marxist in origin, Said's version of ideology critique is influenced
by French structuralism and poststructuralism, especially the work of Michel Foucault, who plays a prominent role in *Beginnings*, Said's first book of theory, and
Orientalism, his first attempt to apply that theory to Western discourse about the
Middle East. Whether Marxist ideology critique is compatible with the Foucauldian concept of the power-knowledge relation is, however, doubtful.

7. More recently, in an interesting paper on the idea of holy war in ancient
Israel, Walzer has developed the first of these arguments at some length. Noting
that "there are two very different versions of the conquest in the Bible—one based
on the idea of holy war, the other on the idea of limited war—he concludes that
"the religious doctrine of holy war does not seem to have any intrinsic connection
to Israel's covental faith" ("Idea" 216–17).

8. Said's review and the subsequent exchange with Walzer appeared originally
in the New York journal *Grand Street*. The review alone is reprinted in *Blaming
the Victims: Spurious Scholarship and the Palestinian Question*, edited by Said and
Christopher Hitchens. Said had mentioned Walzer briefly in "An Ideology of
Difference."

9. In addition to *Blaming the Victims*, this project has produced *The Question of
Palestine* and, most recently, *After the Last Sky: Palestinian Lives*, a montage of
photos and text based on personal experience and its theoretical implications.

10. In *The Question of Palestine*, Said praises "the notion of a state based on
secular human rights, not on religious or minority exclusivity," as "the only possible and acceptable destiny for the multicommunal Middle East" (220). At the
same time, he seems to accept the necessity of partition. "On occasion after occasion," he recalls, "the PLO [has] stated its willingness to accept a Palestinian state
in the West Bank and Gaza" (224).

11. Walzer seems to set preconditions for negotiation, however. "I support the
peace movement in Israel (Peace Now)," he says, "and keep looking for a similar
movement among the Palestinians. . . . I defend national liberation [for the Pa-
lestinians]—but insist at the same time that the stocking mask be removed. I want
to be sure . . . that the face of 'liberation' is not the face of a new oppressor"
(Walzer and Said, "Exchange" 252). Said's response is that the Israelis have no
right to impose preconditions (see "Ideology" 51). Clearly, this obstacle to dia-

logue is not to be minimized. One would like to see Walzer and his fellow liberals accept the PLO as a negotiating partner; the recent negotiations between Pretoria and the ANC might serve as a precedent.

12. See Mandela 32–35. Interestingly, Umkonto we Sizwe, the military wing of the ANC established by Mandela and his colleagues in the aftermath of the Sharpeville massacre, was modeled after the Zionist defense organizations Haganah and Palmah, the official predecessors of the Israeli Defence Forces, as well as the underground Irgun. See Mandela 162–89 passim.

13. An earlier version of this essay was first published in *Soundings* (74.3–4 [1991]: 327–50).

Works Cited

Abrams, M. H. "English Romanticism: The Spirit of the Age." *Romanticism Reconsidered*. Ed. Northrop Frye. New York: Columbia UP, 1963. 26–72.

Achebe, Chinua. *Hopes and Impediments: Selected Essays*. 1988. New York: Doubleday, 1989.

———. *Morning Yet on Creation Day*. New York: Doubleday, 1975.

———. *Things Fall Apart*. New York: Fawcett, 1959.

Ahmad, Aijaz. "Jameson's Rhetoric of Otherness and the 'National Allegory.' " *Social Text* 17 (1987): 3–27.

Alazraki, Jaime. *En busca del unicornio: Los cuentos de Julio Cortázar*. Madrid: Ed. Gredos, 1983.

Alexander, Edward. "Professor of Terror." *Commentary* Aug. 1989: 49–50.

———. Reply to Letters. *Commentary* Dec. 1989: 12–15.

Allende, Isabel. *Las casa de los espíritus*. Barcelona: Plaza & Janes Ed., S.A., 1982.

———. *The House of the Spirits*. Trans. Magda Bogin. New York: Bantam, 1986.

———. "Writing as an Act of Hope." *Paths of Resistance: The Art and Craft of the Political Novel*. Ed. William Zinsser. Boston: Houghton, 1989. 39–63.

Alter, Robert. *The Art of Biblical Narrative*. New York: Basic, 1981.

———. *The Literary Guide to the Bible*. Cambridge: Harvard UP, 1987.

Amnesty International Report. *Torture in the Eighties*. London: Amnesty International Publications, 1984.

Appiah, Kwame Anthony. *In My Father's House: Africa in the Philosophy of Culture*. New York: Oxford UP, 1992.

Arguedas, José María. *Deep Rivers*. Austin: U of Texas P, 1978.

———. "Palabras de José María Arguedas." *Recopilacion de textos sobre José María Arguedas*. Ed. Juan Larco. Havana: Casa de las Americas, 1976.

Arrupe, Pedro. "Marxist Analysis by Christians." Hennelly 307–14.

Ashcroft, Bill, Gareth Griffiths, and Helen Tiffin. *The Empire Writes Back: Theory and Practice in Post-Colonial Literatures*. London: Routledge, 1989.

Assman, Hugo. *Practical Theology of Liberation*. London: Search P, 1975.

Baëta, C. G. "Missionary and Humanitarian Interests, 1914 to 1960." Gann and Duignan. Vol. 2. 422–59.

Bakhtin, Mikhail M. *Art and Answerability: Early Philosophical Essays*. Ed. Michael Holquist and Vadim Liapunov. Austin: U of Texas P, 1990.

————. *The Dialogic Imagination: Four Essays by M. M. Bakhtin*. Ed. Michael Holquist. Trans. Gary Saul Morson and Caryl Emerson. Evanston: Northwestern UP, 1989.

————. *Problems of Dostoevsky's Poetics*. 1963. Ed. and trans. Caryl Emerson. Minneapolis: U of Minnesota P, 1984.

————. *Speech Genres and Other Late Essays*. Trans. Vern W. McGee. Ed. Caryl Emerson and Michael Holquist. U of Texas P Slavic Series, No. 8. Austin: U of Texas P, 1986.

Bareiro, Rubén, and Jacqueline Baldran. "Las dos caras del mito en *Hijo de hombre* de Augusto Roa Bastos." *Revista cultural de Excelsior* 204 (1988): 38–47.

Bascom, Tim. "The Black African and the 'White Man's God' in *Things Fall Apart:* Cultural Repression or Liberation?" *Commonwealth Essays and Studies* 11 (1988): 70–76.

Batson, E. Beatrice. *John Bunyan: Allegory and Imagination*. London: Croom Helm, 1984.

Beier, U. *Yoruba Poetry*. Cambridge: Cambridge UP, 1970.

Bellah, Robert, et al. *Habits of the Heart: Individualism and Commitment in American Life*. Berkeley: U of California P, 1985.

Bell-Villada, Gene H. *García Márquez: The Man and His Work*. Chapel Hill: U of North Carolina P, 1990.

Berkhofer, Robert F., Jr. *The White Man's Indian: Images of the Indian from Columbus to the Present*. New York: Knopf, 1976.

Beverley, John. *Del 'Lazarillo' al sandinismo: Estudios sobre la función ideológica de la literatura española e hispanoamericana*. Minneapolis: Prisma Institute, 1987.

————. "The Margin at the Center: On *Testimonio* (Testimonial Narrative)" *Modern Fiction Studies* 35 (1989): 11–28.

Beverley, John, and Marc Zimmerman. *Literature and Politics in the Central American Revolutions*. Austin: U of Texas P, 1990.

Bhabha, Homi K. "Signs Taken for Wonders: Questions of Ambivalence and Authority Under a Tree Outside Delhi, May 1817." *Europe and Its Others*. Vol. 1. Ed. Francis Baker et al. Colchester: U of Essex, 1978. 89–106.

Bishop, Jonathan. "Emerson and Christianity." *Renascence* 38 (1986): 183–99.

Black Elk. *Black Elk Speaks: Being the Life Story of a Holy Man of the Oglala Sioux*. Ed. John G. Neihardt. 1932. Lincoln: U of Nebraska P, 1979.

————. *The Sacred Pipe: Black Elk's Account of the Seven Rites of the Oglala Sioux*. Ed. Joseph Epes Brown. Norman: U of Oklahoma P, 1953.

Bloch, Ernst. *The Principle of Hope*. 2 vols. Cambridge: MIT P, 1986.

Boahen, A. Adu. "The Colonial Era: Conquest to Independence." Gann and Duignan. Vol. 2. 503–20.

Boesak, Allan. *Black and Reformed: Apartheid, Liberation and the Calvinist Tradition*. Ed. Leonard Sweetman. Maryknoll, NY: Orbis, 1984.

Boff, Leonardo. "Vatican Instruction Reflects European Mind-Set." Hennelly 415–19.

Boldy, Steven. *The Novels of Julio Cortázar*. Cambridge: Cambridge UP, 1980.

Boyarin, Jonathan. "Reading Exodus into History." *New Literary History* 23 (1992): 523–54.

Brathwaite, Edward. "The African Presence in Caribbean Literature. *Daedalus* 103 (1974): 73–109.

———. Introduction. *Brother Man*. By Roger Mais. London: Heinemann, 1974. v–xxi.

Brennan, Timothy. "Preface." *Modern Fiction Studies* 35 (1989): 3–8.

Breytenbach, Breyten. *The True Confessions of an Albino Terrorist*. London: Faber & Faber, 1984.

Brink, André. *An Instant in the Wind*. 1976. Harmondsworth, Eng.: Penguin, 1985.

———. *Writing in a State of Siege*. New York: Summit, 1983.

Brown, David Maughan. "*Matigari* and the Rehabilitation of Religion." *Research in African Literatures* 22 (1991): 173–80.

Brown, Lloyd W. "Cultural Norms and Modes of Perception in Achebe's Fiction." Innes and Lindfors 22–36.

Brownstein, Marilyn L. "Accidental Feature, Emergent Grammars, and Women's Writing." MLA, Washington, DC, 1989.

Brueggemann, Walter. *The Message of the Psalms*. Minneapolis: Ausburg, 1984.

Brumble, David H. *American Indian Autobiography*. Berkeley: U of California P, 1988.

Brydon, Diana. "The Myths that Write Us: Decolonising the Mind." *The Journal of Commonwealth Literature* 10 (1987): 1–14.

Buber, Martin. "The Contradiction." *The Writings of Martin Buber*. Ed. Will Herberg. New York: Meridian, 1956. 209–217.

———. *The Prophetic Faith*. New York: MacMillan, 1949.

Buchanan, Rhonda L. "The Cycle of Rage and Order in García Márquez' *El otoño del patriarca*." *Perspectives on Contemporary Literature* 10 (1984): 75–85.

Buechner, Frederick. *Now and Then*. New York: Harper, 1983.

Bühlmann, Walbert. *The Coming of the Third Church*. Maryknoll, NY: Orbis, 1977.

Bunyan, John. *The Pilgrim's Progress*. Ed. Roger Sharrock. Harmondsworth, Eng.: Penguin, 1986.

Cachia, Pierre. "Themes Related to Christianity and Judaism in Modern Egyptian Drama and Fiction." *Journal of Arab Literature* 2 (1971): 178–94.

Callan, Edward. Introduction. *Cry, the Beloved Country.* By Alan Paton. New York: Scribner's 1987. xv–xxvii.

Canfield, Martha L. "El patriarca de García Márquez: Padre, poeta, tirano." *Revista iberoamericana* 50.128–129 (1984): 1017–56.

Cardenal, Ernesto. *Canto nacional.* Buenos Aires: Ed. Carlos Lohlé, 1973.

———. *En Cuba.* Buenos Aires: Ed. Carlos Lohlé, 1972.

———. *El evangelio de Solentiname.* Salamanca: Ed. Sígueme, 1975.

———. *La democratización del la cultura.* Managua: Ministerio de la Cultura, 1982.

———. *Nueva antología poética.* Mexico City: Siglo XXI, 1980.

———. *Poesía nueva de Nicaragua.* Managua: Ed. Nueva Nicaragua, 1981.

———. *Salmos.* Buenos Aires: Ed. Carlos Lohlé, 1969.

———. *Tocar el cielo.* Ed. Benjamín Forcano. Managua: Ed. Monimbó, n.d.

Carroll, David. *Chinua Achebe.* 2nd ed. New York: St. Martin's, 1980.

Carusi, Annamaria. "Post, Post and Post, Or, Where is South African Literature in All This?" *Ariel* 20.4 (1989): 79–95.

Cary, Norman R. "Religion and the West Indian Novel." *Commonwealth Essays and Studies* 10.2 (1988): 98–106.

Castro-Klarén, Sara. "Ontological Fabulation: Toward Cortázar's Theory of Literature." *The Final Island.* Ed. Jaime Alazraki and Ivar Ivask. Norman: U of Oklahoma P, 1976. 140–50.

Chamberlain, Daniel Frank. *Narrative Perspective in Fiction: A Phenomenological Mediation of Reader, Text, and World.* Toronto: U of Toronto P, 1990.

Chevigny, Bell Gale and Gari Laguardia. Introduction. *Reinventing the Americas: Comparative Studies of Literature of the United States and Spanish America.* Ed. Bell Gale Chevigny and Gari Laguardia. New York: Cambridge UP, 1986. 3–39.

Chinweizu, Onwuchekwa Jemie, and Ihechukwu Madubuike. *Toward the Decolonization of African Literature.* Washington, DC: Howard UP, 1983.

Clark, Katerina, and Michael Holquist. *Mikhail Bakhtin.* Cambridge: Harvard UP, 1984.

Clarke, Thomas E. "Spirituality, Justice, and Cultural Evangelization." *Religious Education* 83.1 (1988): 53–66.

Clifford, James. *The Predicament of Culture: Twentieth-Century Ethnography, Literature, and Art.* Cambridge: Harvard UP, 1988.

Cobham, Rhonda. "Making Men and History: Achebe and the Politics of Revisionism." Lindfors, *Approaches* 91–100.

Coetzee, J. M. "Simple Language, Simple People: Smith, Paton, Mikro." *White Writing: On the Culture of Letters in South Africa.* New Haven: Yale UP, 1988. 115–35.

———. "Too Late the Liberal." *New Republic* 8–15 Jan. 1990: 39–41.

———. *Waiting for the Barbarians.* 1980. Harmondsworth, Eng.: Penguin, 1982.

Columbus, Claudette Kemper. *Mythological Consciousness and the Future*. New York: Peter Lang, 1986.

Cortázar, Julio. *A Certain Lucas*. New York: Knopf, 1984.

———. *A Change of Light and Other Stories*. Trans. Gregory Rabassa. New York: Knopf, 1980. 119–27.

———. *Deshoras*. Mexico City: Ed. Nueva Imagen, 1983.

———. *Hopscotch*. Trans. Gregory Rabassa. New York: Avon, 1966.

———. *A Manual for Manuel*. New York: Pantheon, 1978.

———. *Nicaraguan Sketches*. Trans. Kathleen Weaver. New York: Norton, 1989.

———. *Territorios*. Mexico City: Siglo XXI, 1978.

———. *"We Love Glenda So Much" and Other Tales*. Trans. Gregory Rabassa. New York: Vintage, 1983. 81–96.

Cowell, Alan. "Pope Challenges Brazil's Authorities." *New York Times* 15 Oct. 1991: A4.

———. "Pope Asks Amends of Brazil's Indians." *New York Times* 17 Oct. 1991: A3.

Crapanzano, Vincent. *Waiting: The Whites of South Africa*. New York: Vintage, 1986.

Culbertson, Diana. *The Poetics of Revelation: Recognition and the Narrative Tradition*. Macon: Mercer UP, 1989.

Damrosch, Leopold. *God's Plot and Man's Stories: Studies in the Fictional Imagination from Milton to Fielding*. Chicago: U of Chicago P, 1985.

Darby, Phillip. *Three Faces of Imperialism: British and American Approaches to Asia and Africa 1870–1970*. New Haven: Yale UP, 1987.

Dathorne, Oscar R. "Roger Mais: The Man on the Cross." *Studies in the Novel* 4 (1974): 275–84.

de Certeau, Michel. *The Practice of Everyday Life*. Trans. Steven Rendall. Berkeley: U of California P, 1984.

de Gruchy, John W., and Charles Villa-Vicencio, eds. *Apartheid is a Heresy*. Grand Rapids, MI: Eerdmans, 1983.

de Klerk, Willem Abraham. *The Puritans in Africa: A Story of Afrikanerdom*. Harmondsworth, Eng.: Penguin, 1975.

DeLillo, Don. *Mao II*. New York: Viking, 1991.

DeMallie, Raymond J., ed. *The Sixth Grandfather: Black Elk's Teachings Given to John G. Neihardt*. Lincoln: U of Nebraska P, 1984.

Diawara, Manthia. *African Cinema, Politics and Culture*. Bloomington: Indiana UP, 1992.

Dickson, Kwesi A. *Theology in Africa*. London: Barton, Longman and Todd, 1984.

Dodd, C. H. *The Authority of the Bible*. 2nd ed. New York: Harper, 1962.

Donahue, John R. "Biblical Perspectives on Justice." *The Faith that Does Justice*. Ed. John C. Haughey. New York: Paulist P, 1977.

Donovan, Vincent J. *Christianity Rediscovered.* 2nd ed. Maryknoll, NY: Orbis, 1978.

Douglass, Frederick. *Narrative of the Life of Frederick Douglass, an American Slave.* 1945. New York: Penguin, 1982.

Duerdon, Dennis, and Cosmo Pieterse, eds. *African Writers Talking.* London: Heinemann, 1972.

Dunne, John S. *A Search for God in Time and Memory.* 1969. Notre Dame, IN: U of Notre Dame P, 1977.

During, Simon. "Postmodernism or Postcolonialism?" *Landfall* 39 (1985): 366–80.

———. "Postmodernism or post-colonialism today." *Textual Practice* 1 (1987): 32–47.

———. "Waiting for the Past: Some Relations Between Modernity, Colonization, and Writing." *Ariel* 20.4 (1989): 31–61.

Dworkin, Ronald. "Report from Hell." *The New York Review of Books,* 17 July 1986: 11–16.

Eagleton, Terry. *Literary Theory: An Introduction.* Minneapolis: U of Minnesota P, 1983.

Eastman, Charles Alexander (Ohiyesa). *From the Deep Woods to Civilization: Chapters in the Autobiography of an Indian.* 1916. Lincoln: U of Nebraska P, 1977.

———. *Indian Boyhood.* 1902. New York: Dover, 1971.

Eco, Umberto. "The Sacred is Not Just a Fashion." *Travels in Hyperreality.* New York: Harcourt, 1973. 8–94.

Egejuru, Phanuel Akubueze, ed. *Towards African Literary Independence: A Dialogue with Contemporary African Writers.* Westport, CT: Greenwood, 1980.

Éla, Jean-Marc. *My Faith as an African.* New York: Orbis, 1988.

El-Gabalawy, Saad. "The Allegorical Significance of Naguib Mahfouz's *Children of Our Alley.*" *International Fiction Review* 16.2 (1989): 91–97.

Elphick, Richard. *Khoikhoi and the Founding of White South Africa.* New Haven: Yale UP, 1977.

Emerson, Caryl. "Russian Orthodoxy and the Early Bakhtin." *Religion & Literature* 22.2–3 (1990): 109–31.

Emerson, Ralph Waldo. *Essays and Lectures.* New York: Library of America, 1983.

Eyoh, Hansel Nolumbe. "Ngũgĩ wa Thiong'o Interviewed." *Journal of Commonwealth Literature* 21 (1986): 162–66.

Fanon, Frantz. *The Wretched of the Earth.* Trans. Constance Farrington. New York: Grove P, 1963.

Ferlinghetti, Lawrence. *Seven Days in Nicaragua Libre.* San Francisco: City Lights, 1984.

Fiddian, Robin W. "Two Aspects of Technique in *El coronel no tiene quien le escribe.*" *Neophilologus* 69.1 (1985): 386–93.

Fiedler, Leslie A. *The Return of the Vanishing American*. New York: Stein and Day, 1968.

Fiorenza, Elisabeth Schüssler. *In Memory of Her*. New York: Crossroad P, 1989.

Forcano, Benjamin. Introduction. *Tocar el cielo*. By Ernesto Cardenal. Managua: Ed. Monimbó, n.d.

Forsyth, Neil. *The Combat Myth*. New Haven: Yale UP, 1990.

Foster, David W. *Augusto Roa Bastos*. Boston: Twayne, 1978.

———. *The Myth of Paraguay in the Fiction of Augusto Roa Bastos*. U of North Carolina Studies in the Romance Languages and Literatures 80. Chapel Hill: U of North Carolina P, 1969.

Foster, Douglas. "Isabel Allende Unveiled." *Mother Jones*. Dec. 1988: 42–46.

Foucault, Michel. "The Subject and Power." *Michel Foucault: Beyond Structuralism and Hermeneutics*. Ed. Hubert L. Dreyfus and Paul Rabinov. 2nd ed. Chicago: U of Chicago P, 1983. 208–26.

Frye, Northrop. *Anatomy of Criticism: Four Essays*. Princeton: Princeton UP, 1957.

Fugard, Athol. *"Master Harold"*. . . *and the Boys*. New York: Penguin, 1982.

Gann, L. H., and Peter Duignan, eds. *Colonialism in Africa: 1870–1960*. 5 vols. London: Cambridge UP, 1969–75.

García, Matías. *La iglesia, el cristiano y la política*. Madrid: Ed. HOAC, 1968.

García Márquez, Gabriel. *The Autumn of the Patriarch*. Trans. Gregory Rabassa. New York: Harper, 1976.

———. *Love in the Time of Cholera*. New York: Knopf, 1988.

———. *No One Writes to the Colonel*. Trans. J. S. Bernstein. New York: Harper, 1968.

Gelpi, Donald L., ed. *Beyond Individualism: Toward a Retrieval of Moral Discourse in America*. Notre Dame, IN: U of Notre Dame P, 1989.

Gikandi, Simon. *Reading Chinua Achebe*. London: James Currey, 1991.

Girard, René. *"To double business bound": Essays on Literature, Mimesis, and Anthropology*. Baltimore: Johns Hopkins UP, 1978.

González Bermejo, Ernesto. *Conversaciones con Cortázar*. Mexico City: Ed. Hermes, 1978.

Gordimer, Nadine. *My Son's Story*. New York: Farrar, 1990.

———. *A Sport of Nature*. New York: Penguin, 1988.

Griffin, Keith. "Underdevelopment in History." *The Political Economy of Development and Underdevelopment*. Ed. Charles K. Wilber. New York: Random, 1973. 15–25.

Groves, Charles Pelham. "Missionary and Humanitarian Aspects of Colonialism from 1870 to 1914." Gann and Duignan. Vol. 1. 462–96.

Gurnah, Abdulrazak. *"Matigari*: A Tract of Resistance." *Research in African Literatures* 22 (1991): 161–80.

Gutiérrez, Gustavo. "Criticism Will Deepen, Clarify Liberation Theology." Hennelly 419–25.

―――. *Entre las calandrias: Un ensayo sobre José María Arguedas.* Lima: Instituto Bartolomé de Las Casas, 1989.

―――. *On Job: God-Talk and the Suffering of the Innocent.* Maryknoll, NY: Orbis, 1987.

―――. *Teología de la liberación: perspectivas.* Salamanca: Ed. Sígueme, 1972.

―――. *A Theology of Liberation: History, Politics and Salvation.* Trans. and ed. Caridad Inda and John Eagleson. Maryknoll, NY: Orbis, 1973.

Hargreaves, John D. *Decolonization in Africa.* London: Longman, 1988.

Häring, Bernard. "Justice." *New Catholic Encyclopedia.* Vol. 8. New York: McGraw, 1967.

Harlow, Barbara. "Narrative in Prison: Stories from the Palestinian Intifada." *Modern Fiction Studies* 35 (1989): 29–46.

―――. *Resistance Literature.* New York: Methuen, 1987.

Hennelly, Alfred T., ed. *Liberation Theology: A Documentary History.* Maryknoll, NY: Orbis, 1990.

Herreshoff, David. "Marxist Perspectives on Bunyan." *Bunyan in Our Time.* Ed. Robert G. Collmer. Kent, OH: Kent State UP, 1989. 161–85.

Hirsch, Edward. *The Night Parade.* New York: Knopf, 1989.

Holler, Clyde. "Black Elk's Relationship to Christianity." *American Indian Quarterly* 8 (1984): 37–49.

―――. "Lakota Religion and Tragedy: The Theology of *Black Elk Speaks.*" *Journal of the American Academy of Religion* 52 (1984): 19–45.

Hourani, Albert. *A History of the Arab Peoples.* Cambridge: Harvard UP, 1991.

Howard, W. J. "Themes and Development in the Novels of Ngũgĩ." E. Wright 95–120.

Huggan, Graham. "Philomela's Retold Story: Silence, Music, and the Post-Colonial Text." *The Journal of Commonwealth Literature* 25 (1990): 12–23.

Hunter, J. Paul. *Before Novels: The Cultural Contexts of Eighteenth Century English Fiction.* London: Norton, 1990.

Hutcheon, Linda. "Circling the Downspout of Empire." *Past the Last Post: Theorizing Post-Colonialism and Post-Modernism.* Ed. Ian Adam and Helen Tiffin. Calgary: U of Calgary P, 1990.

―――. *A Poetics of Postmodernism: History, Theory, Fiction.* New York: Routledge, 1988.

Innes, C. L. *Chinua Achebe.* Cambridge: Cambridge UP, 1990.

―――, and Bernth Lindfors, eds. *Critical Perspectives on Chinua Achebe.* Washington: Three Continents, 1978.

Jabbi, Bu-Buakei. "The Structure of Symbolism in *A Grain of Wheat.*" *Research in African Literatures* 16.2 (1985): 210–42.

Jaffé, Aniela. "Symbolism in the Visual Arts." Jung, *Man* 230–71.

Jahner, Elaine A. "Transitional Narratives and Cultural Continuity." *boundary 2* 19.3 (1992): 148–79.

Jameson, Frederic. "A Brief Response." *Social Text* 17 (1987): 26–27.

———. "Third World Literature in an Era of Multinational Capitalism." *Social Text* 15 (1986): 65–88.

———. "World Literature in an Age of Multinational Capitalism." *The Current in Criticism: Essays on the Present and Future of Literary Theory.* Ed. Clayton Koelb and Virgil Lokke. West Lafayette, IN: Purdue UP, 1987. 139–58.

Janes, Regina. *Gabriel García Márquez: Revolutions in Wonderland.* Columbia: U of Missouri P, 1981.

JanMohamed, Abdul R. "Sophisticated Primitivism: The Syncretism of Oral and Literate Modes in Achebe's *Things Fall Apart.*" *Ariel* 15.4 (1984): 19–39.

Jennings, Francis. *The Invasion of America: Indians, Colonialism, and the Cant of Conquest.* Chapel Hill: U of North Carolina P, 1975.

Jomier, Jacques. *The Bible and the Koran.* Trans. Edward P. Arbez. New York: Desclee, 1964.

Jung, Carl G., ed. *Man and his Symbols.* New York: Doubleday, 1964.

———. "Psychology and Literature." 1930. Trans. and rpt. *Twentieth-Century Literary Criticism.* Ed. David Lodge. London: Longman, 1972. 175–88.

Jussawalla, Feroza, and Reed Way Dasenbrock, eds. *Interviews with Writers of the Post-Colonial World.* Jackson: UP of Mississippi, 1992.

"Justice." *Dictionary of the History of Ideas.* Vol. 2. New York: Scribner's, 1973. 652–53.

Kandinsky, Wassily. "Concerning the Spiritual in Art." *Art, Creativity and the Sacred: An Anthology in Religion and Art.* Ed. Diane Apostolos-Cappadona. New York: Crossroad P, 1986. 3–7.

Kane, Cheikh Hamidou. *Ambiguous Adventure.* Portsmouth, NH: Heinemann, 1963.

Katrak, Ketu H. "Decolonizing Culture: Toward a Theory for Postcolonial Women's Texts." *Modern Fiction Studies* 35 (1989): 157–79.

"Kenya Riots Spread." *The Manchester Guardian Weekly* 15 July 1990: 7.

Kermode, Frank. *The Sense of an Ending.* New York: Oxford UP, 1967.

Kierkegaard, Søren. *Fear and Trembling/Repetition.* Ed. and trans. Howard V. Hong and Edna H. Hong. Princeton: Princeton UP, 1983.

Killam, G. D. *An Introduction to the Writings of Ngũgĩ.* London: Heinemann, 1980.

———. *The Writings of Chinua Achebe.* London: Heinemann, 1977.

The Koran. Trans. N. J. Dawood. 4th rev. ed. Harmondsworth, Eng.: Penguin, 1973.

Kriesteva, Julia. "Semiotics of Biblical Abomination." *Powers of Horror: An Essay on Abjection.* Trans. Leon S. Roudiez. New York: Columbia UP, 1982. 90–112.

Krupat, Arnold. *For Those Who Come After: A Study of Native American Autobiography.* Berkeley: U of California P, 1985.

————. *The Voice in the Margin: Native American Literature and the Canon*. Berkeley: U of California P, 1989.

Krupnick, Mark. "The Critic and His Connections: The Case of Michael Walzer." *American Literary History* 1.3 (1989): 689–98.

————. "Edward Said: Discourse and Palestinian Rage." *Tikkun* 4.6 (Nov.–Dec. 1989): 21–24.

Kundera, Milan. *The Art of the Novel*. New York: Grove P, 1988.

————. *The Unbearable Lightness of Being*. New York: Harper, 1984.

Kunene, Mazisi. *Emperor Shaka the Great*. London: Heinemann, 1979.

Kuyper, Abraham. *Christianity and the Class Struggle*. Trans. Dirk Jellema. Grand Rapids, MI: Piet Hein, 1950.

Langan, John P. "What Jerusalem Says to Athens." *The Faith that Does Justice*. Ed. John C. Haughey. New York: Paulist P, 1977.

Laye, Camara. *The Guardian of the Word*. Trans. James Kirkup. New York: Vintage/Aventura, 1984.

Le Gassick, Trevor. Introduction. *Critical Perspectives on Naguib Mahfouz*. Ed. Trevor Le Gassick. Washington: Three Continents, 1991. 1–8.

León-Portilla, Miguel. *Fifteen Poets of the Aztec World*. Norman: U of Oklahoma P, 1992.

Lincoln, Kenneth. *Native American Renaissance*. Berkeley: U of California P, 1983.

Lindfors, Bernth, ed. *Approaches to Teaching Achebe's* Things Fall Apart. New York: Modern Language Association, 1991.

————. "The Palm-Oil with which Achebe's Words Are Eaten." Innes and Lindfors 47–66.

Lovesey, Oliver. "Accommodation and Revolt: Ngũgĩ wa Thiong'o's *Devil on the Cross*." *From Commonwealth to Post-Colonial*. Ed. Anna Rutherford. Sydney: Dangaroo, 1992. 151–59.

————. "Ngũgĩ wa Thiong'o's *Devil on the Cross* and *Matigari*: Writing the Female Subject." *World Literature Written in English*. Forthcoming.

McAnay, Emily. G., trans. *The Psalms of Struggle and Liberation*. By Ernest Cardenal. New York: Herder and Herder, 1971.

MacCabe, Colin. "Foreward." *In Other Worlds: Essays in Cultural Politics*. By Gayatri Chakravorty Spivak. New York: Methuen, 1987.

McCallister, Richard. "Nomenklatura in *La casa de los espíritus*." *Critical Approaches to Isabel Allende's Novels*. Ed. Sonia Riquelme Rojas and Edna Aguirre Rehbein. American University Studies, Series XXII, Latin American Literature. Vol. 14. New York: Peter Lang, 1991.

McCluskey, Sally. "*Black Elk Speaks:* And So Does John Neihardt." *Western American Literature* 6.4 (1972): 231–42.

MacIntyre, Alasdair. *Whose Justice? Which Rationality?* Notre Dame, IN: U of Notre Dame P, 1988.

Mahfouz, Naguib. *Children of Gebelaawi*. 1959. Trans. Philip Stewart. London: Heinemann, 1981.

Mais, Roger. *Brother Man*. London: Heinemann, 1974.

Mandela, Nelson. *No Easy Walk to Freedom*. Oxford: Heinemann, 1965.

Manley, Norman W. Introduction. *The Three Novels of Roger Mais*. By Roger Mais. London: Cape, 1953. v–viii.

Mariátegui, José Carlos. *Seven Interpretive Essays on Peruvian Reality*. Austin: U of Texas P, 1971.

Martínez Andrade, Marina. "Ernesto Cardenal: denuncia profética." *Plural: Revista Cultural de Excelsor* 130 (1982): 24–34.

Memmi, Albert. *The Colonizer and the Colonized*. 1957. New York: Orion P, 1965.

Mendoza, Plinio Apuleyo. *El olor a la guayaba*. Buenos Aires: Ed. Sudamericana, 1982.

Menkiti, Ifeanyi A. "Person and Community in African Traditional Thought." *African Philosophy: An Introduction*. Ed. Richard A. Wright. Washington, DC: UP of America, 1979. 157–67.

Menton, Seymour. *Magic Realism Rediscovered: 1918–1981*. Philadelphia: Art Alliance P, 1983.

Merleau-Ponty, Maurice. "Eye and Mind." 1961. *The Primacy of Perception*. Trans. Carleton Dallery. Ed. James M. Edie. Evanston: Northwestern UP, 1964. 159–90.

———. *Phenomenology of Perception*. 1945. Trans. Colin Smith. London: Routledge and Kegan Paul, 1962.

———. *The Visible and the Invisible*. Trans. Richard C. McCleary. Evanston: Northwestern UP, 1968.

Miller, J. Hillis. *The Disappearance of God: Five Nineteenth-Century Writers*. Cambridge: Harvard UP, 1968.

Milson, Menahem. "Reality, Allegory and Myth in the Work of Najib Mahfouz." *Asian and African Studies* 4 (1976): 157–79.

Minta, Stephen. *Gabriel García Márquez: Writer of Colombia*. London: Jonathan Cape, 1987.

Miranda, Jose Porfirio. *Marx y la Biblia*. Salamanca: Ed. Sígueme, 1972.

Moodie, T. Dunbar. *The Rise of Afrikanerdom: Power, Apartheid, and the Afrikaner*. Berkeley: U of California P, 1975.

Moore, Gerald. *Twelve African Writers*. Bloomington: Indiana UP, 1980.

Morish, Ivor. *Obeah, Christ and Rastaman: Jamaica and Its Religion*. Cambridge: James Clarke, 1982.

Morris, Donald R. *The Washing of the Spears*. New York: Simon, 1965.

Morson, Gary Saul, and Caryl Emerson. *Mikhail Bakhtin: Creation of a Prosaics*. Stanford: Stanford UP, 1990.

Motthabi, Mokgethi. "Liberation Theology: An Introduction." *Liberation The-*

ology and the Bible. Ed. Pieter G. R. de Villiers. Pretoria: U of South Africa P, 1987.

Mukherjee, Bharati. *Jasmine*. New York: Ballantine, 1989.

Ngũgĩ wa Thiong'o. *Barrel of a Pen: Resistance to Repression in Neo-Colonial Kenya*. London: New Beacon Books, 1983.

———. *Decolonising the Mind: The Politics of Language in African Literature*. London: James Currey/Heinemann, 1986.

———. *Detained: A Writer's Prison Diary*. London: Heinemann, 1981.

———. *Devil on the Cross*. Trans. by the author. London: Heinemann, 1982.

———. *A Grain of Wheat*. 1967. Rev. ed. London: Heinemann, 1986.

———. "Literature and Society." *Writers in Politics*. London: Heinemann, 1981. 3–33.

———. *Matigari*. Trans. Wangui wa Goto. Oxford: Heinemann, 1987.

———. *Moving the Centre: The Struggle for Cultural Freedoms*. London: James Currey/Heinemann, 1993.

———. "On Writing in Gikuyu." *Research in African Literature* 16 (1985): 151–56.

———. "Preface." *Secret Lives, and Other Stories*. London: Heinemann, 1975.

———. *The River Between*. London: Heinemann, 1965.

———. *Writers in Politics*. London: Heinemann, 1981.

Niebuhr, Reinhold. "The Church and the South African Tragedy." *Christianity and Crisis* 2 May 1960: 53–54.

———. "Our Stake in the State of Israel." *New Republic* 4 Feb. 1957: 9–12.

Nijland, C. "Najib Mahfouz and Islam: An Analysis of Some Novels." *Die Welt des Islams* 123–24 (1984): 136–55.

Oduyoye, Mercy Amba. *Hearing and Knowing: Theological Reflections on Christianity in Africa*. Maryknoll, NY: Orbis, 1986.

Ogot, Bethwell A., and Tiyambe Zeleza. "Kenya: the Road to Independence and After." *Decolonization and African Independence, 1960–1980*. Ed. Prosser Gifford and William Roger Louis. New Haven: Yale UP, 1988.

Ojeda, Jose Promís. "Los Salmos de Ernesto Cardenal." *Ernest Cardenal: poeta de la liberación latino-americana*. Ed. Elisa Callabrese. Buenos Aires: Fernando García Cambeiro, 1975.

Opata, Damian U. "Eternal Sacred Order Versus Conventional Wisdom: A Consideration of Moral Culpability in the Killing of Ikemefuna in *Things Fall Apart*." *Research in African Literatures* 18 (1987): 71–79.

Parker, Kenneth. "The South African Novel in English." *The South African Novel in English: Essays in Criticism and Society*. Ed. Kenneth Parker. New York: Africana, 1978. 1–26.

Parrinder, Edward G. *Jesus in the Qu'ran*. New York: Barnes, 1965.

Paton, Alan. *Cry, the Beloved Country*. 1948. New York: Scribner's, 1987.

Pearce, Roy Harvey. *Savagism and Civilization: A Study of the Indian and the American Mind*. 1953. Baltimore: Johns Hopkins UP, 1975.

Pechey, Graham. "On The Borders of Bakhtin: Dialogization, Decolonization." *Oxford Literary Review* 9 (1987): 59–84.

Perelman, Chaim. *Justice.* New York: Random, 1967.

Pieris, Aloysius. *An Asian Theology of Liberation.* New York: Orbis, 1988.

Pratt, Annis, et al. *Archetypal Patterns in Women's Fiction.* Bloomington: Indiana UP, 1981.

Pratt, Mary Louise. *Imperial Eyes: Travel Writing and Transculturation.* London: Routledge, 1992.

Puebla bishops. "Evangelization in Latin America's Present and Future." Hennelly 225–59.

Pynchon, Thomas. "The Heart's Eternal Vow." Rev. of *Love in the Time of Cholera.* By Gabriel García Márquez. *New York Times Book Review* 10 April 1988: 47.

Randall, Margaret. *Christians in the Nicaraguan Revolution.* Vancouver, BC: New Star Books, 1983.

Ramchand, Kenneth. Introduction. *Listen, the Wind.* By Roger Mais. Burnt Mill: Longman, 1986. vi–xxx.

Rich, Paul. "Tradition and Revolt in South African Fiction: The Novels of André Brink, Nadine Gordimer, and J. M. Coetzee." *Journal of Southern African Studies* 9 (1982): 54–73.

Roa Bastos, Augusto. *Son of Man.* 1961. Trans. Rachel Caffyn. London: Gollancz, 1965.

Robertson, P. J. M. "*Things Fall Apart* and *Heart of Darkness:* A Creative Dialogue." *International Fiction Review* 7 (1980): 106–11.

Ruether, Rosemary. *Liberation Theology: Human Hope Confronts Christian History and American Power.* New York: Paulist P, 1972.

Said, Edward W. *After the Last Sky: Palestinian Lives.* New York: Pantheon, 1986

———. "Arafat's Deal." *The Nation* 20 Sept. 1993: 269–70.

———. *Beginnings: Intention and Method.* Baltimore: Johns Hopkins UP, 1975.

———. *Covering Islam: How the Media and the Experts Determine How We See the Rest of the World.* New York: Pantheon, 1981.

———. "Foucault and the Imagination of Power." *Foucault: A Critical Reader.* Ed. David Couzens Hoy. Oxford: Blackwell, 1986. 149–55.

———. "An Ideology of Difference." *Critical Inquiry* 12.1 (1985): 38–58.

———. "Michael Walzer's *Exodus and Revolution:* A Canaanite Reading." *Grand Street* 5.2 (1986). Rpt. Edward W. Said and Christopher Hitchens, eds. *Blaming the Victim: Spurious Scholarship and the Palestinian Question.* London: Verso, 1988. 161–78.

———. *Orientalism.* New York: Pantheon Books, 1978.

———. "Permission to Narrate." *Journal of Palestine Studies* 13.3 (1984): 27–48.

———. *The Question of Palestine.* New York: Times Books, 1979.

———. "A Tragic Convergence." *New York Times* 11 Jan. 1991: A19.

Said, Edward, et al. "An Exchange on Edward Said and Difference." *Critical Inquiry* 15.3 (1989): 611–46.

Scarry, Elaine. *The Body in Pain: The Making and Unmaking of the World.* New York: Oxford UP, 1985.

Scharper, Philip, and Sally Scharper. *The Gospel in Art by the Peasants of Solentiname.* Maryknoll, NY: Orbis, 1982.

Schöckel, L. Alonso. *Job. Comentario teológico y literario.* Madrid: Cristiandad, 1983.

Schwerdt, Dianne. "Leading the People Home: Matigari as Redeemer in Ngũgĩ wa Thiong'o's Latest Novel." *CRNLE Reviews Journal* 2 (1989): 10–17.

Segal, Charles M., and David C. Stineback. *Puritans, Indians, and Manifest Destiny.* New York: Putnam, 1977.

Serote, Mongane. *To Every Birth Its Blood.* London: Heinemann, 1981.

Sharma, Govind Narain. "Ngũgĩ's Christian Vision: Theme and Pattern in *A Grain of Wheat*." *Critical Perspectives on Ngũgĩ wa Thiong'o.* Ed. G. D. Killam. Washington: Three Continents, 1984. 201–10.

———. "Socialism and Civiliation: The Revolutionary Traditionalism of Ngũgĩ wa Thiong'o.' *Ariel* 19 (1988): 21–30.

Shumway, David R. *Michel Foucault.* Boston: Twayne, 1989.

Sicherman, Carol M. "Ngũgĩ wa Thiong'o and the Writing of Kenyan History." *Research in African Literatures* 20.1 (1989): 347–70.

———, ed. *Ngũgĩ wa Thiong'o: The Making of a Rebel, A Source Book in Kenyan Literature and Resistance.* London: Hans Zell, 1990.

Siemens, William L. "The Antichrist-Figure in Three Latin American Novels." *The Power of Myth in Literature and Film.* Ed. Victor Carrabino. Tallahassee: UP of Florida, 1980. 113–21.

Simpson, John, and Jana Bennett. *The Disappeared and the Mothers of the Plaza: The Story of the 11,000 Argentinians Who Vanished.* New York: St. Martin's, 1985.

Slemon, Stephen. "Cultural Alterity and Colonial Discourse." *Southern Review* 21 (1987): 102–07.

———. "Magic Realism as Post-Colonial Discourse." *Canadian Literature* 116 (1988): 9–23.

———. "Modernism's Last Post." *Ariel* 20.4 (1989): 3–17.

———. "Post-Colonial Allegory and the Transformation of History." *Journal of Commonwealth Literature* 23.1 (1988): 157–68.

Slotkin, Richard. *Regeneration through Violence: The Mythology of the American Frontier, 1600–1800.* Middletown, CT: Wesleyan UP, 1973.

Somekh, Sasson. *The Changing Rhythm: A Study of Najib Mahfuz' Novels.* London: Brill, 1973.

———. "The Sad Millenarian: An Examination of Awlad Haratina." *Critical Perspectives on Naguib Mahfouz.* Ed. Trevor Le Gassick. Washington: Three Continents, 1991. 101–15.

Soyinka, Wole. *Myth, Literature, and the African World*. Cambridge: Cambridge UP, 1976.

Spykman, Gordon, et al. *Let My People Live: Faith and Struggle in Central America*. Grand Rapids, MI: Eerdmans, 1988.

Steinberg, Leo. *The Sexuality of Christ in Renaissance Art and in Modern Oblivion*. New York: Pantheon, 1983.

Stewart, Philip. Introduction. *Children of Gebelaawi*. By Naguib Mahfouz. 1959. London: Heinemann, 1981. vii–ix.

Suchocki, Marjorie Hewitt. *The End of Evil: Process Eschatology in Historical Context*. Albany: State U of New York P, 1988.

———. "In Search of Justice: Religious Pluralism From a Feminist Perspective." *The Myth of Christian Uniqueness: Toward a Pluralistic Theology of Religions*. Ed. John Hick and Paul F. Knitter. Maryknoll, NY: Orbis, 1987.

Sullivan, Zohreh T. "The Postcolonial African Novel and the Dialogic Imagination." Lindfors, *Approaches* 101–06.

Terry, Don. "Accord a Bittersweet Occasion for Arabs in U.S." *New York Times* 8 Sept. 1993: A1, 8.

Thistlethwaite, Susan Brooks, and Mary Potter Engel, eds. *Lift Every Voice: Constructing Christian Theologies from the Underside*. San Francisco: Harper, 1990.

Thompson, Leonard. *The Political Mythology of Apartheid*. New Haven: Yale UP, 1985.

Tiffin, Helen. "Post-Colonialism, Post-Modernism and the Rehabilitation of Post-Colonial History." *Journal of Commonwealth Literature* 23 (1988): 169–81.

Todorov, Tzvetan. *Mikhail Bakhtin: The Dialogical Principle*. 1981. Trans. Wlad Godzich. Minneapolis: U of Minnesota P, 1984.

Trigo, Pedro. *Arguedas, mito, historia y religion*. Lima: Centro de estudio y publicaciones, 1982.

Urdanivia Bertarelli, Eduardo. *La poesía de Ernesto Cardenal: cristianismo y revolution*. Lima: Latinoamericana Ed., 1984.

Vargas Llosa, Mario. Interview. *Die Zeit* 30 March 1990: 17–18.

———. *The Real Life of Alejandro Mayta*. New York: Farrar, 1986.

———. *The Storyteller*. New York: Farrar, 1989.

von Balthasar, Hans Urs. *The Balthasar Reader*. Philadelphia: Crossroads P, 1982.

———. *Engagement with God*. London: SPCK, 1975.

Walzer, Michael. *The Company of Critics: Social Criticism and Political Commitment in the Twentieth Century*. New York: Basic, 1988.

———. *Exodus and Revolution*. New York: Basic, 1985.

———. "The Idea of Holy War in Ancient Israel." *Journal of Religious Ethics* 20.2 (1992): 215–28.

———. *Interpretation and Social Criticism*. Cambridge: Harvard UP, 1987.

———. *Just and Unjust Wars*. New York: Basic, 1977.

———. "On the Road." *New Republic* 4 Oct. 1993: 22–26.

———. "Perplexed." *New Republic* 28 Jan. 1991: 13–15.

———. *The Revolution of the Saints: A Study in the Origins of Radical Politics.* Cambridge: Harvard UP, 1965.

———. *Spheres of Justice.* New York: Basic, 1983.

———. "What Kind of State is a Jewish State?" *Tikkun* 4.4 (1989): 34–37, 126–28.

Walzer, Michael, and Edward W. Said. "An Exchange." *Grand Street* 5.4 (1986): 246–59.

Watts, Cedric. "'A Bloody Racist': About Achebe's View of Conrad." *Yearbook of English Studies* 13 (1983): 196–209.

Weil, Simone. *Oppression and Liberty.* Trans. Arthur Wills and John Petrie. Amherst: U of Massachusetts P, 1973.

Weinstock, Donald J. "Achebe's Christ-Figure." *Journal of the New African Literature and the Arts* 5–6 (1968): 20–26.

Weinstock, Donald J., and Cathy Ramadan. "Symbolic Structure in *Things Fall Apart.*" Innes and Lindfors 126–34.

Weschler, Lawrence. "The Great Exception." *The New Yorker,* 3 April 1989: 43–85; 10 April 1989: 85–108.

Wessels, A. "Naguib Mahfouz and Secular Man." *Humaniora Islamica* 2 (1974): 105–19.

White, Steven. *Culture and Politics in Nicaragua: Testimonies of Poets and Writers.* New York: Lumen Books, 1986.

Wilkinson, Jane. *Talking with African Writers.* London: James Currey/Heinemann, 1992.

Williams, Raymond. *Marxism and Literature.* New York: Oxford UP, 1985.

Wilson, Raymond. *Ohiyesa: Charles Alexander Eastman, Santee Sioux.* Urbana: U of Illinois P, 1983.

Winks, Robin W., ed. *British Imperialism: Gold, God, Glory.* New York: Holt, 1963.

Wolterstorff, Nicholas. "Can Scholarship and Christian Commitment Mix? A New Look at the Integration of Knowledge." *Universitas* Forum. Messiah College. 25 May 1993.

———. *Until Justice and Peace Embrace.* Grand Rapids, MI: Eerdmans, 1983.

Wong, Hertha Dawn. *Sending My Heart Back Across the Years: Tradition and Innovation in Native American Autobiography.* New York: Oxford UP, 1992.

Wood, Forrest G. *The Arrogance of Faith: Christianity and Race in America from the Colonial Era to the Twentieth Century.* Boston: Northeastern UP, 1990.

Wood, Michael. "Ah, the Fredonna Tree." *New York Review of Books* 18 July 1985: 33–35.

Wren, Christopher S. "Apartheid a Sin, Clergy Conference Says." *New York Times* 10 Nov. 1990: A3.

Wright, Edgar, ed. *The Critical Evaluation of African Literature.* London: Heinemann, 1982.

Wright, T. R. *Theology and Literature*. Oxford: Basil Blackwell, 1988.

Zamora, Lois Parkinson. *Writing the Apocalypse: Historical Vision in Contemporary U.S. and Latin American Fiction*. Cambridge: Cambridge UP, 1989.

Zell, Hans M., and Helene Silver, eds. *A Reader's Guide to African Literature*. London: Heinemann, 1972.

Ziolkowski, Theodore. *Fictional Transfigurations of Jesus*. Princeton: Princeton UP, 1972.

Contributors

Ed Block, Jr., is Associate Professor of English at Marquette University, Milwaukee, Wisconsin. He is author of *Rituals of Dis-Integration* (Garland, 1993) and editor of *Critical Essays on John Henry Newman* (ELS, 1992). Associate editor of the journal *Renascence*, he has also published on Victorian literature, philosophical hermeneutics, and the relation of science, literature, and values.

Norman R. Cary is Professor of English at Wright State University, Dayton, Ohio. He is series editor for *Studies of World Literature in English* (Peter Lang) and has published in the areas of religion and literature and postcolonial literature.

Terry DeHay is Assistant Professor of English at Southern Oregon State College. She teaches Latin American literature in translation and postcolonial literatures, and has published essays in those areas.

Susan VanZanten Gallagher is Professor of English at Seattle Pacific University and the author of *A Story of South Africa: J.M. Coetzee's Fiction in Context* (Harvard, 1992). She is also coauthor of *Literature Through the Eyes of Faith* (HarperCollins, 1989) and has published essays on feminist criticism, African literature, and American literature.

John C. Hawley, S.J., is Associate Professor of English at Santa Clara University, and the editor of *Reform and Counterreform* (Mouton de Gruyter, 1994) and *Through a Glass Darkly* (Fordham, 1995). He chairs the Modern Language Association's Executive Committee on Religious Approaches to Literature, and has published in *ARIEL* and *Research in African Literatures*.

Alan Jacobs is Associate Professor of English at Wheaton College in Wheaton, Illinois, and the author of essays on modern literature, culture, and literary theory. He is currently completing a book on W. H. Auden.

Claudia Marie Kovach is Professor of English and French at Neumann College and has published articles on Margery Kempe, the Tristan corpus, Voltaire, ethnic American literature, and literary theory. She has a book in progress on the work of Isabel Allende.

Oliver Lovesey is Professor of English at Okanagan University College in Kelowna, British Columbia, Canada. He has published *The Clerical Character in George Eliot's Fiction* (University of Victoria: ELS Monograph Series, 1991) and a number of essays on postcolonial and Victorian narrative.

Bradley J. Monsma is a graduate student at the University of Southern California. His dissertation on trickster narratives and literary theories focuses on the work of Gerald Vizenor, Maxine Hong Kingston, and Ishmael Reed.

Lourdes Elena Morales-Gudmundsson is Assistant Professor of Spanish at the University of Connecticut at Stamford. After publishing an article on parody and biblical imagery in García Márquez' *Love in the Time of Cholera,* she has been working on a book on the role of the Bible and liberation theology in the Latin American novel of the "Boom" generation.

Mark Walhout is Associate Professor of English at Seattle Pacific University. For the last five years he has been an associate editor of *Christianity and Literature.* His most recent publication is "Critical Theory" (in *Contemporary Literary Theory: A Christian Appraisal* [Eerdmans, 1991]).

Lois Parkinson Zamora is Professor of English at the University of Houston. Her area of specialization is comparative literary relations in the Americas, particularly contemporary U.S. and Latin American fiction. Her books include *Writing the Apocalypse: Historical Vision in Contemporary U.S. and Latin American Fiction* (Cambridge, 1989), *Image and Memory: Latin American Photography, 1880–1992* (Rice, 1994), and an edited collection of essays, *Magical Realism: Theory, History, Community* (Duke, 1994).

Index

www.ingramcontent.com/pod-product-compliance
Lightning Source LLC
Chambersburg PA
CBHW060344030726
47497CB00003B/595